Psychoanalysis in China

Psychoanalysis in China

Literary Transformations

1919-1949

Jingyuan Zhang

East Asia Program
Cornell University
Ithaca, New York 14853

The *Cornell East Asia Series* publishes manuscripts on a wide variety of scholarly topics pertaining to East Asia. Manuscripts are published on the basis of camera-ready copy provided by the volume author or editor.

Inquiries should be addressed to Editorial Board, Cornell East Asia Series, East Asia Program, Cornell University, 140 Uris Hall, Ithaca, New York 14853.

ISSN 8756-5293
ISBN 0-939657-55-4

TABLE OF CONTENTS

ACKNOWLEDGEMENTS

This study has grown out of my Ph.D. thesis, which was completed in 1988. It is interesting to recall the start of this project: in 1984, while searching for a thesis topic, I attended an inspiring course with Professor Cynthia Chase called "Reading Freud as an Imaginative Reader and Writer." Psychoanalysis and literary criticism have a great deal in common, as interpretive enterprises, and for a long time I considered switching my field from Comparative Literature to psychoanalysis--luckily my dream was smashed by the cruel fact that I could not afford to pay the expensive tuition for seven-year psychoanalytic training, nor could I afford the time. Before 1984, I had worked as a research assistant and read widely in dozens of Chinese periodicals between 1915-1925. After I passed my generals, Professor Edward Gunn, knowing my interest in psychoanalysis, asked me whether Freud had any footing in modern China and challenged me to show him proof should I say yes. That initiated my research on Freud in China. At first, I was groping in the dark and tended to read all the pre-1949 Chinese magazines from one bookshelf to another. In this way, I "finished" using Cornell's Wason Collection, the Harvard-Yenching library, the Columbia Asian Collection, the University of Chicago Library, and visited other American libraries as well. I want to express my great appreciation to Beijing Library, Nanjing Library, Shanghai Library, and Chongqing Library for facilitating my research in the summer of 1985.

In January 1989 I returned to Beijing and began working at the Institute of Comparative Literature, Peking University. During my absence from China, there had been a great storm of interest in Freud, which had then died down as quickly as it had arisen. Research on Freud could not go further. With the development of my other academic interests, I have changed my focus of studies. The present study basically rests on the original research, having undergone some revisions thanks to the invaluable suggestions of the anonymous readers.

I owe special debts to my former advisers at Cornell: Walter Cohen, Edward Gunn, Sandra Siegel, and Jonathan Culler. Genuine gratitude goes to Nancy Glazener and William Haines, whose unremitting friendship has time and again proved an incalculable resource. I wish to express my sincere thanks to Professor Yue Daiyun, whose consistent faith in me and in the importance of this topic has helped more than I can say.

INTRODUCTION

This study covers roughly the thirty-year period in Chinese literary history between 1919 and 1949, two turning points in Chinese history. The May Fourth Movement of 1919 came to be celebrated as marking a cultural and literary revolution, a movement in which the younger generation of Chinese intellectuals took an active part in the social and political affairs of the nation.[1] The year 1949 witnessed the founding of the People's Republic of China. Between 1919 and 1949, there was relatively free intellectual exchange between China and the rest of the world. Foreign ideas were imported, contested, and assimilated. The literature of this period was rich, diverse, and experimental. Indeed, the shift from classical to vernacular Chinese in literature, to cite just one example, indicates the significant and far-reaching transformations of Chinese culture that took place during this time. Although the thirty years in question constitute a short interval in Chinese history, they laid down the political and cultural foundation for modern China.

At the turn of the twentieth century, following foreign military invasions of China, many Chinese intellectuals believed that the nation needed political, economic, and social reforms to survive. In literature, Confucian ideology and traditional literary forms were attacked for being narrow and outdated. Chinese intellectuals turned to the West and Japan for usable revolutionary theories and ideas. They had a strong sense of being pioneers, often explicitly comparing themselves to Prometheus stealing fire from heaven for the people on earth. Many of their writings reflect their felt obligation to awaken the whole nation. They sought reforms in literature commensurate with the political, social, and economic reforms that were underway.

---

1. For details, see Chow Tse-Tung, *The May Fourth Movement: Intellectual Revolution in Modern China* (Cambridge: Harvard University Press, 1960).

1

Freudianism [Fuluoyide zhuyi] was introduced to China at the same time that Darwinism, Marxism, pragmatism, and other Western philosophies began to influence Chinese intellectuals. In literature, realism, naturalism, expressionism, aestheticism, and other literary modes and forms were also imported. It has commonly been assumed that foreign literary trends did not have much impact on Chinese writers, because the writers only borrowed the slogans and flourishes of these "isms" and then freely changed their substance to conform to the Chinese cultural heritage. I shall argue that Freudian theory, unlike a number of other Western literary influences, such as futurism and expressionism (which indeed appeared in only a few articles in Chinese journals), has had a genuine and important impact on modern Chinese literature, although it never became a dominant ideology or shaped mainstream literary forms.[2]

The present study will examine the reception of Freudian theory in Chinese literature and the particular ways in which Freudianism was expressed, displaced, transformed, and reproduced in the course of being appropriated by Chinese intellectuals. This study will also examine the reasons why certain parts of Freudian theory were rejected by Chinese intellectuals. My subject is, in a way, a problem of intellectual history--an attempt to establish the role that Freudian theory played in China during the period I have named. Although I will focus mainly on literary uses and revisions of Freud, I will also draw on the work of psychologists and intellectuals. Since, however, materials about Freud and more or less Freudian writings available from this era are legion, my study of them is necessarily selective.

This book is not, however, a study of influences in the traditional sense. Traditional influence studies were based upon the concept that certain great thinkers (usually male) or great works shaped their eras. Not only did such studies ignore the broader context of intellectual and social history within which the single masterpiece had meaning or the great thinker worked, they implied that other thinkers or works were passively shaped rather than that these receivers re-thought what they received. What I am doing may resemble an influence study insofar as psychoanalytic theory, especially during the early twentieth century, was identified overwhelmingly with the single figure of Sigmund Freud. Freud's was the name that virtually meant psychoanalysis in both West and East. As I concentrate on

---

2. Some scholars have noticed occasional Chinese literary interest in Freudian theory, but dismissed it as superficial. See, for instance, Marián Gálik, *The Genesis of Modern Chinese Literary Criticism (1917-1930)* (London: Curzon Press, 1980), p. 33.

the reception of all the ideas associated with Freud and his work, I am concerned with his influence. Yet Freudian theory was not transmitted in a single coherent form, but rather in bits and pieces over time and in changing social contexts. It was altered in the course of being translated and explained in China, and it took on a different significance as a result of being grafted onto the country's own rich tradition of psychological explanation in literature. I am interested in evaluating the Chinese understanding of psychology and its relationship to literature both before and after Freud, in order to understand how this environment was hospitable and inhospitable to Freud. I want to stress the important ways in which Chinese transformed Freudian theory rather than merely passively received it. These transformations are not just misreadings or perversions of Freud but rather are significant interpretations and elaborations of Freud.

The present study comprises five chapters, fusing an account of the historical reception of Freud's own writings in China with an interpretation of the interchange between Freudian theory and Chinese literature. Chapter One traces the routes by which Freudian theory gained currency in China, emphasizing the impact these ideas had on the disciplines most affected by Freud's work. Chapter Two considers the problems of translation. As the introduction of any new idea from one culture into another is essentially a translation, this chapter attends especially carefully to the linguistic problems that arose, and continue to arise, in China's assimilation of Freud. Chapter Three offers my interpretation of some major themes from Freudian psychoanalysis as they are engaged by Chinese literature: theories of artistic creativity, the Oedipus complex, and the interpretation of dreams. In my view, this strategic selection covers the most important aspects of the interpretation of Freudian theory by and for twentieth-century Chinese literature. And in order to explore the far-reaching implications of Freudian literary theory for Chinese literature, Chapter Four concentrates on the work of one particular group of Chinese modernists known as "psychoanalytic novelists." Finally, Chapter Five examines the importation and development of psychoanalytic criticism by both professional psychologists and literary critics in China. Through these selective analyses, I hope not only to delineate the relationship between Freud and China, but also to explore the possible fruits of such a marriage.

Chapter 1

A BRIEF ACCOUNT OF THE LITERATURE OF
FREUDIAN PSYCHOANALYSIS IN CHINA

Any study of a comparative nature should take into account not only the indebtedness of intellectual or literary works to each other, but also the ways in which social, political, and economic situations shape such relationships. It is easy to claim in the abstract that one particular set of ideas has influenced and affected a culture: to claim, as I shall, that the assimilation of Freudian theory had some effect on Chinese literature. It is more difficult to uncover the precise channels through which China assimilated Freud and to understand the reasons why the Chinese accepted some Freudian ideas more readily than others.

This chapter, therefore, establishes some crucial historical background for discussing the relationship between Freud and twentieth-century Chinese literature. I shall minimize discussion of the specifically literary impact of Freudian theory at this stage because I wish to convey the broad outlines of how Freudian theory was disseminated in China. Because literature never exists in a social vacuum, it is necessary to examine the environment that framed and fostered the literature under investigation. Referring to the relationship between psychoanalysis and literature, Shoshana Felman has suggested that the notion of the "application" of psychoanalysis to literature, and vice versa, should be replaced by "implication"--"each one finding itself enlightened, informed, but also affected, displaced, by the other."[1] The beginning of this implication of Freudian theory with Chinese literature may be traced to a letter from Sigmund Freud, which is the only record of direct contact between Freud and Chinese scholars.

---

1.   Shoshana Felman, ed., *Literature and Psychoanalysis* (Baltimore: Johns Hopkins University Press, 1982), pp. 8-9.

On May 27, 1929, Freud wrote a short note to Zhang Shizhao, an ex-Minister of Education in Beiping then touring Europe, in response to a letter of Zhang's that has been lost:

Hochgeehrter Herr Professor
Ich bin überaus erfreut durch Ihre Absicht, in welcher Art immer Sie sie ausführen wollen, sei es daß Sie die Kenntnis der Psychoanalyse in Ihrem Heimatlande China anbahnen, sei es daß Sie uns Beiträge für unsere Zeitschrift *Imago* geben, in denen Sie unsere Vermutungen über archaische Ausdrucksformen am Material Ihrer Sprache messen. Was ich in den Vorlesungen aus dem Chinesischen anführte, war aus einem Artikel der Enzyklop. Britannica (11th edit) genommen.
In vorzüglicher Hochachtung, Ihr Freud.

[I am much pleased by your intention, in whatever manner you care to carry it out, be it that you introduce psychoanalysis to your native country China, or be it that you make contributions to our periodical *Imago* in which you test our hunches concerning archaic forms of expression against the material of your language. What I said about Chinese in my lectures was taken from an article in the *Encyclopedia Britannica* (11th ed).][2]

Amid extended argument and controversy, psychoanalysis had become an established field of study in the human sciences by 1929. The International Psychoanalytic Association that Freud had organized included no participants from China, although his letter to Zhang indicates that he welcomed Chinese interest. There is no record of what Zhang had written to ask Freud. We can, however, infer from Freud's response a few of the questions that Zhang must have raised: he apparently asked Freud about his knowledge of Chinese and informed Freud of his intention to introduce psychoanalysis to China and/or to write for the journal of psychoanalysis *Imago* from a Chinese viewpoint. Subsequently, Zhang translated Freud's *Selbstdarstellung*, but he did not contribute any articles to *Imago*. As a matter of fact, during that time, there were few contributions to *Imago* from Oriental scholars.[3]

---

2.   Zhang Shizhao, trans., Sigmund Freud, *Selbstdarstellung* [Fuluoyide xuzhuan], (Shanghai: The Commercial Press, October, 1930), p. 1

3.   The Indian Psycho-Analytical Society was founded in 1922 in Calcutta, but few of its members wrote for *Imago*. See T. C. Sinha, "Development of Psycho-analysis in India," in *International Journal of Psycho-Analysis*, No. 47, 1966.

In the twenty-four volumes of his complete psychological works, Freud refers to China or Chinese culture four times: once he describes the social custom of foot-binding in China; another time he refers to a book on Chinese ways of interpreting dreams; a third time he talks about Chinese script; and the last time he offers ideas about the Chinese language. Of course, Freud's knowledge of things Chinese was by no means confined to such idiosyncratic materials. As is well known, Freud drew broadly on materials that fascinated him and enabled him to advance his own hypotheses. Nor was his thought untouched by the Orientalism prevalent among European intellectuals in his time.

In his article "Fetishism" (1927), Freud, after discussing the fetish as a substitute for the mother's phallus, a way of repressing the threat of castration, comes to the subject of a race-psychological parallel to fetishism:

> Another variant, which is also a parallel to fetishism in social psychology, might be seen in the Chinese custom of mutilating the female foot and then revering it, like a fetish, after it has been mutilated. It seems as though the Chinese male wants to thank the woman for having submitted to being castrated.[4]

His conclusion that the prototype of all fetishes is the male sexual organ may seem a bit hasty, but it is consistent with his hypothesis that the physical marking of sexual difference has profound psychic and cultural consequences. Fetishism, the worship of a metonymic object, has existed from time immemorial, but it was not until the mid-nineteenth century that anthropological and sociological studies of this phenomenon were begun. Marx discusses the fetishistic relation to commodities which arises from the peculiar social character of the labor that has produced them. But Freud considers fetishism within a different economy: a libidinal one. For Freud, a fetish object substitutes for the penis that a boy (and later a man) fears to lose and that a mother (and by extension any woman) seems to lack. Not confining his analysis to the individual psychology of fetishism, however, Freud expands his theory to the sphere of ethnopsychology--in this case, footbinding in China.

Freud's interpretation of this custom was different from all the other new interpretations in China at the time. Footbinding was usually seen as a barbarous method of enslaving women. In China, this custom

---

4.   *The Standard Edition of the Complete Psychological Works of Sigmund Freud* (London: The Hogarth Press and the Institute of Psycho-Analysis, 1981), Vol. 14, p. 157.

was criticized severely from the late nineteenth century to the early twentieth century for the practical reason that it weakened the nation. The mutilation of half of its population kept China from modernizing itself. The movement to abolish footbinding was initiated by Liang Qichao, whose main purpose was to "build up the nation and foster strong offspring" [qiangguo baozhong].[5] Among Chinese scholars, Lin Yutang, a graduate of Harvard University, attributed a sexual meaning to this custom:

> Actually, footbinding was sexual in its nature throughout. Its origin was undoubtedly in the court of licentious kings, its popularity with men was based on the worship of women's feet and shoes as a love fetish and on the feminine gait which naturally followed, and its popularity with women was based on their desire to curry men's favor.[6]

Freud's link between fetishism and the fear of castration, though more extreme than Lin Yutang's treatment, has some pertinence to Chinese history. Castration is symbolic in Freudian theory, but it was a common practice in Chinese imperial palaces where male servants were castrated to preserve the purity of palace women, who belonged solely to the rulers. Freud's suggestion that fetishism for the bound foot is an expression of man's gratitude for woman's submission opens up a new and disturbing vista on the subject of men's sexual control of women by means of symbolic castration. Freud's pertinence for a different culture is, however, not confined to the discussion of fetishism.

In his masterpiece, *The Interpretation of Dreams*, Freud refers in a footnote to "the further history of dream-interpretation among the Chinese by Secker (1909-10)." He also cites various views and traditions on the interpretations of dreams held by the Jews, the Arabs, the Japanese, and the Indians.[7] Evidently Freud gathered extensive materials about dream interpretation in Asia before launching his own theory. Freud describes his aim as that of elaborating "a method by which the unintelligible content of a dream might be replaced by one that was comprehensible and significant,"[8]

---

5. Chen Dongyuan, *A History of Chinese Women's Life* [Zhongguo funü shenghuo shi] (Shanghai: The Commercial Press, 1926), p. 324.

6. Lin Yutang, *My Country and My People* (New York: John Day Company, 1935), pp. 165-166.

7. James Strachey, ed., *The Complete Psychological Works of Sigmund Freud* (London: Hogarth Press, 1959), Vol. 4, p. 4 (hereafter *TCPWOSF*).

8. Freud, *The Interpretation of Dreams* (New York: Avon Books, 1965), p.38 (hereafter *TIOD*).

the method being mainly that of free association by the dreamer. Departing from previous theories that proposed universal interpretations for the symbolic contents of dreams, Freud insists that dream interpretation be mediated by the context in which it is found: "as with Chinese script, the correct interpretation can only be arrived at on each occasion from the context."[9] Thus Freud not only showed passing familiarity with Chinese theories of dream interpretation but also considered the Chinese language itself to be a model for his own interpretive strategies.

Indeed, Freud's most extensive discussion of Chinese matters concerns the Chinese language. It is likely that this discussion was the cause of Zhang's inquiry, since in his letter to Zhang, Freud replied honestly that all his knowledge about the Chinese language came from the eleventh edition of the *Encyclopedia Britannica*. In his *Introductory Lectures on Psychoanalysis*, Freud implies that the indeterminacy characteristic of dreams is a regular feature of all primitive systems of expression. But the ancient tongues and scripts, however imprecise or figurative they may be, are designed as means of communication. The scripts in dreams, in contrast, are merely self-expressive, and are not intended to be understood. This is the crucial difference between a dream and an archaic language, Freud thinks. Freud's interest in the Chinese language arises from his wish to find a parallel between an archaic language and dream interpretation.

His findings, he claims, are not disappointing, "for Chinese is [so] full of uncertainties as positively to terrify one." He marvels at Chinese syllabic sounds, which have an average of ten different meanings each; he also admires the devices used in Chinese to avoid ambiguity, such as combining two sounds into a single word and speaking syllables in any of four different "tones." Informed only by the encyclopedia, he thinks that it must be hard to tell whether single-syllable words, when standing alone, are nouns, verbs or adjectives. Freud is equally amazed that there are no inflections to show gender, number, case, tense, or mood. "The language consists ... of the raw materials only. ... Wherever there is any uncertainty in Chinese the decision is left to the intelligence of the listener, who is guided by the text." This listener's job, Freud finds, is very similar to the task of a dream-interpreter. In spite of the apparent indeterminacy of the Chinese language, Freud is assured and wants to assure his audience and readers that "the Chinese language is a quite exceptionally good medium of

---

9.   Freud, *TIOD*, p.388.

expression; so it is clear that indefiniteness does not necessarily lead to ambiguity."[10]

Freud's interest is not so much in the Chinese language as in proving his point that although dream content is uncertain, not intended to "tell anyone anything," psychoanalysts who interpret it in the proper context can find it very expressive and meaningful.[11] His view of the Chinese language was not his own innovation. It was apparently influenced by nineteenth-century Western linguists, such as Wilhelm von Humboldt, who believed that Chinese was devoid of formal grammatical classes or distinctions, but for that reason had its own particular excellence as a language.[12] Freud's knowledge of Chinese culture and language was therefore enhanced by his psychoanalytic insight but constrained by his social and historical environment.

Just as Freud made use of the Chinese language and culture for his own theoretical purposes, the Chinese who promoted Freud's ideas turned those ideas to their own purposes. Their approach was to borrow from foreign cultures by "depending on our own eyes to choose what is beneficial."[13] Foreign scholars who toured China and discussed Freudian concepts in passing helped the spread of Freudian psychoanalysis in China. For example, around 1920, Bertrand Russell delivered a series of lectures in Beiping entitled "The Analysis of Mind," which were published as a book in London and New York in the following year (1921).

Russell argues that progress in physics and psychology has rendered the debate between materialist and idealist metaphysics increasingly obsolete, as physics undermines the idea of matter as fundamental and psychology learns more about the bodily basis of mind. Russell finds a congenial view in William James, who holds that the "stuff of the world is neither mental nor material, but a 'neutral stuff,' out of which both are constructed."[14] Russell wishes to defend this view. Approaching psychoanalysis from a background in mathematical logic and skeptical empiricism, Russell takes a very critical stance toward Freud. He criticizes Freudian theory for being invested with "an air of mystery and mythology

10. James Strachey, ed., *TCPWOSF*, Vol. 15, p. 230.

11. Ibid., p. 231.

12. R. H. Robins, *A Short History of Linguistics* (London: Longmans, 1969), p.177.

13. Wu Zimin, ed., *Lu Xun on Literature and Art* [Lu Xun lun wenxue yu yishu] (Beijing: Renmin, 1980), p. 691.

14. Bertrand Russell, *The Analysis of Mind* (London: George Allen and Unwin, 1921), p. 6.

which forms a large part of its popular attractiveness."[15] He expresses
concern that the Freudian view of human nature is an exaggeration which is
having an unfortunate effect on people's conceptions of themselves. "We
used to be full of virtuous wishes, but since Freud, our wishes have
become, in the words of the Prophet Jeremiah, 'deceitful above all things
and desperately wicked.'"[16]

A prime purpose of Russell is to attack the idea that
"consciousness" is the name of a distinct entity or stuff, rather than merely a
loose general term for a variety of relations such as seeing, knowing and
remembering.[17] He criticizes some psychoanalysts' notions of the
unconscious and of unconscious desires on the grounds that they build on a
mistaken view of consciousness. It is normal, Russell says, that we desire
what we desire without consciously thinking to ourselves, "I desire that."
Sometimes we have such thoughts about what our desires are, sometimes
these thoughts are mistaken, and sometimes the mistakes are themselves
strongly motivated and psychologically disastrous. Learning the truth about
these desires can cure mental illness. Russell readily states that in this
sense of "the unconscious," Freud and his followers have demonstrated
beyond dispute the importance of the unconscious. But they are wrong to
say that all desires are originally "conscious," that unconsciousness is the
abnormal state for a desire. And they are wrong to say that the powerful
motives we refuse to recognize must be mainly sexual rather than including
desires for, say, power or honor. In making the unconscious thus abnormal
and wicked, and speaking of "the unconscious" as a distinct entity, Freudians
encourage an almost mythological view, that within us there is "an
underground prisoner, living in a dungeon, breaking in at long intervals
upon our daylight respectability with dark groans and maledictions and
strange, atavistic lusts."[18]

Russell hopes that his lectures can remove the atmosphere of
mystery from the phenomena brought to light by psychoanalysts. He
intentionally avoids using the two terms "consciousness" and "the
unconscious" in his discussions, because these concepts are not "the essence
of life or mind." In fact, consciousness is treated, in his lectures, as
"mainly a trivial and unimportant outcome of linguistic habits."[19]

---

15. Russell, p. 37.
16. Russell, p. 39.
17. Russell, pp. 10-14.
18. Russell, pp. 31-40.
19. Russell, p. 40.

Russell borrows extensively from William James's theory of psychology. Although James proposed "streams of thoughts" in his *Principles of Psychology* (1890), a notion which later influenced modernist literature significantly, he remained solidly within the tradition of empiricism, holding that people can experience the world directly and reliably.[20] In light of James's theory of psychology, Russell loses no time in dissecting psychoanalysis, focusing on the concepts of instinct, desire, introspection, sensations, and images. For instance, in discussing the concept of desire, he states, "Most psycho-analysts pay little attention to the analysis of desire, being interested in discovering by observation what it is that people desire, rather than in discovering what actually constitutes desire."[21] Russell demands from psychoanalysis "a re-statement of what constitutes desire, exhibiting it as a causal law of our actions, not as something actually existing in our minds."[22] Only one aspect of psychoanalysis appeals to him: "The whole tendency of psycho-analysis is to trust the outside observer rather than the testimony of introspection. I believe this tendency to be entirely right."[23] This is, however, an erroneous reading of Freud.

Russell's view of Freudian theory was one-sided and, on the whole, prejudiced. Unfortunately, he was facing an audience who had very little knowledge of Freudian theory. Russell's views were taken seriously by Chinese intellectuals, and he made a deep impression on them. In fact, his speeches were repeatedly translated into Chinese, appeared in a number of newspapers and journals, and were published as books in Chinese by different translators.[24]

Prior to Russell's talks about Freud, some scattered writings about psychoanalysis had appeared in Chinese journals and newspapers, most notable among which are Zhang Xichen's article, "The Characteristics of Mass Psychology," in 1913,[25] and Lu Kefeng's article, "Chinese Methods of

---

20. Henry James, ed., *The Letters of William James* (Boston: Atlantic Monthly Press, 1920), Vol. 2, p. 328.

21. Russell, p. 59.

22. Russell, p. 60.

23. Russell, p. 59.

24. For instance, Sun Fuyu, trans., Russell's lectures, *The Analysis of Mind* [Xin zhi fenxi] (Beiping: Xinzhi, 1922); Ji Ji, trans., Russell, *The Analysis of Mind* [Xin de fenxi] (Shanghai: Zhonghua, 1947); Russell, "Xin de fenxi" in *National Daily* [Guomin ribao] 1920-1921; Russell, "Xin de fenxi," in *Daily News* [Shishi xinbao], March-April 1921.

25. Zhang Xichen, "Qunzhong xinli zhi tezheng," in *Dongfang zazhi*, Vol. 10, No. 4, October 1, 1913.

Hypnosis," in 1917.[26] Wang Guowei translated Harold Höffding's *Outlines of Psychology* from English into Chinese as *Xinlixue gailun* (1907); in this work Höffding discussed the concepts of consciousness and the unconscious. In 1919, the concept of the "stream of consciousness" was discussed in *New Tide*.[27] Nevertheless, widespread discussion about Freud did not occur until after 1920, following Russell's lectures. It is beyond any doubt that Russell, by denouncing Freudian theory and promoting behaviorism and a Jamesian psychology, generated an enthusiasm among Chinese intellectuals for the study of various schools in Western psychology.

Another Western thinker who had a considerable impact on Chinese intellectuals during that time was John Dewey, who went to China in 1919. In the course of his two years there, he spoke at universities in eleven provinces on topics ranging from philosophy to education and social reforms. As a philosopher, he paid no attention to Freudian theory. He introduced only three of his contemporaries to the Chinese audience: William James, Henri Bergson, and Bertrand Russell.[28] But interest in these figures inevitably led Chinese intellectuals to the general arena of psychological controversy dominated by Freud.

During the thirty years from 1919 to 1949, many books, translations, expositions, and criticisms, both foreign and Chinese, appeared in China on the subject of Freudian psychoanalysis. I shall consider this huge body of material in two major sections: foreign views of Freudian theory available in Chinese and Chinese reactions to Freudian theory. I do not discuss the Chinese bibliography in chronological order but arrange it by subject matter instead, so that I can examine the impact in China of various individual topics within Freudian theory.

1.1 Translated Criticisms of Freudian Theory

According to my research, five works by Freud were translated into Chinese before 1949: *An Autobiographical Study*, *Introductory Lectures on Psychoanalysis*, *Group Psychology and the Analysis of the Ego*, *New*

---

26.   Lu Kefeng, "Zhongguo cuimian shu," in *Dongfang zazhi*, Vol. 14, No. 3, March 15, 1917.

27.   Chen Jia'ai, "The New" [Xin], in *The New Tide* [Xin chao], Vol. 1, No. 1, December 31, 1919.

28.   John Dewey, *Additional Lectures in China 1919-1921*. Robert W. Clopton and Tsun-Chen Ou, trans. and eds. (University of Hawaii, Microfilm, 1971).

Introductory Lectures on Psychoanalysis, and *The Interpretation of Dreams*. Freud's lectures at Clark University were also translated into Chinese. These works provided Chinese intellectuals with their only direct contact with Freudian theory, aside from Freud's works in German and the translations into English and Japanese that were available. Apart from these translations, Chinese intellectuals also had access to translated expositions and criticisms of Freudian psychoanalysis by foreign theoreticians. Most of the critical materials were translated from Western languages, especially from German and English, into Chinese. There were also secondhand translations of Western criticisms of psychoanalysis from Japanese into Chinese. I shall discuss in this section how some of the major points made by these foreign critics influenced the Chinese perception of Freudian theory.[29]

Several of the important secondary works were favorable toward Freudian theory. In 1927, Zhao Yan translated Barbara Low's *Psycho-Analysis: A Brief Account of the Freudian Theory* into Chinese.[30] Barbara Low was a member of the British Psychoanalytical Society and had worked as a training college lecturer in London.[31] Ernest Jones wrote a preface to her work, but the preface was not translated into Chinese because it was aimed at an English audience. Jones explained that there were two practical reasons why psychoanalysis spread slowly in England: the relative inaccessibility of the standard works on the subject and the lack of introductory works giving a clear and simple account of psychoanalysis. In his judgment, Low presented "all aspects of the psycho-analytical theory fairly and straight forwardly, and yet [brought] them within reach of those

---

29. Some of the translated criticisms of Freud available to Chinese readers were: D. H. Bonus, *How to Psychoanalyze Yourself* (Hao Yaodong, trans., *Zi zhi zhi shu*, 1925); Barbara Low, *Psycho-Analysis: A Brief Account of the Freudian Theory* [Zhao Yan, trans., *Fuluote xinli fenxi* (Shanghai: The Commercial Press, 1927)]; John Carl Flugel, "Theories of Psychoanalysis" (Chen Derong, trans., *Jie xin shu xueshuo*, 1934); Wilhelm Reich, "Dialektischer Materialismus und Psychoanalyse," and W. Jurinetz, "Psychoanalyse und Marxismus" in *Criticisms of Psychoanalysis* [Yu Xinyuan, trans., *Jingshen fenxi xue pipan* (Shanghai: Xinken shuju, March 1936]; Reuben Osborn, *Freud and Marx: A Dialectic Study* [the Chinese translation is *Psychoanalysis and Historical Materialism* [Jingshen fenxi yu weiwu shi guan] (Shanghai: Shijie, first edition in November 1940 and second edition in June 1949). Some of the journals also carried translated articles on the subject; for instance, W. Fritche's "Freudianism and Art" appeared as "Jingshen fenxi xue yu yishu" (translated by Hu Qiuyuan) in *Dushu zazhi*, Vol. 2, No. 6, 1932, and as "Fuluoyite zhuyi yu yishu" (translated by Zhou Qiying) in *Wenxue yuebao* , June 10, 1932.

30. Zhao Yan, trans., *Fuluote xinli fenxi* (Shanghai: The Commercial Press, 1927).

31. B. Low, *Psychoanalysis: A Brief Account of the Freudian Theory* (New York: Harcourt, Brace and Company, 1921), p. 1.

who have made no previous study of the subject."[32] Low was not the first to attempt to give a clear and simple account of psychoanalysis, but she had the advantage of "having beforehand made an immediate study of the subject with the purpose of adequately qualifying herself for such a task."[33] Since Jones was at this time already president of the British Psychoanalytic Society and editor of the *International Journal of Medical Psychoanalysis*, we can trust that Barbara Low's work was of some importance in England at that time. Just as Low's work played a role in introducing Freudian theory to English readers, so it provided the Chinese with insight into the problems it raised.

In her book, Low stresses the importance of viewing psychoanalysis as a science and not as a philosophy or metapsychology or ethics, because she feels that its opponents and supporters alike tend to derive questionable inferences from Freud's theories. Low defines psychoanalysis as a science not only because it is based on phenomena observed and theories tested "with exhaustive patience and judgment,"[34] and because its continuing method is empirical, but also because it is shaped by some of the assumptions of pragmatism. Both psychoanalysis and pragmatism oppose rationalism as a pretension. However, Low feels compelled to acknowledge that in a broad sense psychoanalysis hovers between science and philosophy. According to her, the major contribution of Freud's research is to prove that all psychological life is unified and continuous. It is impossible to separate mind into several functions. Psychic life is a continuous unity because no consciousness at any particular time is causally separate from previous events and present happenings.

A psychoanalyst herself, Low understands the clinical practice of psychoanalysis. She pays special attention to the roles of analyst and patient, but she seems to overestimate the importance of the analyst and underestimate that of the patient. She emphasizes the lofty qualifications of a psychoanalyst--talent, wide and varied experience of life and thought, a power of quick intuitive insight and human compassion. The psychoanalyst is to observe all the manifestations of the patient in his or her free association. The analyst's attention is not confined to what patients say, but also includes trifling physical habits, sudden bodily and facial movements, sighs, smiles, hesitations, and so forth. The analyst attends to the patient's impulse to select and coordinate his or her narration, to ignore

---

32. Low, p. 7.
33. Low, p. 5.
34. Low, p. 21.

irrelevancies, and to rationalize things. Omniscient and superior, the analyst enables the patient to recover for the first time experiences that are unobtainable in any other way. The analyst is to be prepared for the patient's displacement of feelings towards him or her, an inevitable process in the treatment. Through this transference, the patient relives in feelings directed toward the analyst many of their forgotten or unrecognized feelings, thereby gaining an understanding of himself and achieving a therapeutic effect. Neither a teacher nor a confessor, the psychoanalyst works with the patient as a scientist. Low counsels the patient, on the other hand, to cultivate infinite patience and self-renunciation. "He must suspend all intellectual work--selection, criticism, and so forth--and simply use himself as a receptacle to admit the incoming tide of thoughts, fancies, emotions, of any and every reaction, in short--a task to which he is left by the analyst."[35] Assuming a passive role, the patient in the course of analysis has to turn from his fantasies, from his pleasurable childish desires, and from his unconscious gratifications, and adapt himself to present reality. Low's position, however, underscores the complicated process of psychoanalysis and makes the role of the analyst resemble the role of confessor.

Low also discusses the potential significance of applying psychoanalysis to social issues, such as education, family relations, and social systems. Once the rational conscious life is understood as only part of the whole psyche, Low expects that social systems will allow some freedom and satisfaction to the primitive instincts, and when this happens, "the undue exaltation of the ultra-civilized ideals will cease."[36] Ideally, this understanding will also bring a revolution in people's methods of child-training and education, which hitherto have dealt almost exclusively with consciousness. She therefore believes that psychoanalysis offers a way to transform conventional values and provide greater individual freedom.

In 1934, Chen Derong, a psychologist, translated another introduction to psychoanalysis, John C. Flugel's article "Theories of Psycho-analysis," in a book entitled *Jie xin shu xueshuo*.[37] Flugel was an assistant professor of psychology in University College, University of London. In his article, he clarifies the term "psychoanalysis" and distinguishes it from the term "psychology," which is a broader study of the mind and traditionally derived from philosophy. According to him, "psychoanalysis" can have several meanings: it can refer to a method of

---

35. Low, p. 149.

36. Low, p. 165.

37. John C. Flugel, "Theories of Psycho-analysis," in William Rose, ed., *An Outline of Modern Knowledge* (London: Victor Gollancz, 1931), pp. 349-393.

psychological study, to a therapeutic practice, and to the theories that are used to explain psychological processes. He acknowledges that psychoanalysis is not a theoretically complete structure. Freud and his followers start with no fixed conceptions of the nature and function of the human mind or of its disorders. They modify their theories over time, in keeping with their belief that the mind is "dynamic."[38] Moreover, Flugel considers Freud a scientific successor of the great pessimistic philosophers Schopenhauer and E. Hartmann. He holds that the leading difference between Freud and these other philosophers is that Freud's outlook is more empirical.

Flugel offers a comparative study of the different schools of psychoanalysis organized around the figures of Sigmund Freud, Alfred Adler, and Carl G. Jung. He summarizes the difference between Freud and other schools: Adler concentrates on the frustration of individual self-assertion, whereas Freud tends to emphasize sexuality; Jung considers the unconscious itself to be collective or universal, but Freud refuses to get involved in mysticism. Flugel is more sympathetic to Freud than to Adler and Jung, especially on the question of human sexuality:

> Freud has, time and again, emphatically stated his belief that sexual tendencies, though of immense importance, do not exhaust the instinctive equipment of man, and that psycho-analysis has in the course of its development continually broadened the range of its observations and its theories, without thereby sacrificing the earlier acquisitions. Adler's Individual Psychology on the other hand has become more and more rigid in its accent on aggressiveness as an all-pervading and all-important factor, and has, with ever greater determination, set its sail against the intrusion of sexual or other influences.[39]

Similarly, Flugel criticizes both the form and content of Jung's theory of the "collective unconscious" as determined by heredity. He points out that Jung's theory of symbols is designed to fend off the sensuality and infantilism of the unconscious as revealed by Freud. Jung's analytical psychology, according to Flugel, is not "in any sense a product of psycho-analysis or a feature of psycho-analytic theory."[40] Flugel concludes that psychoanalytic theory has positive consequences for human culture as a

---

38. Flugel, p. 357.
39. Flugel, pp. 361-362.
40. Flugel, p. 367.

whole because it enables people to become more conscious of themselves and thus extends human powers of rational insight and control.[41]

In the West at that time, Freudian theory was often measured against Marxism. Indeed, some psychoanalysts and cultural critics attempted to synthesize psychoanalysis and Marxism.[42] As China was enthusiastically embracing Western ideas, Chinese intellectuals also showed an interest in combining the two theories. Several books and articles on the relationship between Marxism and Freudianism were translated into Chinese. In March 1936, Yu Xinyuan published his translations of Wilhelm Reich's "Dialektischer Materialismus und Psychoanalyse" and W. Jurinetz's "Psychoanalyse und Marxismus" together under the title *A Critique of Psychoanalysis* [Jingshen fenxi xue pipan]. This dual work was translated from a Japanese translation of the German texts: Imai Sueo, *Dialectical Materialism and Psychoanalysis* [Bensho yuibutsu shugi to seishin bunsekigaku]. The German texts were from a magazine, *Unter dem Banner des Marxismus*.[43] (The Chinese translation is awkward, due to Yu's difficulties with the Japanese language.) Both of the articles attempt to establish a philosophical dialogue between psychoanalysis and the Hegelian dialectics of Marxism.

Jurinetz considers Freudian theory to be binaristic, deterministic, and dialectical, and therefore somewhat compatible with Marxist accounts of historical processes. Freudian concepts are presented as pairs of opposites: the pleasure principle and the reality principle, the id and the ego, sadism and masochism, and so on. Jurinetz also points out that the Freudian theory of the repetition compulsion is similar to Nietzsche's concept of the "eternal return of the same"--which phrase is transformed to "all things converge" by the time it reaches Chinese. He considers Freudian theory pessimistic because it supposes that the aim of life is death--and therefore similar to the philosophy of Arthur Schopenhauer. Freud holds that an emotion can transfer energy to its opposite: Jurinetz considers this to be a dialectical notion. However, Jurinetz finds Freud's social theory unconvincing in that Freud tries to apply individual psychology to mass psychology. Psychoanalysis cannot explain class psychology and the origin of human society, in Jurinetz' view.

---

41. Flugel, p. 392.

42. Reuben Fine, *A History of Psychoanalysis* (New York: Columbia University Press, 1979), p. 108.

43. Yu Xinyuan, trans., W. Jurinetz and W. Reich, *A Critique of Psychoanalysis* [Jingshen fenxi xue zhi pipan] (Shanghai: Xinken, 1936), p. 3.

Wilhelm Reich, who wrote the other work translated in the volume *A Critique of Psychoanalysis*, was expelled from the International Psychoanalytic Association for attempting to merge psychoanalysis with Marxism.[44] Reich views the two as complementary: psychoanalysis is useful for interpreting psychological phenomena, whereas Marxism is useful for understanding social phenomena. Marxism cannot explain the psychological cause of neurosis, and psychoanalysis cannot entirely explain the reasons for social changes. Each, however, can enrich the other. Reich countered charges made by some Marxists that the birth of psychoanalysis signalled the decline of the bourgeois class by pointing out that Freud was isolated and hated not only in academic circles, but also in bourgeois society as a whole, because he analyzed the core of conservative ideology: the origin of bourgeois morality in sexual repression. Reich insisted that Freud's version of psychoanalysis was correct and that his successors, such as Jung and Adler, distorted his intentions.

In 1940, Reuben Osborn's *Freud and Marx: A Dialectical Study* was translated into Chinese by Chu Zhi. In the English edition, the book has a preface by John Strachey, who praises the significance of Osborn's book as the first step in England toward combining Marxism and Freudianism. He criticizes the tendency of Marxists to dismiss psychoanalytic theory and speculates that if Engels were alive, he would have paid close attention to Freud's theory and would have "digested it, criticized it, sifted it," unlike the contemporary Marxists, who ignore it.[45] Strachey posits that the proper relationship of Marxism to psychoanalysis is dialectical: "By means of their very oppositeness, by means of their sharply contradictory character, [Marxism and Freudianism] provide, when taken together, a unity of opposites adequately described."[46]

Osborn claims that the purpose of his book is to illustrate the interrelationship between the subjective life of man, as described by Freud, and the objective world of economic processes, as described by Marx. He reiterates at the end of each chapter that if Freudianism is combined with Marxism, people can learn more about the truth of human society and about themselves. If Marxists understand Freud's scientific inquiry into the nature of mental activities, they will know how to combat those undesirable mental tendencies that are expressed in social movements. If psychoanalysts

---

44. Reuben Fine, p. 108.

45. Reuben Osborn, *Freud and Marx: A Dialectical Study* (New York: Equinox Co-Operative Press, no date), p. 6.

46. Osborn, p. 8.

study Marxism, they will be able to have a fuller view of the causes of their patients' symptoms.

Osborn's attempt to connect Freudian with Marxist theories begins with a consideration of primitive society, a subject that interests both psychoanalysts and Marxists. Freud bases his theory on Darwin's view of the character of the first human groups in *The Origin of Man*. Darwin speculates that men "originally lived in small communities, each with a single wife, or, if powerful, with several, whom he jealously defended against all other men."[47] Freud then develops the Darwinian view into his theory of the primal horde. His version of the origin of totemism is this: the primitive horde was dominated by a powerful male, who kept all the females for himself. The young males were compelled by the threat of castration to stay away from the females. One day the expelled brothers joined together to slay and eat the father. Afterward they felt remorseful and guilty. They undid their deed by declaring that the killing of the Father was not allowed; they renounced the fruit of their deed by denying themselves the liberated women. Osborn compares this notion with Engels's ideas in *The Origin of the Family*. Engels uses "group marriage" to show that women in one totem belonged sexually to males of another totem. Drawing on C. H. Morgan's *Ancient Society*, Engels thinks there was a period of "unrestricted sexual intercourse," right after the slaying of the primal father. The remarkable similarity between Engels and Freud, Osborn says, is that both of them believe that the prevention of mutual rivalry between males is the main motivation for forming large social groups.

Osborn holds that Engels anticipated the Freudian notion of repression as a condition for stability in social life. Freud believes that civilization is built under the pressure of the struggle for existence as a result of people's sacrifice of some of their primitive gratifications. Similarly, Engels correlates the development of the labor process with the decline of the dominance of sexual ties. Man becomes a working animal and represses his individual sexual urges because social cooperation requires such repression. Freud also indicates that repression is a response to social and economic needs. Occasionally, Freud sounds rather like a Marxist, as in this significant passage that Osborn quotes:

> At bottom society's motive [for restraining the instinctive life] is economic; since it has not means enough to support life for its members without work on their part, it must see to it that the

---

47. Osborn, p. 113.

number of these members is restricted and their energies directed away from sexual activities on to their work--the eternal primordial struggle for existence, therefore persisting to the present day.[48]

Both Freud and Engels emphasize the importance of sexual factors in social organization. Engels praises Morgan's rediscovery of the sexual foundation of human history and says that Morgan's findings about the sexual organization of the North American Indians can be the key to opening all "the insoluble riddles" of the most ancient history.[49] Although Engels pays more attention to the productivity of labor than to sexual instincts themselves, based on sexual relationships, his theories are not incompatible with Freud's libidinal ones: according to Freud, too, instinctual energy can be displaced, sublimated, or expressed in some other indirect way. Osborn holds that Freud also outlines the transformation of sexual motives into social ones in his account of the origin of language, which began, he proposes, as a means of summoning a sexual mate and was later developed into a rhythmic stimulus for work.

Osborn's picture is that psychoanalysis is the science of human desires and drives, whereas Marxism can be defined as the science dealing with external conditions that either fulfill or frustrate those desires. He thinks that a Marxist can easily accept the concept of the unconscious. According to him, Marx and Engels knew that behind human consciousness, there are other motives, that is, unconscious ones. These unconscious motives are the most fundamental psychic activities, "causative factors." One piece of evidence Osborn shows for Engels's receptivity to some concept of an unconscious occurs in a letter written in 1893 in which Engels remarks, "[I]deology was consciously created by the so-called thinkers. This might be true, but it is made in the false consciousness. They did not know their real motives. Otherwise it was not an ideological process."[50] False consciousness is equated by Osborn with the Freudian concept of the unconscious.

Osborn believes that psychoanalysis emerged dialectically as a response to previous systems of thought, not as a final truth. Here of course he agrees with Freud, who always thought of his researches as work

---

48. Freud, *Introductory Lectures on Psychoanalysis* (London: Allen and Unwin), p. 262.

49. Frederick Engels, *The Origin of the Family, Private Property and the State in the Light of the Research of Lewis H. Morgan* (New York: International Publishers, 1972), p. 72.

50. Quoted in Osborn, p. 173.

in progress. Arguing for a combination of Marxist economic theory with Freudian psychoanalysis, Osborn holds that sublimation transfers instinctual drives to social functions whose significance cannot be understood through the study of the individual alone. Although Osborn does not answer the question of the relationship between Marxism and psychoanalytic theory, his service is, in John Strachey's words, to have "propounded it." Paralleling Strachey's enthusiasm, the Chinese edition has a favorable introduction by a reviewer who agrees with Osborn that Marxism and Freudian theory can reinforce each other.

The materials on both Freudian and Marxist theories translated into Chinese suggest that German and British Marxist critics of this era were usually rather sympathetic to Freudian psychoanalysis. They tended to criticize parts of it and affirm other parts. Such was not, however, the case with Soviet critics, who tended to reject Freudo-Marxism; the Soviet government took an antagonistic position against psychoanalysis in the late 1920s.[51] For example, a Marxist literary critic, W. Fritche, criticizes Freud in his article, "Freudianism and Art," which was published in the fifth volume of *Literature of the World Revolution* (Moscow: State Publishing House, 1931). The article, which analyzes the specific social and political milieu in which Freudianism arose, was twice translated into Chinese by leftist literary critics and published in two separate magazines.[52]

> Freudianism was born in Vienna and Budapest, which had not been nourished by the traditions of the heroic epoch of capitalism. Its bourgeoisie had, without making any great effort, prospered on the back of the Croatian, Slovenian, Dalmatian and Serbian peasants, who have had their marrows sucked dry. Freudianism absorbed a great deal of the spirit of that capitalism.[53]

Fritche argues that the Viennese bourgeois intelligentsia were characterized by eroticism, aestheticism, and individualism. He focuses on Freud's treatment of the arts. Although Freud's school did not subject all forms of art to analysis--they omitted, for instance, music and architecture--Freudians had from the start devoted much attention to poetic creation. Fritche

---

51. See Martin A. Miller, "Freudian Theory Under Bolshevik Rule: The Theoretical Controversy During the 1920s," in *Slavic Review*, Winter 1985.

52. Zhou Qiying, trans., "Fuluoyite zhuyi yu yishu," in *Wenxue yuebao*, No. 1, July 10, 1932. Hu Qiuyuan, trans., "Jingshen fenxi xue yu yishu," in *Dushu zazhi*, Vol. 2, No. 6, 1932.

53. W. Fritche, "Freudianism and Art," in *Literature of the World Revolution*, Vol. 5, 1931, p. 80.

criticizes Freudian psychoanalysis of literature for having stripped it of all serious social significance; in particular, he criticizes the Freudian habit of looking for Oedipus complexes in literature. He feels repelled by the idea that the root impulse of every revolt against monarchy is nothing but the enmity of son for father, the result of a mother-fixation, as in Otto Rank's analysis of Shakespeare's *Hamlet*. He notices that although Freud attempts to analyze the psychology of the artist, he cannot explain the artist's unusual capacity for sublimating his sexual cravings. He itemizes ten major shortcomings of Freudian interpretations of literature and art, the most important of which are the Freudian reduction of the artistic act to sublimation of the incest complex; Freud's excessive preoccupation with sexual factors in general; Freud's depriving art of its social significance and isolating the artist from all historical, cultural, social and literary influences; and Freud's dilettantism. Fritche's article, which reduces Freudian theory to a few disjoined practices, exemplifies the Soviet Marxist critique of psychoanalysis at that time.

More sympathetic to Freudianism were Japanese intellectuals, several of whose discussions of Freudian theory were translated into Chinese, such as Matsumura Takeo, *Literature and Sexuality* [Bungei to seiai], translated by Xie Liuyi.[54] Most of them were appreciations of Freudian theory, or applications of Freudianism to literary criticism. Because Japan was also newly eager to engage foreign theories, Japanese scholars tended to address Western critics' viewpoints on Freudian theory when they synthesized and adapted it.[55]

In summary, foreign discussions of Freud were varied: some favored Freud; some opposed him. The translated discussions fall into three general categories: expositions by psychoanalysts who were enthusiastic about Freud and practiced psychoanalysis themselves, discussions by intellectuals who were sympathetic to Freud, and Soviet criticisms that utterly rejected Freudian theory. As there was such a diversity among the foreign discussions, one can expect that there could very well be mixed views about Freud among Chinese intellectuals.

---

54. Matsumura Takeo, *Literature and Sexuality*, translated by Xie Liuyi (Shanghai: Xinyue, 1927).

55. For reference on the Japanese reception of psychoanalysis, see Akira Kawada Shuizuoka, "Psychoanalyse und Psychotherapie in Japan," in *Psyche* (Stuttgart), Vol. 31, 1977, pp. 272-285.

1.2 Chinese Reactions to Freudian Theory

In the early 1920s, Chinese intellectuals began to formulate their own responses to Freud. The earliest records I have found on Freud were not translations of his works, but articles introducing his life and theories. During the thirty years I am examining, many journals and magazines published articles on Freud: newspapers and news magazines such as *National Daily* [Guomin ribao] and *Eastern Miscellany* [Dongfang zazhi]; general magazines of commentary such as *Yiban* and *New China* [Xin Zhonghua]; psychology journals such as *Semi-Annual Psychology Magazine* [Xinli ban nian kan]; education journals such as *Education Magazine* [Jiaoyu zazhi]; university journals such as *China-France University Monthly* [Zhongfa daxue yuekan] and *Students Magazine* [Xuesheng zazhi]; and literary magazines such as *Arts and Letters Monthly* [Wenyi yuekan], *New North Monthly* [Beixin yuebao], and *Literary Monthly* [Wenxue yuebao]. Chinese scholars also published books on Freudian theory, since many intellectuals were able to read foreign languages and therefore could examine Freudian texts that had not been translated into Chinese. In addition, Chinese scholars who had been trained in the West or in Japan had access to firsthand information about psychoanalysis.

The volume of publication about Freudian psychoanalysis in China kept pace with the tide of other publications in psychology. According to Zhang Yaoxiang's statistics, during 1917-1921, the average rate of publication of articles on psychology was two articles per month; during 1922-1926, seven articles per month; and during 1927-1931, five articles per month.[56] Another researcher, Zhang Depei, showed that, between 1930 and 1934, there were about twenty articles published every month on psychology.[57] According to my research, the frequency with which articles on Freudian theory were published was approximately the same. Publication on Freud steadily increased from 1920 and in the mid-1930s reached its height. It came to a decline during the Second World War, as the whole nation was plunged into a life-or-death resistance to the Japanese invasion. During the war, the object of psychological study understandably shifted from individual sexuality to social and national themes. A few titles of the articles on psychology from that period demonstrate this shift: Gao

---

56. Zhang Yaoxiang, "An Observation of Recent Chinese Psychology from Publications" [Zhushu shang guancha wan jin Zhongguo xinlixue zhi yanjiu], in *Tushu pinglun*, Vol. 2, No. 1.

57. Zhang Depei, "An Observation of the Tendency of Chinese Psychology from Magazine Articles in the Past Four Years" [Cong jin si nian zazhi lunwen shang guancha Zhongguo xinlixue de qushi], in *Shida yuekan*, No. 16, Dec. 30, 1934.

Juefu, "Fascism and Psychological Experiments";[58] He Bang, "Wartime Psycho-Neurosis";[59] Gao Juefu, "The Mobilization of Psychologists";[60] Qian Nengxin, "Psychological War and Quick War";[61] and Liu Yonghe, "Psychological Elements in Aggressive Behaviors."[62] It should be noted that, in keeping with this trend, the translation of Reuben Osborn's *Freud and Marx: A Dialectical Study* was reprinted in July 1949, two months before the founding of the People's Republic of China. Throughout the thirty-year period of the present study, however, discussions of Freudian theory ranged from the abstract and theoretical level to that of common sense. Because it is unnecessary and impossible to list all the opinions presented in Chinese articles, I shall concentrate on the general climates of reception afforded to Freudian theory by three Chinese academic disciplines (psychology, philosophy and education), as well as by ordinary readers and the political parties.

1.2.1   Freudian Theory and Psychology

Psychoanalysis never became a professional field in China. Chinese psychologists trained in the United States were the dominant force in the field when they returned, and they usually criticized Freud sternly for lacking sufficient evidential support. At that time, the American academic psychological community was enamored of behaviorism. It set itself determinedly against psychoanalysis, which it castigated as unscientific "hokum."[63] For example, one representative of the American-trained behaviorist psychologists in China, Guo Renyuan, promoted a complete separation of psychology from philosophy. He criticized traditional Western psychology as being "poisoned" by philosophy. Because psychology was a new field in China, Guo decided to try to have it classed as a field of natural science from the outset. In China, he predicted, resistance to a scientific psychology would be weaker than in America

---

58.   Gao Juefu, "Faxisidi zhuyi yu xinli ceyan," in *Dongfang zazhi*, Vol. 35, No. 16, August 16, 1938.

59.   He Bang, "Zhanshi de xinli shenjing bing," in *Dongfang zazhi*, Vol. 35, No. 22, November 16, 1938.

60.   Gao Juefu, "Xinlixuejia de dongyuan," in *Dongfang zazhi*, Vol. 35, No. 13, July 1, 1938.

61.   Qian Nengxin, "Xinli zhan yu shanji zhan," in *New China*, Vol. 1, No. 6, June, 1943.

62.   Liu Yonghe, "Qinlüe xingwei de xinli yinsu," in *Dongfang zazhi*, Vol. 42, No. 12, June 15, 1946.

63.   Reuben Fine, p. 112.

because the forces of old psychology--that is, Western, philosophically oriented psychology--had not entered China. He wanted Chinese psychology to be built upon laboratory experiments. He not only refused to have anything to do with Western traditional psychology, but also repudiated the traditional Chinese study of the mind. He held that psychology as a new field should be separated from traditional views of "xin," as the Chinese study was known, held by metaphysicians, Sinologists, and Buddhists. The new psychology should ignore these people's "nonsense" about "xinxing" (the nature of the mind). Guo insisted that all issues of psychology should and could be solved within the laboratory, and that those who had not worked a few years in the laboratory had no qualification to talk about psychology. "This is the real psychology, which is different from the psychology of dreamers like Russell, Dewey and Bergson," Guo maintained. It was not, he particularly stressed, "like the mysterious Freudian psychoanalysis, which relied on a pack of lies such as the unconscious to mystify human behavior."[64] Influenced heavily by the behaviorist theory of John B. Watson, Guo wrote "Giving up Instincts in Psychology"[65] and "How Are Our Instincts Acquired,"[66] which were published in American journals. He deemed Freudian psychoanalysis unworthy of his attention and called Freud "Jianghu pai dawang"(king of quacks).[67]

Another American-trained psychologist, Huang Weirong, was also a behaviorist. He criticized Freudian psychoanalysis as unscientific, metaphysical [xuanxue], and unsubstantiated and proposed to get rid of Freudian psychoanalysis altogether. He explained the popularity of Freudian theory in China by suggesting that "because Freud has discussed extensively the issue of sexuality, people who have had no scientific training find him attractive."[68] This view contrasted with Russell's accounting for the popularity of Freudian theory in Europe by its "air of mystery and mythology." Huang criticized Freudian theories of the unconscious, wish-fulfillment, libido, sublimation, infantile sexuality, fixation, and so on. In sum, he completely rejected Freudian theory. He went so far as even to regret the emergence of psychoanalysis, asserting that but for psychoanalysis the field of psychology could have developed much

---

64. Guo Renyuan, *Human Behavior* [Renlei de xingwei] (Shanghai: The Commercial Press, 193?), p.4.

65. Guo, "Giving up Instincts in Psychology," in *Journal of Philosophy*, 1921.

66. Guo, "How Are Our Instincts Acquired," in *Psychological Review*, 1922.

67. Guo, *Beginning Psychology* [Xinlixue rumen] (Shanghai: Qiming, no date), p. 3.

68. Huang Weirong, *ABCs of Abnormal Psychology* [Biantai xinli ABC] (Shanghai: Shijie, 1929), p. 19.

faster than it had. Sharing the prejudice that some Western-trained Chinese had against their own folk culture, Huang downgraded Freudian theory by comparing it with Chinese herbal medicine, which he thought also had no scientific proof.[69]

Other psychologists and intellectuals who had not been trained in the United States and were not strongly influenced by the behaviorist school were more receptive to Freudian theory. Chinese intellectuals, like their Western counterparts, produced general introductions to Freud as well as more specific critiques of his work. Most of the articles on Freudian psychoanalysis were of an introductory nature. In these articles, authors usually focused on summarizing Freudian theory and refrained from giving their own criticisms until the end of the articles, not because they were uncritical but rather because they intended to be open-minded about new ideas.

One of these intellectuals, Zhu Guangqian, not only kept an open mind about Freud but also problematized the criterion of scientificity that was often used to discredit psychoanalysis. In *Abnormal Psychology*, Zhu questions the concept of a unified "science" and argues that a question should have as many answers as possible: "The term 'science,' strictly speaking, should be written in plurals." He holds that "sciences" have two major characteristics: their answers are usually hypotheses and their conclusions need to be tested against the facts. No science should make exclusive claims to truth. The field of psychology must be especially provisional because it is still a new field.[70] His treatment of Freudian theory is well balanced, but because his main interest is in the aesthetic implications of Freudian theory, I shall leave his discussions of psychoanalysis for another chapter.

Xiao Xiaorong, a psychologist, adopted a pluralist attitude toward abnormal psychology. In one article, he introduced all the schools of abnormal psychology, from American behaviorist theory and French sensationist theory (Janet) to Freudian psychoanalytic theory. Amid such an all-embracing account, though, he mentioned only that Freudian theory had two obvious shortcomings, simplification and mystery, because of its reductive method and "unscientificity."[71]

---

69. Huang Weirong, p. 29.

70. Zhu Guangqian, *The Schools of Abnormal Psychology* [Biantai xinlixue paibie] (Shanghai: Kaiming, 1930).

71. Xiao Xiaorong, "Analysis of Modern Abnormal Psychology" [Xiandai biantai xinli xueshuo zhi fenxi jiqi piping], in *Semi-Annual Psychology Journal* [Xinli ban nian kan], Vol. 1, No. 1, January, 1934.

Gao Juefu, an education major and a self-made psychologist, sought to be objective about Freudian theory. He held that until the question "What is Man?" had been answered satisfactorily, the huge mansion of psychology remained built upon sand and could easily be blown away. However, he also believed that people who had not studied all schools of psychology should reserve judgment about any particular school.[72] It was mainly through his painstaking effort in translating Freud's works and his careful criticisms of Freudian theory that the Chinese came to understand Freudian psychoanalysis. A real intellectual, Gao was critical of Freudian theory, but his criticisms were not obtuse and did not degenerate into personal attacks, as some articles tended to do. He was able to address Freudian theory intellectually and to point out contradictory elements in Freudian texts. He believed that the main contributions of Freudian theory to the field of psychology were its powerful argument against conventional psychology, its scientific analysis of cause and effect, and its combination of abstract theory with concrete linguistic and behavioral data. He criticized some people's abuse of psychoanalysis, manifested by reductively sexual explanations and the arbitrary analysis of symbolism in dreams, but he also questioned the omniscient role of psychoanalysts in the actual analysis. For instance, he found the stances of Freud and of little Hans's father in the treatment of little Hans suspicious. He criticized Freud for having preconceptions about his patients, and he emphasized the danger of finding only what was sought and forcing the view of the analyst upon the patient. He also proposed that there were other causes for neurotic symptoms besides sexual repression. Although I must reserve a fuller discussion of Gao Juefu's work for a later chapter, it should be clear that his engagement with Freud was one of the most profound among Chinese intellectuals.

In spite of the fact that there were no professional psychoanalysts in China, some people tried informally to treat themselves or their friends by its methods. For instance, Feng Hong, in his article "The Unconscious and Neurosis," states that from his self-analysis and psychoanalysis of others he has become convinced that the key to Freudian psychoanalysis is the transference achieved through the patient's suggestibility.[73] In Qian Pin's article, "A Study of a Case of Child Depression,"[74] she carefully records her use of psychoanalysis in the treatment of a twelve-year-old girl.

---

72. Gao Juefu, *Essays on Psychology* [Xinlixue lunwen ji] (Shanghai: The Commercial Press, December, 1926), p. 3.

73. Feng Hong, "The Unconscious and Neurosis" [Xia yishi yu jingshengbing], in *New China*, Vol. 6, No. 8, pp. 40-41.

74. Qian Pin, "A Study of a Child Depression Case" [Yiyu ertong zhi ge an yanjiu], in *Semi-Annual Psychology Journal*, Vol. 2, No. 2, June 1, 1935.

The materials, such as the girl's repeated dreams of snakes, water, and a vase of smoke [yanping], lend themselves to Freudian interpretations. But Qian refuses to apply a Freudian interpretation to that particular case. She states that her purpose in using the method of psychoanalysis is to let the girl have a chance to express all her "complexes" so as to lessen her depression. Even though Qian's aim is therapeutic--the alleviation of the girl's anxieties to prevent them from becoming fixations--the effect of the treatment is never explored on a theoretical level, and therefore the child's recovery is never given any analytic explanation. Qian Pin emphasizes as well that a successful cure also depends on factors outside of the analytic setting, such as social and familial cooperation. In fact, her observations of the child were conducted outside of the clinical room: she befriended the girl and kept her parents informed of the progress in the treatment.

As Qian Pin's adaptation of psychoanalysis suggests, the fact that clinical psychoanalysis never became established as a therapeutic profession in China need not be taken to indicate a lack of interest in Freudian psychological views. A successful clinical practice needs a clientele familiar with the concept of professional treatment for psychological disorders. Chinese people looked rather to family and other societal support and discipline for their emotional problems.[75]

1.2.2 Freudian Theory and Philosophy

Most of the Chinese introductory articles on Freudian theory pointed out that psychoanalysis was a theory of the abnormal as well as of the normal. Psychoanalysis as a theory about the working of the psyche entailed certain ethical, physical, and metaphysical assumptions. Furthermore, both psychoanalysis and philosophy studied the mind, although from different perspectives. Xu Qingyu, who studied psychology at Oxford, claimed that he had taken the study of psychology as his starting point for studying philosophy.[76]

There were not many Chinese articles on philosophical aspects of Freudian theory, and none offered any critique of Freudian psychoanalysis from the traditional Chinese view of "xin." Furthermore, there was only

---

75. See Wen-Shing Tseng and Jing Hsu, "Chinese Culture, Personality Formation and Mental Illness," in *The International Journal of Social Psychiatry*, Vol. 16, No. 1, Winter 1969/70.

76. Xu Qingyu, "Is the Heart the Product of the Mind?" [Xin shi nao de chanwu ma?], in *Dongfang zazhi*, Vol. 23, No. 24, December 1926.

one person who tried to explore Freudian theory in light of Western philosophy-- Ye Qing, a polemical writer who was once a leader of the Communist Youth League but later severed his relationship with the Communists. He published three articles on the philosophical aspects of Freudian theory: "A Critique of the Freudian Interpretation of Dreams,"[77] "A Philosophical Conclusion about Freudian Psychoanalysis,"[78] and "A Critique of Psychoanalysis."[79]

Ye argues that Freud's theories of the pleasure principle and reality principle, the id and the ego, and consciousness and the unconscious show the dialectical unity of opposites and posit that all apparent opposites are really implicated in each other. He suggests that the departure of Freud, as the founder of psychoanalysis, from psychology is marked by his rejecting certain kinds of mechanistic explanations offered by behaviorists. However, Ye also views Freud as a determinist who applies the law of cause and effect to his analysis of abnormal psychology. Apparently, Ye is very familiar with the terminology of Western philosophy, which he uses with disarming ease. Freudian theory, in his view, is in general a combination of dialectics and teleology in a Kantian dualism. He claims that this is the philosophical foundation of psychoanalysis, and he believes that Freud's limitation lies in his inability to promote revolution or to provide any other solution to the conflict between society and individuals. But he grants Freudian theory two major contributions to philosophy: Freud's criticism of rationalism and his reinforcement of determinism. In addition, in Ye's view, Freudian theory has a carefully worked-out logic and a complete system of abnormal psychology. Nevertheless, Ye does not think that sexual repression is the sole cause of mental illness, as he mistakenly thinks Freud does. He points out that economic relations can also affect people's mental health. After all, he argues, politics, law, morality and social customs are all built upon the economic base. Abnormal psychological behavior may be plausibly shaped by these superstructures. Ye shrewdly (though wrongly) points out that Freud refuses to blame human suffering on society, because he realizes that if he did, he would turn psychoanalysis into a theory of social revolution. Therefore, Ye maintains, Freud is an observer, not a reformer or a revolutionary. Psychoanalysis is good for analyzing abnormal behavior internally, but it is insufficient for analyzing the social problems that

---

77. Ye Qing, "Fuluoyide menglun pipan," in *New China*, Vol. 2, No. 9/10, 1934.

78   Ye, "Fuluoyide xinlixue zhi zhexue de jielun," in *Essays on Sciences* [Kexue luncong], Vol. 3, 1935.

79.   Ye, "Jingshen fenxi pai xinlixue pipan," in *New China*, Vol. 3, Nos. 15 and 17, 1935.

produce or affect that behavior. Ye considers his own preferred use of psychoanalysis and its application to sociology to be a kind of mechanistic materialism.

One of Ye Qing's philosophical conclusions about Freudian psychoanalysis is that Freud has contributed greatly to philosophy by discovering that psychic life can cause biological disorders and that individual psychologies can influence the shape of society. This accords with the view of dialectic materialism that matter determines spirit, but that spirit also has its countereffect on matter. In general, Ye Ying's philosophical views of Freud have their parallels in foreign criticisms of Freud, such as Osborn's and Reich's.

1.2.3 Freudian Theory and Education

Traditional Chinese education tended to consider human desires and instincts harmful to the growth of man. Accordingly, the entire educational system tried to keep instincts under control. It also served the old by teaching the young how to obey orders. Many modern writers protested against this traditional education, charging it with ignoring children's dispositions and treating them as mere receptacles into which to pour whatever knowledge the teacher thought was important. They advocated an education that would enable children to dare to laugh, cry, speak, and act. They emphasized the importance of physical health and a certain amount of sexual education.

Some of these critics found Freudian theory instructive and enlightening for their purpose. Wu Fuyuan, in his article "Major Theories of Freudian Psychoanalysis and Their Contributions to Education,"[80] relates four contributions of Freudian theory to education: (1) The Freudian theory of sexuality shows that rational education about human sexuality is necessary to human health. Wu sharply criticizes traditional Chinese education for completely avoiding of the topics of sex and sexuality. (2) Freudian theories about children teach educators to pay special attention to children's emotions. Wu criticizes the fact that Chinese education is based on rigid rationality and pays no attention to children's developing emotions. This bias ultimately harms the interest of the state. Wu thinks that if educators understand the Freudian theory of child psychology and if children are allowed to express their own sentiments, they will be able to learn more

---

80. Wu Fuyuan, "Fuluoyite xinlixue de zhongyao lilun jiqi duiyu jiaoyu shang de gongxian," in *Semi-Annual Psychology Journal*, Vol. 1, No. 1, January 1, 1934.

at school. (3) Freudian theory can teach educators to channel students' desires in the right way and lead students to discover their own methods of sublimation. Freud believes that education is a tool for self-development that encourages people to control their own pleasure principles and adjust them to the reality principle. (4) Most generally, Freudian theory indicates the need to reform the whole educational system. The traditional educational system is a failure, having succeeded only at forcing students to memorize texts. In light of Freudian theory, teachers can reevaluate their way of teaching and take students' individual psychologies into consideration. Wu believes that Freudian theory has opened up a branch of new knowledge and that this knowledge can bring changes for the better.

Zhu Guangqian also points out that since the Freudian theory of the unconscious holds that the unconscious originated in childhood, Freudian theory has profound implications for education. Pernicious secrecy about sexuality should be abolished. Indeed, Zhu alleges that the strict demarcation between the sexes in itself induces children to fantasize unprofitably about sex. Society measures the success of the educational system by the extent to which children repress their sexual curiosity and desire. Zhu points out, however, that this repression is where the trouble lies. Citing an example, Zhu says that every time he reads poems, essays, and novels written by young people, he finds that the pages are filled with melancholy and a "sour" smell, which show the dissatisfaction created by this repression. He proposes education about aesthetics and proper guidance for students in sublimating their desires, preferably through the cultivation of interests in art and literature.[81]

Zhang Dongsun believes that Freudian theory productively makes people aware of the importance of infant education. Freud makes it clear that the crucial period of a child's education is between the ages of one and five, from the oral stage to the genital stage. Since preschool education is the task of the parents, parents should know something about the basic principles of psychoanalysis. He particularly criticizes Chinese parents' practice of forbidding children to play games. Games, he argues, are beneficial for children's growth. Through games, children learn cooperation. Zhang thinks that the most important thing psychoanalysis reveals to people is that desires can be directed, not just followed or ignored. Human beings have the tendency to pursue pleasure because they are governed by the pleasure principle, but the reality principle can guide their instincts to

---

81. Zhu Guangqian, "Freudian Theory of the Unconscious and Psychoanalysis" [Fulude de yin yishi shuo yu xinli fenxi], in *Dongfang zazhi*, Vol 18, No. 14, July 25, 1921.

other outlets, notably through sublimation.[82] Evidently, Freud's theory about the importance of sexuality--including infantile sexuality--was taken seriously by Chinese educators during the early twentieth century.

1.2.4 The Reaction of the General Reading Public to Freud

Freud was studied mainly by intellectuals. However, Freudian theory also reached a wider audience in popularized versions. Commercial publishers even borrowed Freud's name to increase their sales. For instance, one advertisement of a translated book, *The Diary of a Young Girl*, capitalized on Freud's name by advertising the fact that Freud had written a preface to the book in which he praised it highly for revealing the psychology of a young girl's sexual desire.[83] Freud's name became a sensation and was closely linked with sex. As a result, the common people as well as professional educators worried about the bad influence that over-simplified Freudian theories might have on young people. Some self-righteous moralists attributed the popularity of cheap, sub-literary love stories to the influence of Freudian theory. Even Gao Juefu, the translator of two books by Freud, believed that popular versions of Freud tended to corrupt young people.[84] Whether he was applauded or attacked, Freud was associated by most common readers with the promotion of sexual liberty.

1.2.5 The Political Parties' Reactions to Freud

It is impossible to discuss Freudian theory in China without mentioning the attitudes toward Freud taken by the two major parties, the Nationalist Party and the Communist Party, because the political parties have influenced and shaped modern Chinese thinking in profound ways. When Freud was first introduced into China, neither party was yet very strong. During the 1930s and 1940s, though, when they expanded their influence and territory, both tended to criticize the romantic or liberal ideas

---

82.   Zhang Dongsun, *ABCs of Psychoanalysis* [Jingshen fenxi xue ABC] (Shanghai: Shijie, 1929).

83.   Zhang Yiping and Zhang Tiemin, trans., *The Diary of a Young Girl* [Shaonü riji], prefaced by Sigmund Freud (Shanghai: Xiandai, 1934); see the advertisement in *Xiandai*, Vol. 4, No. 4, 1934.

84.   Gao Juefu, "Psychology and the Education of the Young" [Qingnian xinli yu jiaoyu], in *Essays on Psychology* [Xinlixue lunwen ji] (Shanghai: The Commercial Press, 1926), p. 157.

and behavior of the young. Although Freud did not yet pose a significant threat to either party and failed to inspire official attacks by the central party organizations, Freudian theory was frowned upon by individual members of the parties. For instance, some writers who were initially sympathetic toward Freudian theory tended to renounce it when they later affiliated themselves with political parties. The journals published by the Left-Wing Association, affiliated with the Communist Party, carried unfavorable articles about Freudian theory by Soviet critics and by members of the Association, although their criticism was directed less at Freudian theory per se than at the bourgeois ideology of which it was taken as just one prominent representative. There were, however, some attempts to combine Freudian theories with Marxism. Nevertheless, the parties did not particularly emphasize attacks on Freud; they had many other intellectual priorities.

Overall, Freud's impact on Chinese political culture seems minimal, as compared with the Chinese literary reception of Freud. In fact, the chief advocate of Freudianism was a nonaligned, liberal journal called *Xiandai*, with a French term, *Les Contemporains*, co-listed as its front-page title (1932-1935). Its main function was to introduce foreign literary trends and experimental writings by both foreign and Chinese writers to a Chinese audience.

1.3   Conclusion

By the mid-1930s, Freudian theories were familiar to many Chinese intellectuals and, in reductive forms, to a surprisingly broad sector of the non-intellectual population. Of course, it would be impossible to estimate the number of people who actually read or heard of Freud and his theories during these thirty years. Given the range of publications on Freud, from ordinary journals to professional publications and several reprints of Freudian works (for instance, Freud's *Introductory Lectures on Psychoanalysis* was reprinted at least three times), we can conclude that Freudian theory was known fairly widely to the Chinese public. The reaction to Freudian psychoanalysis ranged from strong criticism to wholehearted welcome. Freud was both praised as a second Charles Darwin or Nicolaus Copernicus and defamed as a liar or a quack-doctor. Most of the articles that tackled Freudian theory tended to be moderate, though, pointing out strong as well as weak points of the theory. Foreign discussions of Freudian theory, from Germany, England, America, Japan, and the Soviet Union, influenced the Chinese reception of Freudian theory, and there was consequently a discernible similarity between the Chinese and the foreign writers in their discussions of philosophical aspects of Freudian theory. In some fields--education, for instance--Freudian theory was promoted as a possible basis for broad programs of reform. The intentions of those who introduced Freudian theory also varied: to introduce it as a science, to use it for interpreting dreams, to employ it against superstitions, to present it as a new philosophy, to feed the growing interest in the knowledge of the human mind and of sexuality, and to shed light on the roles of pleasure and power in literature.

The most prominent impact of Freudian theory was not, paradoxically enough, on the fields of psychology, philosophy, or education, although people discussed many possible applications and implications of Freudian psychoanalysis to these fields. During the thirty years in question, the dominant school in psychology was behaviorism;[85] in philosophy, it was John Dewey's pragmatism and Marxist materialism; in education, it was one organized around the development of intellectual skills and the inculcation of moral rules. Although Freudian theories in their limited way helped catalyze discussions in these fields, their most visible effect was on literature.

Psychoanalysis was introduced and understood mostly in terms of Freudian theory, the so-called "orthodox" branch of psychoanalysis. Jung's and Adler's schools of psychoanalysis were also discussed, but they were often merely appended to the main texts of Freudian theory. Significantly, Freudian psychoanalysis addressed itself more than the other schools did to problems of language, and since the relationship of Chinese readers to Freud has been shaped by acts of translation and linguistic interchange, we must take a closer look at ways in which Freudian theory was transformed by its transmission.

---

85.   O. Briére, *Fifty Years of Chinese Philosophy, 1898-1948* (New York: Frederick A. Praeger, 1965), p. 94.

Chapter 2

SEARCHING FOR THE RIGHT WORDS

In this chapter, I shall discuss the significance of how Freudian works were translated into Chinese, and some of the main problems and solutions found by Chinese translators. Translation, as both selection and interpretation of materials, has played an important part in introducing Western psychology into China. Before the late nineteenth century there was no special field of psychology in the country, nor was there in the West a psychology distinct from philosophy. Although metaphysical inquiries and ideas about the human mind had fascinated scholars for centuries, psychology as a science did not exist. Even the term "xinli xue," which was the Chinese translation for "psychology," did not enter Chinese usage until shortly before 1900. "Xin" and "li," taken separately, refer to mind and reason respectively. Traditionally, the two words were rarely put together. Even when they were used together, they referred to "li xue," a Confucian school of idealist philosophy of the Song and Ming dynasties, something quite different from their modern sense of referring to mental processes or the "psyche".[1]

As Zhang Yaoxiang, a noted psychologist, observed in 1941, Western psychology came to China as part of a massive importation of elements of Western culture.[2] The first translated book on psychology appeared in 1889, when Joseph Haven's *Mental Philosophy: Including the Intellect, Sensibilities and Will* (Boston: Gould and Lincoln, 1857) was translated and published by Yan Yongjing under the Chinese title *Xinling xue*, meaning "study of the soul" (in a somewhat supernatural sense).

---

1. The combination of "xin" and "li" was rare and denoted Neoconfucianism. See Zhao Liru, "A Study on *Philosophy of the Mind* " [Youguan *Xing ling xue* yi shu de yanjiu], in *Xinli xuebao*, No. 4, 1983, p. 387.

2. Zhang Yaoxiang, "A Brief History of Chinese Psychology" [Zhongguo xinlixue fazhanshi lüe], in *Jiaoyu xinli yanjiu*, Vol. 1, No. 3, 1941.

Haven's book was also the first book of psychology translated into Japanese (1875). Although the Japanese translation appeared fourteen years earlier than the Chinese one, Zhao Liru, a contemporary researcher, carefully studied the choice of words and sentence structures of both translations and concluded that there was no direct relationship between them.[3] It is difficult to estimate how well-known Haven's book was to the Chinese audience at that time, but it marked the beginning of Western psychology in China.

In 1903, during the Reform, Emperor Guangxu announced that preparatory schools, teachers' colleges, and universities [da xue tang] should initiate courses on general psychology. Thus, China began to introduce the new Western field of psychology officially.[4] To start this new field, Chinese intellectuals faced an enormous obstacle: translation. Yan Yongjing mentions this problem in his preface to *Xinling xue* :

> Many ideas have not been discussed in China and have no compatible Chinese terminology. All I could do is to connect words together to give them new meanings. Outwardly, it may look ambiguous, but if one studies it with care, one can find the logic in it. If a reader finds this book awkward in its expressions or imprecise in its meanings, that is because the translator had to create new terms.[5]

As Yan's explanation suggests, translation presented a major problem for those who tried to introduce new foreign theories. Translators had enormous freedom, since there were no unified rules for the translation of foreign names and specialized terms. To rectify this messy situation, the Commercial Press issued a dictionary called *Proper Names with Standard Chinese Equivalents*,[6] and in March 1937, the Ministry of Education issued a book, *The Terminology of Ordinary Psychology*.[7] It does not seem, however, that many translators of psychological works strictly followed the standard translations provided by the dictionaries. For instance, translations have produced more than ten versions even of the name of Freud:

---

3.   Zhao Liru, p. 386.

4.   Shu Xincheng, ed., *Materials on the History of Modern Chinese Education* [Zhongguo jindai jiaoyushi ziliao] (Beijing: People's Education Publishing House, 1961), pp. 569, 595, 695, 698.

5.   Yan Yongjing, trans., Josheph Haven, *Mental Philosophy: Including the Intellect, Sensibilities and Will* (Shangai: Yuzhi shuhui, 1889).

6.   *Biaozhun hanyi waiguo renming diming biao* (Shanghai: The Commercial Press, 1924, 1934, 1935).

7.   *Putong xinlixue mingci,* issued by the Ministry of Education in March 1937 (Changsha: The Commercial Press, 1939).

佛洛以特　弗洛一特　**佛洛伊德**　弗洛依德　弗羅依德

佛羅依德　莆羅乙德；　　佛洛特　　弗洛特　　福洛特

弗勞特　福魯德　佛洛德

Considered linguistically, the translations fall into two groups: (1) "fuluoyide/fuluoyite"; (2) "fuluode/fuluote." The first group is a transliteration either of Japanese katakana--"furoyito"--or of the German name "Freud." The second group seems to be a mispronunciation. The variation of "te" and "de" was very common in Chinese transcription of foreign names. In the 1948 edition of *A Comprehensive English-Chinese Dictionary*, the name "Freud" was transcribed as "froit."[8] Chinese translators do not always stick to the same transcription of a foreign name. For instance, Gao Juefu used "fuluote" and "fuluoyide" interchangeably for "Freud" in his *Essays on Psychology*.

Many scholars on China have assumed that most of the terms for the physical and social sciences were borrowed from Japan at the beginning of the twentieth century. In 1919, Zhu Ziqing, a poet, flatly stated:

> Nowadays, eighty per cent of the terminology of every subject is borrowed from the Japanese, due to the fact that the nouns in Japanese books are written in Chinese. The Japanese have also translated foreign terminology with Chinese characters. Now that they have translated Western languages into Chinese characters, we may as well get the ready-made terminology from Japan, so as to save us the trouble of translation.[9]

In the field of psychology, many Chinese terms were taken directly from Japanese. For instance, the following terms, though pronounced differently, are written in exactly the same way in the two languages:

psychology: 心理學　　　　　taboo: 禁忌

regression: 退化　　　　　　illusion: 錯覺

resistance: 抵抗　　　　　　ego: 自我

8.　*A Comprehensive English-Chinese Dictionary* (Shanghai: The Commercial Press, 1948), p. 1000.

9.　Zhu Ziqing, "Translation of Nouns" [Fanyi mingci], in *New China*, Vol. 1, No. 7, 1919. Reprinted in *Essays on the Study of Translation 1894-1948* [Fanyi yanjiu wenji] (Beijing: Waiyu jiaoxue yu yanjiu chubanshe, 1984), p. 55.

There was a problem with taking terms directly from the Japanese, though. Since languages are culturally defined and used, the Japanese had already developed new meanings for the existing kanji (Chinese characters) and had different uses for them, especially those of "ateji" [phonetic equivalents] in Japanese. For instance, two Japanese translations of the word "repetition" were 繰返 and 繰言 , which would make very little sense in Chinese. Chinese equivalents for "repetition" were "chongfu" and "fanfu"; 重複 , 反復 . (反復 is now the common term in Japanese.)

It is very difficult to distinguish Japanese influences from direct Western influences in the introduction of Freudian terms. Robert Chin and Ai-li S. Chin state that the field of psychology in China before 1949 was entirely Western.[10] However, in the early teens, most works on psychology were translated into Chinese from Japanese. It was only after 1920, when many students of psychology returned to China from Europe and America, that Chinese psychology opened direct communication with the West.

Although Japan acted as a bridge for the entry of Western psychology into China, the bulk of Freudian theory was introduced into China at almost the same time as it was to Japan. During 1929-1936, more than twenty books by Freud were translated into Japanese. There was even a psychoanalytic institute in Tokyo at that time.[11] We can assume that in translating Freudian works, it might have been convenient for Chinese translators to borrow some useful terms from the Japanese translations. Nevertheless, my research shows that at least four out of the five Chinese translations of whole books by Freud had no direct relationship to the Japanese translations: Zhang Shizhao translated Freud's *Selbstdarstellung* from German into Chinese; Gao Juefu translated Freud's *Introductory Lectures on Psychoanalysis* and *New Introductory Lectures on Psychoanalysis* from English into Chinese; Zhang Jingsheng translated Freud's *The Interpretation of Dreams* from either French or English into Chinese. Only the fifth, Xia Fuxin's edition of Freud's *Group Psychology and the Analysis of the Ego*, was translated from Japanese. Otherwise, some psychological terms may have been borrowed from Japanese formulations, but there is no evidence that the Chinese translations were based on the Japanese translations. For this reason, I shall not presuppose

---

10. Robert Chin and Ai-li S. Chin, *Psychological Research in Communist China 1949-1966* (Cambridge: MIT Press, 1969), p. 5.

11. See Akira Kawada Shizuoka, "Psychoanalyse und Psychotherapie in Japan," in *Psyche* (Stuttgart), Vol. 31, 1977, and Tokyo do hen, *Shuppan nenkan* (1929-1935).

Japanese mediation when I explore how China assimilated Freudian theory in translation.

I shall approach the issue of translation with three objectives: (1) to ascertain whether the translations of some major Freudian terms were of Japanese origin or were the invention of the Chinese writers themselves; (2) to examine the actual transformations that translation wrought in books by Freud; (3) to discuss the problems of selecting and editing that emerged when Freudian texts were introduced to China.

2.1 Translating Freudian terms

The first step in translation is to select suitable key words to substitute for those in the original texts. When a term representing a new idea is to be rendered in Chinese, there is a difference between coining a new word to serve as an equivalent and translating the word. Words never exist in isolation. They are not pure signs. In the Chinese language that Freud once admired because he speculated that it best represented unconscious images (due to its similarity to the indefiniteness of dreams),[12] the meaning of a word can be grasped only by its combination or association with other words. Moreover, even where one term renders the central meaning of another well enough, the less central associations of the two terms in the two languages may be quite different.

Mao Dun's "Discussion on the Methods of Translation," written in 1921, stresses the importance of choosing words carefully. He quotes from *The Literary Mind and the Carving of Dragons* (Liu Xie, *Wenxin diaolong*, completed before 502 A.D.):

> Words form sentences; sentences form paragraphs; paragraphs form complete compositions. A good literary piece depends on the faultlessness of each paragraph; the clarity of the paragraph depends on the faultlessness of each sentence; and the purity of the sentence depends on a precise choice of words.

Mao Dun proposes that "zi bu wang" (precise wording) should be the motto not only for creative writers, but also for translators.[13] The importance of searching for the right words when introducing foreign theories into China

---

12. James Strachey, ed., *TCPWOSF*, Vol. 15, pp. 230-231.
13. Shen Yanbing, "Yi wenxueshu fangfa de taolun," in *Xiaoshuo yuebao*, Vol. 12, No. 4, 1921, p. 2.

was also highlighted by Qu Qiubai, a founder of the Chinese Communist Party, in a 1931 letter to Lu Xun: "The function of translation, in addition to introducing the contents in the original texts to Chinese readers, has an important role, that is, to help us create a modern Chinese vocabulary."[14] Although Chinese intellectuals learned from the West and Japan in their attempt to enrich modern Chinese written language, they rendered their own independent judgments and created a Chinese psychological vocabulary.

A wide variety of translations were tried for every major Freudian term, thereby creating problems of consistency. Needless to say, in expressing one's own ideas, it is suitable and preferable to diversify one's language, but in translation, because each word has its own distinct function, another word, even a synonym, may be different in semantic color and range. It was no easy matter, indeed, for translators to reach general agreement about the translation of Freudian terms. Some serious-minded translators were aware that multiple styles of translation could create confusion. They discussed this issue earnestly in an attempt to achieve relatively precise Chinese terms for Freudian concepts. Erich Fromm has proposed, "If we grasp the meaning of a word in all its ramifications and connotations, then we can often better understand certain problems that are circumscribed by that word."[15] I shall illustrate the difficulties of this task by examining the various translations of several key Freudian terms: "psychoanalysis," "the unconscious," "sexuality," "the Oedipus complex," and "hysteria."

(a) "Psychoanalysis": The commonly accepted term was "jingshen fenxi"; less common was "xinli fenxi." Both of these terms were borrowed from the Japanese. ("Fenxi" is roughly equivalent to the general-purpose English term "analysis.") It appears that "jingshen" stemmed from the term "psychiatry" [jingshenbingxue] rather than "psychology" [xinlixue]. Nevertheless, people tended to use "xinli fenxi" and "jingshen fenxi" interchangeably. Some psychologists also made no distinction between the two terms; indeed, Zhang Yaoxiang has pointed out that psychoanalysis was called "xinli fenxi" and "jingshen fenxi" interchangeably.[16] This conflation was quite widespread. For instance, in his introduction to psychoanalysis,

---

14. Qu Qiubai, "Guanyu fanyi" (December 5, 1931), in *Essays on the Study of Translation 1894-1948*, p. 216.

15. Erich Fromm, *For the Love of Life* (New York: The Free Press, 1986), translated by Robert and Rita Kimber, p. 1.

16. Zhang Yaoxiang, "The Schools of Psychology" [Xinlixue de paibie, 1945], in *Essays on Psychology* [Xinlixue wenji] (Shanghai: Renmin, 1983), p. 169.

Ye Qing said that the two terms had the same meaning.[17] When the terms were differentiated, however, the choice between "jingshen fenxi" and "xinli fenxi" corresponded to a preference either to treat psychoanalysis as a study concentrating on abnormal psychology or to treat it as a study of mental processes in general, including normal ones. In Chinese book catalogs, psychoanalysis was always listed under the heading "abnormal psychology" [biantai xinlixue], and by 1948, most of the English-Chinese dictionaries listed "psychoanalysis" as "jingshen fenxi," thus confirming the position of psychoanalysis as a specialized field of science.

(b) "The unconscious": One of the essential concepts in Freudian theory is the theory of the unconscious. Freud himself carefully separated the term "unconscious" from "preconscious" and "subconscious." He attempted to give a very broad meaning to the word "unconscious" and confined "preconscious" to a small part of the unconscious. Freud refused to use the term "subconscious" because it suggested a level right below the conscious, which therefore could be called to consciousness very easily. Given the Freudian meaning of the word "unconscious," it was indeed very difficult to find a Chinese equivalent for a term so significant and yet so general. The Japanese way of translating the term was "muishiki" [無意識], which means, in Chinese, "without consciousness or non-conscious," an erroneous way of understanding the Freudian concept of the unconscious.

Chinese translators debated about whether to use the Japanese coined-word "muishiki" or to create a new term. There were several Chinese translations for the Freudian term "the unconscious": 1) "qian shi" 潛識 , "yin shi" 隱識 , "yin ji" 隱機 , "qian yishi" 潛意識 ; 2) "xia yishi" 下意識 ; 3) "wu yishi" 無意識 , "bu qi yi shi de" 不起意識的 . The three groups refer to the unconscious, the subconscious, and nonconsciousness, respectively. Some writers pointed out that "wu yishi" (nonconsciousness) originated from Buddhism and had a special connotation of "Manovijnana," the level at which the awareness of self originates and creates evil karma.[18] The word "qian" in "qian yishi" is metaphorical and has a double meaning of "hidden, latent" and "submerged."

Zhu Guangqian initiated discussions specifically about the unconscious in 1921. He says that the English term "unconscious," the German term "das Unbewusste," and the French term "inconscient" can

---

17. Ye Qing, "Jingshen fenxi pai xinlixue pipan," p. 28.
18. Zhang Dongsun, *ABCs of Psychoanalysis* (Shanghai: Shijie, 1929), p. 4. The definition of the Sanskrit word "manovijnana" is taken from *A Dictionary of Buddhist Terms and Concepts* (Tokyo: Nichiren Shoshu International Center, 1983), p. 257.

easily be misunderstood. Each has one meaning in daily usage and another in Freudian psychoanalysis. He thinks that "yin ji" is an ambiguous term for the unconscious, which cannot reflect Freud's intention because instinct and impulse also belong to "yin ji." Freud's use of "unconscious" is different from "nonconsciousness." Zhu cites an example to show this difference: walking may be an act of nonconsciousness, but talking in one's sleep is an act of the unconscious. He suggests that it is better to use "qian-" (submerged) or "yin-" (hidden) "yishi" than to use the ready-made Japanese term "muishiki."[19] Zhu points out that the unconscious, which originates in childhood, is not directly accessible to consciousness or directly empirically describable. In adult society, human beings have to repress their childhood desires, and the unconscious is what has been repressed. Freud shows that almost nobody knows what lies beyond consciousness. People can only infer what is there by observing dreams, slips of speech and writing, and psychopathological behavior. Qian Zhongshu, who understands the concept of the unconscious very well, also seems to presume that psychoanalytic terms are only indirectly referential. However, he argues that many ideological systems are actually built upon metaphors, such as "zhong" [middle, center] as in "zhongyong" [the Confucian concept of equilibrium], and "qian" [submerge] as in "qian yishi"--the term he uses to represent the "unconscious."[20] In keeping with these understandings, most articles about the unconscious introduce the concept of censorship as a metaphor: the censor is described as a guard standing between the unconscious and consciousness and sifting through the elements pressing from the unconscious toward consciousness. Freudian theory seems more accessible when couched in metaphors and images rather than clinical language.

Although "qian yishi" may seem to be the best term in Chinese for the Freudian concept of the unconscious, the debate for the proper translation of the Freudian term "the unconscious" continues well into 1980s, and people tend to repeat the same questions asked and explored over fifty years ago.

(c) "Sexuality": The general Chinese translation, "xing," followed the Japanese term: "seiyoku" 性慾 . Some Chinese intellectuals disagreed with this adaptation. They argued that Confucius said that hunger and sex were both "xing," that is, that hunger and sex were both human instinctual

---

19. Zhu Guangqian, "Fuluode de qianyishi yu xinli fenxi," pp. 50-51.

20. Qian Zhongshu, "On going home" [Shuo hui jia], in *Guancha*, Vol. 2, No. 1, March 1, 1947.

desires.[21] It was not precise, contended one writer, to use "xing" to describe sex alone. He proposed "seyu" for sexuality and "shiyu" for hunger, so as to separate the two desires. The force of habit has overcome literary precision, however, and "xingyu," a term from Japan, remains standard in Chinese terminology today.

(d) "The Oedipus complex": The Japanese for "Oedipus complex"--"edeipusu konpusitukusu" or 親母復合 . This was incomprehensible in Chinese unless explained in a footnote; the Japanese term 親母復合 is not a permissible phrase in Chinese. Here, therefore, the Chinese translation was not influenced by the Japanese one. A common practice in Chinese translation at that time was to give a full transliteration to a foreign noun in translation. Sometimes, if a foreign term was a compound one--a combination of a name and another noun--it was translated as half transliteration and half paraphrastic translation. So the name "Oedipus" was transliterated, whereas "complex" was translated as "qing jie" (the emotional knot), "nian cong" (the thought cluster), "qing yi zong" (the emotion-idea complex), and so on. All these translations of "Oedipus complex" are fairly euphemistic, except one, "luanlun de cuozong" (incestuous complex), which appeared in a translation of W. Fritche's critique of Freudianism.[22]

(e) "Hysteria": There are two Chinese translations of this term: "xiesidili zheng" (a transliteration) or "yi bing" (from an old term for a broad category of mental disease or attack, including some symptoms characteristic of epilepsy). Several articles introduced Freud's theory of hysteria, but some omitted the vital part of the Freudian theory about the origin of hysteria in women. Freud held that hysteria was the result of a fixation on infantile sexuality, shaped particularly by the castration complex and penis-envy. In the Chinese introductions, all such discussions were omitted. For instance, in an article, "Freudian Psychoanalysis and the Issue of Sexuality," published in the column "Women and Family" in *Dongfang zazhi* in 1936, the author concentrates on the conflict between social pressure and human instinct to suggest the cause of hysteria, a species of neurosis:

> In modern times, the main obstacle to human instincts is the social system itself. Social property is in the hands of a handful of people.

---

21. Xie Xunchu, "Shi se xing hu fei xing hu," in *Education* [Jiaoyu jie], Vol. 1, No. 3, March 15, 1931, p. 54.

22. Zhou Qiying, trans., W. Fritche, "Freudianism and Marxism," in *Literary Monthly*, Vol. 1, No. 1, June 10, 1932.

46

In order to preserve their own privileges, these people have created all kinds of religious doctrines and moral rules, so as to dominate the masses. Those who believe in such social confinements have to model their behavior according to social expectations, but at the same time, their biological instincts cry for satisfaction and fulfillment. When the conflict between the two reaches a certain point, neurosis occurs. Such a situation is particularly common among us women.[23]

The author then concludes that since women are subject to greater social pressure than men, it is easier for women to become neurotic. She argues that the Freudian theory of hysteria is worth studying, especially for women, because most women are at least slightly neurotic and the only way to cure this neurosis is to transform the society that has caused it. It seems to me that in their eagerness to promote Freudian theories, authors willfully cut the materials and arranged them to be politically and socially acceptable. But focusing on the social causes of hysteria does, in fact, transform Freud's original idea, which concentrates on the individual's sexuality. The selections from Freudian theories and their revisions usually arose from practical needs and political demands, as this example demonstrates.

In the process of searching for the right words, Chinese intellectuals were forced to grapple with many of the complexities of Freud's theory. Indeed, the choices made by Freud's interpreters and translators in China had important consequences for the reception of his work.

2.2 Freud's Chinese Translators

Most of the translators of Freud's books were not trained as professional psychologists. For example, Zhang Shizhao was a writer whose diverse activities ranged from advocating revolution and composing romantic poems to serving as an official in the government. His translation of Freud's *Selbstdarstellung* was the only translated book he published. Gao Juefu, who translated two books by Freud, received a bachelor's degree in education, worked as an editor in the Translation Bureau [Yiwen guan], and later taught the history of psychology at various universities. Xia Fuxin was an active contributor to various literary magazines during the 1930s but then disappeared from the publication world. Zhang Jingsheng wrote *A History of Sexuality* [Xing shi] and was compelled to give up his

---

23. Yongqin, "Fuluoyide de jingshen fenxi yu xing wenti," in *Dongfang zazhi*, Vol. 33, No. 7, 1936, p. 252.

university professorship because of his deep involvement with his young female students. Each had a special way of translating Freudian works, and each had a different goal in his translation: Zhang Shizhao wanted to popularize Freud and psychoanalysis in China; Gao intended to maintain a critical stance toward Freud; Xia favored the Freudian theory of mass psychology; and Zhang Jingsheng saw psychoanalysis as a source of sexual enlightenment for the Chinese audience. Their translations sometimes revealed much about themselves, contrary to their claims of objectivity. As strenuous adaptations of the Freudian texts into Chinese, their works present interesting distortions and transferences which deserve a close reading and analysis.

Qian Zhongshu, a leading contemporary literary scholar, once used a Buddhist concept to describe the essence of translation. "Hua" means to dissolve and absorb foreign elements--in this case, ideas--in order to make them communicable to people of a different culture.[24] In the process of "hua"--in choosing the proper or suitable style for the original work--however, translators inevitably express their own outlooks by their very choices of words and style. Zhang Shizhao's translation of Freud's *Selbstdarstellung*, Gao Juefu's translation of Freud's *Introductory Lectures on Psychoanalysis* and Zhang Jingsheng's translation of *The Interpretation of Dreams* provide such revelations.

Zhang Shizhao was well equipped to serve as a translator of Freud, at least as regards his linguistic ability. He frequently travelled to Europe and was fluent in German, English, and Japanese. In his translation of Freud, there are few mistakes resulting from the translator's linguistic misunderstanding of the original text.[25] However, Zhang acknowledges the difficulty in the process of translation: "Given that Freud's books are even hard to translate into English, any attempt at translating his works into Chinese poses a real problem because of the linguistic and cultural barriers."[26]

Zhang's principles of translation make him the most fascinating of the five translators. Displaying the pride of the Chinese literati, he did not employ many of the coinages which were created by the Japanese, although

---

24. Qian Zhongshu, *Four Old Essays* [Jiu wen si pian] (Shanghai: Shanghai guji chubanshe, 1979), pp. 62-63.

25. The one exception is a passage where Freud talked about how he was unable to publish his papers on cocaine because he was busy with the preparation for his marriage: he "bore his fiancée no grudge for the interruption." The Chinese translation reads that Freud "particularly" resented his wife.

26. Zhang, p. 2.

he was well versed in Japanese. He attempted to incorporate into classical "ancient style" Chinese [gu wen] the concepts and categories of psychoanalysis.

In translating Freud's work, Zhang had to create a new terminology for Freudian terms or give new meanings to already existing phrases in Chinese. He used two main devices to naturalize the text in Chinese: traditional Chinese imagery, and references to Chinese culture--to classic Chinese legends and idioms and to the sayings of famous people in Chinese history. As a result, new dimensions of the text emerged. In Zhang's painstaking reproduction of Freud's autobiography, Freud became a Chinese scholar, conversant in Chinese classic literature and history. The historical and national character of Freud's writing was eradicated, or at least deeply muffled.

Zhang's linguistic changes are, however, not errors but creative revisions. His figurative language sometimes helps to explicate the Freudian terms. For instance, the Freudian theory of repression (Theorie der Verdrängung) is translated as "xue cang shuo," which literally means:"hole-hide-theory." This is a free translation of the term, but it grasps the essence of Freud's theory of repression: what is repressed is hidden in a hole.[27] This metaphor, since it uses a conscious act to represent an unconscious one, risks being misleading; but the evocation of the familiar is a clever way of bringing new knowledge to people. In general, Zhang consistently uses references to the Chinese past and to Chinese legends to substitute for Freud's words. He turns Freud's fairly straightforward terms into more allusive and figurative terms in Chinese. Very seldom does Zhang use similes, but he makes lavish use of metaphors.

Freud's use of a Latin term,"coitus interruptus," simply remains untranslated in the English version.[28] Translations from German into English, from one alphabetic language into another, can borrow terms from the original. But a translation from German into Chinese, unless intended solely for an academic audience, cannot have that advantage. Zhang has to create new terms. Nevertheless, he has an ingenious way of getting around this problem. He borrows a term from the oldest book in China, the

---

27. Some might object to this translation on the grounds that when a person hides something in a hole it stays there without further effort by the hider. But "Verdrängung" and "repression" have a strong connotation of pressure, of tension, as if one is holding an inflated ball underwater. Without constant expenditure of energy the ball will emerge, and it is always trying to sneak out sideways.

28. Freud, "An Autobiographical Study," in James Strachey, ed., *TCPWOSF*, Vol. 21, p. 25.

Shijing (The Book of Poetry), Book 4, "The Odes of Yong," to suggest the sexual action: "zhonggou," a term which shares both the classical status of the Latin phrase and its meaning.

Here are a few more examples I have selected and traced of Zhang's use of classical Chinese reference to replace Freud:

1. Kompromiß (compromise)--Zhang thinks that the generally accepted Chinese term "tuoxie" has been abused and is often given a derogatory meaning. He therefore translates "compromise" anew with a reference to an ancient story: "the way of Qiuzi." [Qiuzi zhi dao]. According to *Han Shu* (Ban Gu, 32-92 A.D.), Qiuzi was a small kingdom in Xiyu. In order to survive among the stronger nations, it adopted a policy of appeasement both toward the Han Dynasty and toward the neighboring countries. Zhang uses this historical reference to show that when the repressed can not find an outlet, it then refines itself and takes a different form.

2. Traumentstellung (dream-distortion): Zhang translates Freud's theory of distortion , which occurs in dreams, as "meng ji." This originates from the *Zhou li* (before 221 B.C.) and means "strange dreams." Zhang intends to show that distortion occurs when the unconscious meets censorship and the repressed presents itself in a disguised form.

3. Komplex (complex): Zhang translates "complex" as "zarou," which refers to a mixture of many different things. "Zarou" appeared first in the *Guoyu* and was used in poems by Qu Yuan (340-278 B.C.): "Fragrance and odors mingle in confusion," which, according to Zhu Xi, means "the good and the bad are mixed together, but the fine quality remains undamaged."[29]

4. "Paranoia": Zhang gives this term a Chinese equivalent: "huaxu kuang." The term originated from the *Lie zi/Huang Di* (of uncertain authorship and time of publication, perhaps written between 304 and 439 A.D.). Huang Di, a legendary emperor, has a daydream in which he tours the kingdom of Huaxu shi. Huaxu shi is thousands of miles away from Huang Di's residence. He cannot possibly reach it in a day. "Huaxu" later came to refer to dreamland itself. Building on this reference, Zhang explains "paranoia" this way: a person of "huaxu kuang" is often very egocentric, proud of himself, and apt to imagine all kinds of preposterous situations in which he plays the central part. According to Zhang, the Japanese term for "paranoia" is 榮 華 狂 , which means an obsession with wealth and fame, a term more explicit, unambiguous, and narrow than his own substitute,

29. Zhu Xi, ed., *Chu ci* (Hong Kong: Zhonghua shuju, 1972), p. 10.

"huaxu kuang."[30] Zhang also uses "huaxu" as a verb: "huaxu hua," a Westernized way of adding a suffix to a noun to turn it into a verb. (No wonder Hu Shi once said that Zhang's style had a touch of "Europeanization."[31]) Regardless of Zhang's ingenuity of translation, to translate "paranoia" as an obsession for wealth and fame represents at best a partial picture of Freud's meaning of "paranoia." By definition, "paranoia" also includes delusions of persecution, excessive suspicion, and distrust of others. "Huaxu kuang" can reflect only one symptom of the paranoid psychopathology: a delusion of grandeur.

The net effect of Zhang's use of classic references to replace Freud's terminology is that the Chinese translation dignifies the Freudian text in Chinese eyes. Freud's clinical language, especially the technical terms, are replaced by Chinese historical and cultural references. Zhang's metaphors and allusions were indeed culturally determined and limited to his own culture. It is hard to imagine that when Freud parted with Breuer, they cupped their hands before their chests [gong shou er bie], a classical Chinese ceremonious gesture of departure, and cut off the straw mat [ge xi er qu]. But that is the image of Freud created in Zhang's text. It would be impossible to translate Zhang's text back into the original German because the relationship between content and language is quite different in the original and the translation. This "I" in Chinese and that "I" in German are not identical, although they both signify the very person of Sigmund Freud.

Raymond Williams states that language is the "constitutive element of material social practice," rather than simply a medium of human communication.[32] Translation, a linguistic activity, also can serve to convey and reflect the social values of the translators. Zhang's translation is imbued with his social and ethical outlook, which is manifested in his use of moral language in the translation. Through his careful choice of words, his social views are revealed. For instance, Zhang's translation of "homosexual" as "tongxing jian" shows his aversion for homosexuality because the Chinese word "jian," which implies "rape or illicit sex," is loaded with moral judgment. He also seems to take pleasure in his translation of "perverse" as "gou bian jia." In this phrase, instead of using

---

30. Zhang, p. 40. I can find no Enligh-Japanese dictionary which translates "paranoia" using the same characters as "huaxu kuang." If it existed at all in Japanese, this can at most have been a very uncommon translation.

31. Chen Jingzhi, *Resistance to the New Literary Movement* [Xin wenxue de zuli] (Taibei: Chengwen chubanshe, 1970), p. 145.

32. Raymond Williams, *Marxism and Literature* (London: Oxford University Press, 1978), p. 165.

the common word "zhe" to indicate "person," he uses the word for "master"--"jia"--to refer to somebody who is considered sexually perverse. He thereby suggests that being sexually perverse is better than being homosexual. This is Zhang's view, certainly not Freud's. By foisting his own value-laden language upon Freud, Zhang turns Freud's self-portrait into a self-portrait of Zhang himself.

As we know, the so-called precise or literal translation can never be what it claims, for translation is not simply an act of decoding. Zhang's translation aims at producing a work of high style, and if necessary he does not hesitate to alter or cut the full meaning from the original text. His changes, however, are usually made to aestheticize and acculturate Freud's account, but in this process Freud is transformed.

One might wonder why Zhang did not attempt to translate Freud into vernacular Chinese ("baihua wen"), since he made his translation at the time when the baihua movement had already become popular. Zhang Shizhao was affiliated with a very definite stylistic school, the Tongcheng school, which, in the tradition of the "Old Style" movements of the Tang and Song dynasties looked back to the philosophers of the Zhou dynasty for stylistic models. Zhang's writing style is abstruse and elegant, and his philosophy of style calls for the maximum use of ancient Chinese thought in rendering Freud's concepts. For instance, the concept of "yin-yang," which usually refers to a binary unity, replaces "normal sexuality" in his translation.

Like Kang Youwei, another member of the Tongcheng School, Zhang believes what he advocates is not the adoption of the new civilization of the West, but rather the realization of the ancient and genuine teachings of Confucius. Zhang's translation style resembles that of Yan Fu (1853-1920), who was the first Chinese authority on modern Western thought. In translations by members of the Tongcheng School, works by Spencer, Huxley, Mill, and Freud are converted into Chinese of the most classical style. Zhang, in keeping with this practice, feels that any thought that can be expressed in the classical style is ipso facto as valuable as are the Chinese classical works themselves; even if members of the Tongcheng School cannot make their translations as valuable as the Chinese classical works, at least they have tried to do so.

Notwithstanding the labor that he expended to achieve an elegant style, it is somewhat doubtful whether Zhang's translation served to popularize Freudian theory, because educated people were few at that time and barely literate people could not easily appreciate his style. Nevertheless, among intellectuals his work was hailed as an interesting piece, and it was singled out for special mention by a contemporary writer.[33]

It is well known that China traditionally thought of itself as the center of the world and of the Westerners as "barbarians." Yet as Western thought infiltrated China, the old China faced the loss of its cultural heritage. Zhang's translation was a valuable attempt to preserve Chinese classical language and culture while assimilating Western ideas.

Often, Chinese translations were second or third translations. Freud's works, for example, might be first translated from German into English and then into Japanese and then into Chinese, or they might be translated directly from German. In judging a translated work, one must ask whether a direct translation of the original work is always better than a second translation. Lu Xun holds that a direct translation may not necessarily be better than the second translation if the direct translation is poorly done. He argues that it is easier to do a second translation than to do the original, because the second translation does not have to take the style of the original work into consideration and because the difficult and obscure points in the original work have usually been given explanations in the first translation.[34]

During the same month that Zhang's book appeared, October 1930, another translation of Freud's work became available in Shanghai from the same publisher, the Commercial Press. Freud's *Introductory Lectures on Psychoanalysis* was translated into Chinese by Gao Juefu. Freud's book consisted of twenty-eight lectures delivered at the University of Vienna in two winter sessions in 1915 and 1917. In his lectures Freud discussed three aspects of psychoanalysis: the psychology of parapraxes, dreams, and the general theory of the neuroses. Ernest Jones claimed that Freud's lectures had filled a gap in the literature of psychoanalysis and helped popularize the study of psychoanalysis: "In the future we can unhesitatingly deal with the question so often asked, and say, 'this is the book with which to begin a study of psycho-analysis.'"[35]

Gao Juefu states that his translation of the lectures has been taken from Joan Riviere's English translation.[36] Although some recent scholars

33. Jingquhouren, *Shu yan lie qi lu* (Taiwan: Shuiniu chubanshe, 1966), p. 36.

34. Lu Xun, "On Retranslation" [Lun chong yi] in *The Complete Works of Lu Xun* [Lu Xun quan ji], Vol. 5, p. 504.

35. Ernest Jones, "Preface to English Edition," Freud, *A General Introduction to Psychoanalysis* (New York: Liveright Publishing Corporation, 1920), p. 9.

36. Gao Juefu, trans., Sigmund Freud, *Introductory Lectures on Psychoanalysis* [Jingshen fenxi yin lun] (Shanghai: The Commercial Press, 1930) pp. 42-43.

have complained that the English translations of Freud's writings are seriously defective, most of the English translations completed in Freud's lifetime were authorized by Freud, including Riviere's translation.[37] Gao conscientiously reproduces the English version of Freud's work. If there are words that do not seem very precise in his translation, he provides the English words in parentheses, for instance, "yizhi zuoyong (displacement),"[38] "jiyi de quexian huo yiwang (the memory gaps or amnesias),"[39] and "jiaoji de meng ("impatience" dreams)."[40] He does not risk confusing his readers by making up words that have no previous reference. Such conscientious translation was very rare during the 1920s and 1930s. A cautious translator, Gao does not translate the names of persons and places and other special terms. For example, the English phrase "Wallenstein where Schiller lived" becomes "'Schiller' suo zhu de 'Wallenstein.'"[41] He also carefully preserves the German words in the English translation, especially when Freud uses a linguistic example. But because languages are closely connected with their cultures, a pun in German may induce laughter from a German but seem tasteless to a Chinese (and of course, vice versa). Another language may seem inadequate when it comes to retelling the difference between "ruckhaltslos and ruchgratslos."[42] Hence, there are situations in which Gao cannot follow the English translation at all in its linguistic invention and has to turn to examples that are easily understood in his mother tongue. When it is difficult to illustrate Freud's points in Chinese, Gao invokes Chinese examples. For example, Freud illustrates a speech error of transposition in this way: "In the typical Spoonerism the position of certain letters is interchanged, as when the preacher said: 'How often do we feel a half-warmed fish within us.'"[43] This is hard to convey in Chinese, so the English joke is put there untranslated and Gao adds a note: "The Chinese language is not alphabetic, and therefore can not have examples like this."[44] (Spoken Chinese allows Spoonerisms, of course, but in written Chinese they lose all plausibility.) In cases where a

---

37. Bruno Bettelheim, *Freud and Man's Soul* (New York: Alfred A. Knopf, 1983), p. iii.

38. Gao, Vol. 2, p. 13.

39. Gao, Vol. 3, p. 46.

40. Gao, Vol. 2, p. 59.

41. Gao, Vol. 1, p. 25.

42. Gao, Vol. 1, p. 54.

43. Riviere, trans., Sigmund Freud, *A General Introduction to Psychoanalysis* (New York: Liveright Publishing Corporation, 1920), p. 31.

44. Gao, Vol. 1, p. 20.

literal translation is awkward and meaningless, Gao omits English examples. For instance: "It is a case of anticipation, if anyone says: 'the thought lies heartily...' instead of 'The thought lies heavily on my heart.'"[45] In its place, Zhang gave a Chinese example to show a similar case of anticipation in the speech error: "A man meant to say that he was encouraged to love someone, but actually said that he was loved."[46] This was a good linguistic adaptation, since the communication of a literal translation was impossible. He reproduced the spirit instead of the letter of Freud's text here. In contrast to Zhang Shizhao's translation, Gao's translation was distant and clinical. Yet its lucidity made Freud's basic concepts easily comprehensible by the general Chinese audience.

Just as Ernest Jones claimed in his preface, Freud popularized psychoanalysis by this work, and Gao's translation served to spread Freudian theory in China. His translation was printed three times and was placed in the Wanyou wenku, a book collection of world masterpieces. Encouraged by the reception of the book, Gao went on to translate another book by Freud, *New Introductory Lectures on Psychoanalysis*.

During the early twentieth century, it was a common practice for Chinese translators to abbreviate and edit the original texts and then present them as complete translations. Zhang Jingsheng's translation of Freud's *The Interpretation of Dreams* is a case in point. Highly selective--condensing Freud's thick book of over six hundred pages into fifty-two pages--Zhang's translation simplifies the original book. It is, however, as a Chinese saying explains, "a small sparrow which has all the necessary parts" in that the translation contains the essential ideas of Freud's book. It is difficult to ascertain from which language Zhang translated the book, but clearly it is not from German into Chinese, because Zhang occasionally leaves German words untranslated in the text. Zhang's translation is intended for common readers, and therefore it assumes a casual narrative. Freud in Zhang's translation becomes a story-teller, whose narrative strategy is to stop at the climax before a new section. Hence the ends of sections recall the format of traditional Chinese novels, all but quoting the familiar storytellers' formula, "If you want to know what happened next, please read the next chapter." A raconteur first-person narrator, meant to represent Freud, carries us through his case studies and analysis of dreamwork. As Freud's "libido" becomes the charming "force of

---

45. Joan Riviere, trans., p. 31.
46. Gao, Vol. 1, p. 20.

the heart and the spirit" [xin ling li], this storyteller captivates the hearts of the readers.

2.3 Conclusion

Few people would deny the importance of translation, but ironically, translation has always been held in low esteem. This undervaluation stems from the belief that somehow translation is inferior to creation: that translation simply substitutes words in one language for words in another by way of decoding. Although it is true that a chief concern of translation is linguistic clarity, the textual analysis necessarily for competent translation is very much like that required for literary creation. In creative writing, the writer has to turn his imagination and his experience into written form. Translators face a more complicated situation: they have to mediate between two or more languages, while at the same time they try to keep in control their own independent ideas. The relationship between an original work and its translation is like that of Freudian transference: a translation substitutes for the original text and assumes its authority in a different cultural context.

Such was the situation when Freud's works were translated in China. Translators shouldered a major task in introducing Freudian theory into China, and most of the critical articles published were based on translated materials. On the one hand, Chinese readers' dependence on abridged texts and criticisms of Freudian theory and on secondhand instead of firsthand materials created some misconceptions about Freudian theories. On the other hand, we see that it is only through the selections and revisions of Freudian theory, the inevitable first steps in the act of interpretation, that Freud was made palatable to Chinese audiences. We may say that due to metaphorical resistance and transference, Freudian theory came to China in a form distorted much as Freud described the distortion in the dreamwork:

> Its component parts become condensed, its psychical emphasis becomes displaced, and the whole of it is translated into visual images or dramatized, and completed by a deceptive secondary revision.[47]

47.　Freud, "An Autobiographical Study," in *TCPWOSF*,　Vol. 20, p. 45.

However, a translation assures the survival and the growth of the original; and through dissection, reassembly, and reinvention Freudian ideas found their growth in China.

Chapter 3

FREUDIAN THEMES

This chapter tries to capture the presence of three Freudian themes in Chinese literary scenes: the interpretation of creativity, the Oedipus complex, and the interpretation of dreams. It attends both to the traditional Chinese understandings of the phenomena for which the Freudian theories account, and to how Freudian theories have reinforced or altered these indigenous understandings. Rather than spreading thinly to address the general Chinese reception of these themes, this chapter concentrates on one major writer of 20th-century China--Lu Xun, and in each section gives some space to other writers in order to highlight certain transformations of Freudian materials in Chinese contexts.

3.1 The Symbol of Angst[1]

The search for knowledge about why people engage in creative writing and about the source of creativity itself has fascinated both Chinese and Western intellectuals throughout the centuries. People have offered numerous rational accounts of the creative process. Freud, a prolific writer himself, also takes an interest in the discussion of creativity and contributes to it. His theory of creativity, however, is far from complete, nor is it based on scientific experiments or inventories. His contribution to the

---

1. Kuriyagawa Hakuson's "kumon no shōchō" has been translated into Chinese as "kumen de xiangzheng," which maintains the Japanese words "kumon" and "shōchō." "Kumen de xiangzheng" has had several English translations: symbols of bitterness, symbols of pain, and symbols of anguish. However, I find these translations do not quite convey the meaning of the term, which is not limited to bitterness, pain and anguish. When "ku" [bitter, pain] and "men" [stifling, boredom] are put together, they represent a "modernist syndrome"--a kind of formless unrest and anxiety which is best described by the German term "Angst."

study of creativity is to reaffirm the importance of unconscious processes, especially of unconscious motivations.[2]

It is a common belief that Freud regards artists and writers as neurotics. However, there is a clear distinction in his view between artists and neurotics. Freud sees both neurotics and artists as introverts who are unable to come to grips with life and turn for satisfaction to a life of fantasy. Art, for him, is an outlet for personal frustration, a permissible way of liberating repressed contents of the unconscious. He suggests that writing brings about a reconciliation between the pleasure principle, which represents the claims of the libido, and the reality principle, which represents the influence of the outer world. This sublimation--the process of modifying instinctual impulses to conform to the demands of society--has given birth to literary creativity.

Traditional Chinese literary criticism touches upon the issue of creativity, but focuses more on motivations for creativity than on creative processes. Ideas about the process of creativity can be gleaned instead from the recorded experience of writers, which suggests that many people turn to literary writing to express their emotions, particularly thwarted emotions such as anger and frustration. For instance, as early as 770-476 B.C., the *Book of Poetry* expressed this kind of motive for writing: "I made this fine song /To express fully my restless grief," or "A gentleman made this song to express his sorrows."[3]

Modern literary criticism emerged in China with the introduction of Western psychology and aestheticism in the early twentieth century. Before the 1920s, there were critics who employed Western psychology to explain creativity and whose views were close to Freud's. For instance, Wang Guowei (1877-1927), a philosopher and a literary critic, accepted an amalgam of the philosophies of Schopenhauer, Kant, and Nietzsche as his own theoretical basis. He considered the essence of life to be "yu"(unfulfilled desire). Life is, according to him, a combination of desire and pain. Man turns to art and literature in order to get rid of the pain caused by "yu." Wang held that literature provides a release similar to that of children's games.[4] However, such views of literature were not popular

---

2. Silvano Arieti, *Creativity, the Magic Synthesis* (New York: Basic Books, 1976), p. 21.

3. James Liu, *Chinese Theories of Literature* (Chicago: University of Chicago Press, 1975), p. 68.

4. Yu Min, "A Brief Account of Ancient Chinese Aestheticians" [Zhonguo gudai meixue sixiangjia juyao], in *Meixue xiangdao* (Beijing: Peking University Press, 1982), p. 132.

before the end of the teens. Beginning in the 1920s, the Freudian theory of creativity gained currency among many intellectuals. Writers such as Zhu Guangqian, one of the founders of modern Chinese aesthetics, began to explore the relationship between creativity and the unconscious. He strongly supported the Freudian theory of sublimation.[5] Pan Guangdan, a psychologist, stated in his preface to the translation of Ellis' *Theory of Sexuality* that Freud's explanation for creativity was reasonable. Pan enthusiastically suggested that such a theory offered literary critics a new angle for their observation, interpretation, and analysis of literature.[6]

As I have stated in the previous chapters, many writers during the era I am discussing were able to read foreign languages and therefore had direct access to Freudian theory without the help of translation. Nevertheless, translation did help Freudian theory reach a broader audience. With the translation of Freud's works, the basic concepts of Freud's theory pertaining to creativity--the dream work, resistance and repression, anxiety, the libido theory and narcissism, transference and so on--became readily available to the Chinese audience.

A number of secondhand sources in the form of translated works discussed literary creativity in light of Freudian theory. Of all the books and articles related to the issue of creativity, Kuriyagawa Hakuson's *The Symbol of Angst* (kumon no shōchō) received particular attention. *The Symbol of Angst* serves as a good example of the kind of transformations Freudian theory underwent, and an analysis of the reception of *The Symbol of Angst* in China can reveal much about Chinese reactions to the Freudian theory of creativity.

Kuriyagawa Hakuson was a professor of Western literature and a literary critic in Kyoto. He died during the earthquake in 1923. Although Kuriyagawa was not at all well-known in his own country even after his death, many of his works were translated into Chinese and, as a result, he became one of the Japanese literary critics best known in China at that time. His unfinished book, *The Symbol of Angst*, had three translations into Chinese--one by Lu Xun for the Beixin Bookstore, reprinted five times; another by Feng Zikai for the Literary Association series; the third by Mingchuan for *Study Lamp* [Xue deng] as early as in January, 1921.[7]

---

5.   Zhu Guangqian, "Freudian Theory of the Unsonscious and Psychanalysis," pp. 46-47.

6.   Pan Guangdan, *An Analysis of Xiao Qing* [Xiaoqing zhi fenxi] (Shanghai: Xinyue, 1927), p. 21.

7.   Bonnie S. McDougall, *The Introduction of Western Literary Theories into Modern China 1919-1925* (Tokyo: Center for East Asian Cultural Studies, 1971), p. 108.

In his preface to Kuriyagawa's book, Lu Xun evaluates the book in the following words:

> The author, basing his theory on the Bergsonian philosophy, explains the source of human life in terms of Elan Vital (Vital Impetus), and finds in sciences, such as Freudian theory, the power of this life force to explain literature and art. But his theory is also somewhat different from those old theories--Bergson thinks that the future is unpredictable, whereas Hakuson regards poets as prophets; Freud attributes the life-force to sexuality, whereas Hakuson stresses impetus and leaping force [tujin he tiaoyue] of life. Among contemporary books of the same kind, his essay differs from the reckless assertions of certain scientists and irksome metaphysical discussions by some philosophers. The book is also devoid of the tediousness of ordinary literary critics. Hakuson has original ideas and therefore this book has become a creation itself, which carries a deep understanding of literature.[8]

In retrospect, Lu Xun's evaluation may be more favorable than the book deserves, but it shows that he indeed wished to accept Kuriyagawa's viewpoint. Kuriyagawa's book largely echoed Western theories prevalent during his day; and as Bonnie S. McDougall observes, Japanese literary criticism of that period was itself partly derived from the Anglo-American tradition.[9]

In *The Symbol of Angst*, Kuriyagawa discusses the origins of creativity, the act of literary appreciation, and other issues related to literature. The first two parts of the book were published while he was alive and can be taken as relatively complete in representing his ideas. I shall focus on the first part, his discussion of creativity.

Freud's notion of creativity derives from his libido theory. Kuriyagawa, however, gives creativity a strongly romantic interpretation. He adopts the theory of "shengming li" (life force or Vital Impetus) from the writings of Henri Bergson, Arthur Schopenhauer, Friedrich Nietzsche, and George Bernard Shaw. He borrows Bergson's metaphor of the steam engine to describe the concept. The force of the steam, which has the potential to explode and wreak destruction, is enclosed in the engine. The

---

8.   Lu Xun, *The Complete Works of Lu Xun* (Shanghai: The Memorial Committee of Lu Xun, 1938), Vol. 13, pp. 18-19.

9.   McDougall, p. 251.

steam machine controls the force and yet relies upon this force to operate the whole machine. The nature of steam power is like the life force, which only wants to dash and leap forward. Skillfully, the human machine uses this force by suppressing it. Because of this opposing force, the engine is able to move the whole machine forward. According to him, the joy of life can only be found in creative acts in which this explosive force finds a controlled expression.

Kuriyagawa emphasizes the effect of society on creative writers and holds that because capitalist society has destroyed the joy of work, work becomes merely a means for people to earn a living. The Elan Vital, which seeks to expend itself in leaps and bounds, is opposed by the forces of society and morality. Such conflict creates pain--the pain of living. Literature is an expression of this pure life force, temporarily freed of external pressure, whereas in life the forward-striving energy is bound by its opposing forces: "Our life is like a running stream which is held up by huge rocks, and has therefore to take the path of twists and turns."[10] Kuriyagawa is ambivalent about these social pressures and restrictions. On the one hand, the logic of his steam engine analogy suggests that the force constricting the Elan Vital (society, morality, etc.) is necessary to move humanity as a whole forward. On the other hand, the analogy also suggests that progress will be achieved only at the expense of human beings.

Kuriyagawa specifically discusses Freudian psychoanalysis, but he acknowledges that he does not know much about Freudian theory in the field of psychiatry and psychology because he is just a "layman"--not medically trained. As a literary critic, however, he holds that the current practice of Freudian literary criticism is inadequate. He thinks that Freudian criticisms are often one-sided and fail to touch the essence of literature--its aesthetic value.[11] Nevertheless, his disappointment with Western critics' application of Freudian theory to literary works does not prevent him from borrowing Freudian concepts to enrich his own critical practice. In other words, he likes Freudian theory, but feels it a pity that some Western critics do not apply it well enough. He is attracted to Freudian theory because he sees it as a natural science and believes that natural science is the solution to all human problems. He states, "This branch of psychology [psychoanalysis]

---

10. Lu Xun, p. 31.

11. Some of the Western uses of Freudian criticism he cited were: Albert Mordell, *The Erotic Motive in Literature* (which was translated into Chinese); I. H. Coriat, *The Hysteria of Lady Macbeth* ; and Wilfrid Lay, *H. G. Wells and his Mental Hinterland.*

is different from ordinary literary theories because it contains scientific system and organization. That is what I like."[12]

Using Freudian interpretation to illustrate his views, he discusses the similarity between dreams, which reveal their latent meanings only through symbols and signs, and the content of a thought or an idea which has been rendered in verbal and written forms. The development of an artistic conception into a work of art parallels the transformation of the latent content of the dream into its images. Everyone has daydreams, but only a few can turn their daydreaming into powerful writing. Kuriyagawa, like Freud, deals only with the creative writer's motivations and does not discuss in detail how the writer can turn his fantasy into a writing that will be meaningful and compelling for an audience. He has, perhaps, met the same problem that Freud has: "How the writer accomplishes this [transformation] is his innermost secret; the essential ars poetica lies in the technique of overcoming the feeling of repulsion in us which is undoubtedly connected with the barriers that rise between each single ego and the others."[13]

This creative urge perceived by Kuriyagawa is extraordinary, rare, and hard to describe without the help of literary devices. He quotes Shakespeare to characterize it:

> The poet's eye, in a fine frenzy rolling,
> Doth glance from heaven to earth, from earth to heaven;
> And, as imagination bodies forth
> The forms of things unknown, the poet's pen
> Turns them to shapes, and gives to aery nothing
> A local habitation and a name.[14]

But by this "fine frenzy" Kuriyagawa apparently does not intend to refer to the Freudian notion of sexual drives. It is, rather, a sudden vision or inspiration. Such a romantic notion finds an expression in classical Chinese essays about creativity. Liu Xie describes it in his *Literary Mind and the Carving of Dragons* : "He [the creative writer] observes past and present in a moment, /And covers the four seas in the twinkling of an eye. /He encages Heaven and Earth within Form, /And defeats the myriad things

---

12.   Lu Xun, p. 39.

13.   Freud, "The Relation of the Poet to Daydreaming," in *Delusion and Dream* (Boston: Beacon Press, 1956), p. 133.

14.   *Midsummer's Night Dream*, Act V, Sc. I, quoted in "The Symbol of Angst," *The Complete Works of Lu Xun*, Vol. 13, pp. 59-60.

at the tip of his writing brush."[15] Kuriyagawa relates this creative moment to Freudian theory; he eliminates the mystical element in the description of the creative urge and claims that this is nothing but "Schaffenstimmung" [creative mood], something emerging from the unconscious[16] but not having a specifically sexual content.

Kuriyagawa has his own motives for accepting the Freudian theory of the unconscious. His version of day-dreaming as the pattern of creativity is more like Zen's meditation than like Freud's description of disjointed thoughts and images:

> Our life can be purified and refined through daydreaming because it distances itself from real life. In daydreaming, we can gaze, meditate, criticize, and understand reality. Our life therefore can be deepened, reinforced, and enlarged. Only dreaming can sweep out the dusty ideas of real life and straighten this disordered, disunited, and muddled world into a complete, orderly, unified world. Only in this dream life can we enter a pure, peaceful state of mind and therefore reach the sublimity of Art which reflects life.[17]

Kuriyagawa clearly believes in this model with an almost religious fervor, regarding creativity as a process of purification and enlightenment. It is an idealized representation of the workings of the mind. This description discloses the reason for Kuriyagawa's interest in Freudian theory: he is seeking a remedy for the conflict between society and individuals, and Freud seems to provide a pathway to a peaceful world.

Although he believes passionately in the transcendence of creativity, Kuriyagawa does not make conventional arguments about its moral value. He believes that literature is neither moral nor immoral because it is above the "practical" world of the value system and therefore belongs to the "non-moral."[18] According to him, literature is the result of psychological conflicts:

> In the final analysis, literature originates from the fact that the free-roaming Elan Vital meets with resistance and therefore starts anguish, i.e., psychical trauma. Out of the psychical trauma come

---

15. James Liu, p. 33.
16. Lu Xun, p. 111.
17. Lu Xun, p. 115.
18. Cf. the early modernists' slogan, "Art for art's sake."

the symbolic dreams, which show the unsatisfied desires. These desires are altered and disguised to be presented to the public. Poetry is the individual's dream; myth a nation's dream.[19]

Braving the danger of over-generalized labeling, we may say that this book combines Freudian interpretation of creativity with romantic idealism and fuses Western philosophy with Eastern Buddhism. Freudian interpretation is useful to Kuriyagawa because it generates this discussion, but in fact, Freud never said that the sexual drive is the only drive that motivates human beings to be creative; he put forward a hypothesis that there exists--whether in the ego or in the id--a displaceable energy, a neutral energy that can be used to fuel a qualitatively differentiated erotic or destructive impulse. Freud even speculated that such energy proceeds from the narcissistic store of libido, and is a kind of "desexualized Eros," or in other words, a "sublimated energy."[20] William McDougall suggests that Freudian libido is an equivalent of Bergson's Elan Vital.[21]

In whichever way Freud's theory of creativity may be interpreted, it is true that Kuriyagawa's version of Freudian creativity as the product of angst became popular in China during the 1920s. There are social and historical reasons for such popularity. The country was torn by wars, famine, and natural disasters. Many returning students found that their vision of a beautiful China was destroyed. Wen Yiduo, a poet, found it "a nightmare" and a "horror." Sadly he cried out: "I've come back. With tears and blood, I burst out, 'This is not my China.' No! No!"[22] It was a difficult period both for the returned students who were adjusting to the society and for those who found no way to go after waking up from a dream.

Kuriyagawa's view of the creative power of angst, which appealed to many writers, captured a particular aspect of the Freudian theory of creativity, that is, its emphasis on psychological conflict. Although it seems now that the unconscious sources that Freudians proposed for creativity are over-simple and reductive, sixty years ago, when Freud was first introduced to China, such an idea was considered new and scientific. Writers in the twenties generally agreed that literature was a symbol of

---

19. Lu Xun, pp. 126-127.

20. Freud, *The Ego and the Id* (New York: Norton & Company, 1960), pp. 34-35.

21. Leland E. Hinsie, *Psychiatric Dictionary* (New York: Oxford University Press, 1970), p. 431.

22. Wen Yiduo, "Discovery" [Faxian], in Liu Shousong, ed., *Zhongguo xin wenxueshi chugao* (Beijing: People's Publishing House, 1979), pp. 147-148.

angst, but because the word "angst" in Chinese embodies many meanings, these writers' reactions to the Freudian notion of creativity were various.

As it would be impossible and unnecessary for me to include every discussion of the Freudian theory of creativity, I shall analyze only the reactions of Zhu Guangqian and Lu Xun, whom I consider representative. In particular, both writers participated in transforming Freud's theory of creativity into the belief that every literary work embodies and manifests angst.

Zhu Guangqian was the first Chinese to introduce in detail the Freudian theory of the unconscious to a Chinese audience.[23] He studied in the West, first in England and then in France. His dissertation, later published as *The Psychology of Tragedy: A Critical Study of Various Theories of Tragic Pleasure*, gives an account of the popular notion of vitality:

> Life is...force, energy, "drive," the "will-to-live," "elan vital" or "libido" as it has been baptized by various writers; it is this force which impels life to move on. Life is also its own goal, for regarded in its dynamic aspect, it consists in the ever-going and ever-changing act of realizing itself in willing, striving, doing, moving and all kinds of activities. The force in life urges all living beings toward the same goal of maintaining life. Life is realized in activities and the goal of life is its own self-realization in activities. Feeling is an indicator of the success or failure of life's effort in realizing itself in activities: pleasure results when that effort is unimpeded, pain results when it is thwarted.

He quite pointedly says,

> There is nothing new in this view. It has been repeated in various forms by scholars of all ages from Aristotle to Bergson, Driesch and McDougall. As it is all-embracing, so it is vague.[24]

Zhu agreed with Kuriyagawa Hakuson. In 1956, he wrote a self-criticism, "The Reactionary Aspects of My Literary Thoughts," in which he acknowledged that he had come to know Kuriyagawa's theory in

---

23. Zhu Guangqian, "Freudian Theory of the Unconscious and Psychoanalysis," in *Dongfang zazhi*, Vol. 18, No. 14. July 25, 1921.

24. Chu Kwang-tsien, *The Psychology of Tragedy: A Critical Study of Various Theories of Tragic Pleasure* (Strasbourg: Librairie Universitaire d'Alsace, 1933), p. 195.

the early 1920s. Influenced by Kuriyagawa's theory, he believed that literature was only a "symbol of angst" and that its function was to help the suffering individuals escape from reality. He recounts his version of Freud's ideas as follows: The reality principle restrains human beings from acting freely. People are not satisfied and therefore experience all kinds of pain and boredom. In order to eliminate such pain and boredom, people build palaces in the air. Angst originates from people's dissatisfaction with the "finite," whereas fantasy dramatizes people's pursuit of "infinity." The artist tries to protect himself from the transience of experience by creating in some form a concretization of his personality, thereby immortalizing his mortal life. The function of literature, for its creators and for others, is therefore to free people of the yoke of the real world so that they can find peace, however temporarily.[25] Literature, as a sublimation of unconscious wishes, produces an effect analogous to that of medicine on the body. It is "an alleviating discharge of pent-up emotions which restores the mental equilibrium."[26] Zhu's view of the Freudian theory of creativity was relatively balanced because he was able to compare it with other similar theories, and because his view was not entirely filtered through Kuriyagawa's romantic notion of creativity.

Lu Xun translated Kuriyagawa's *The Symbol of Angst* and used it as part of his school-teaching material.[27] He praised the concept of Vital Impetus and the Freudian interpretation of creation as the "tianma xing kong shi de da jingshen" [uniquely dynamic spirit]. In the early 20s, he was serious about the theory and even wrote a story that used Freudian theory to explain the origin of human creativity. "Mending the Sky" [Bu tian; original title "Buzhou shan"], his first attempt to rewrite a legend, was composed in 1922, two years before he published his translation of *The Symbol of Angst*.

"Mending the Sky" was exalted as a fine piece of literary work by an influential literary critic, Cheng Fangwu from the Literary Association.[28] The story was taken from a Chinese legend of world creation.[29] Lu Xun

---

25. Zhu Guangqian, "The Reactionary Aspects of My Literary Thoughts" [Wo de wenyi sixiang zhong de fandong fangmian], in *Wenyi bao*, June, 1956, No. 12.61

26. Zhu, *The Psychology of Tragedy*, p. 186.

27. Wang Jinyuan, "Foreign Literary Trends and the May Fourth New Literature" [Wailai wenyi sichao he wusi xin wenxue], in *Wenxue pinglun congkan*, Vol. 21, August 1984, p. 13.

28. Lu Xun, preface to "Mending the Sky," in *Lu Xun sanshi nian ji* (Hong Kong: Xinyi, 1967), p. 6.

29. The legend goes like this: After Pan Gu cracked the Cosmic Egg and stood between the two halves to form Heaven and Earth, Nü Wa, a giant goddess, toyed with some

connected the myth of the creation of the world with the Freudian theory of creativity--a rather crude version of it--to show that creation was generated particularly by sexual desires [xing de fadong]. According to Chinese mythology, the Goddess Nü Wa created the world. Lu Xun chose to start his story by making Nü Wa wake up from a dream. "She could not recall the content of her dream and only felt vexed, for there was something too scarce and something too abundant."[30] This unnameable restlessness, proceeding from the delusive unconscious, was the beginning of creativity. Lu Xun suggests that creation starts as quite unintentional play. In an almost random act, Nü Wa forms small human figures with clay. She has never before found such courage and joy in doing a job, even though she is exhausted--"breathing hard and sweating."[31] The process is rewarding: She sees, for the first time, between the heaven and the earth, a smile on the face of her own creature. The creative work tires her out completely, but she continues working. Showing the joy and pain of creation itself, the first part of the story vividly depicts the creative act as a result of boredom and a nameless agitation.

The creative process of the story is worth noting. In his preface to a collection of historical stories, Lu Xun gave an account of the creation of "Mending the Sky": he began work on the story with the serious intention of applying the Freudian theory of creativity to literature, but somehow stopped in the middle of writing and happened to read a newspaper. There he found a certain reader's letter to the paper, in which the reader pleaded "with tears" for young people to stop writing sentimental stuff like Wang Jingzhi's "Hui zhi feng" (a collection of love poems). Lu Xun found this hypocritical plea very comic. Returning to his writing, Lu Xun changed his previous objective.[32]

---

mud and chanced to fashion a little figure. The little creature, being in her own image, pleased her so much that she made many more, both men and women. Things continued in harmonious balance for many years until quite unexpectedly Gong Gong, the Water God, and Zhu Rong, the Fire God, had a falling out and went to battle against each other, shattering the tranquility of the earth. Gong Gong, after losing the battle, dashed his own head against Mount Buzhou, the Pillar of Heaven. As a result, the heavens were rent asunder, leaving an ugly gaping hole; the earth was also cracked in many places. Fires and floods ravaged the earth. Seeing her creation threatened by this holocaust, Nü Wa was deeply distressed. She gathered stones of the five hues in the rivers and lakes and melted them in a huge fire, using the molten liquid to fill the breach of heaven. (See *Chinese Literature*, Autumn 1985, pp. 209-210.)

30. Lu Xun, "Mending the Sky," in *Representative Works of Lu Xun* [Lu Xun daibiao zuo] (Shanghai: Huanqiu, 1939), p. 103.

31. Ibid., p. 104.

32. Lu Xun, *The Complete Works of Lu Xun*, Vol. 2, p. 449.

In the second part of the story, Lu Xun begins to ridicule the creatures made by Nü Wa. There is no real communication between the creator and the created. The created grow very much affected in their manner and speech as years go by. They use archaic language, whereas Nü Wa can only understand vernacular Chinese. The little creatures do not understand Nü Wa even though she has done things for their benefit. When she is collecting stones from the earth to repair the sky, these creatures sneer at her and curse her. Some grab the stones away from her; others bite her hands. They even protest against her nakedness. With the particular incident of the newspaper letter in his mind, Lu Xun adds a little gentleman wearing ancient clothes standing in between Nü Wa's legs and looking upwards. When Nü Wa catches sight of him, he quickly hands to Nü Wa an oblong board which states that nakedness is prohibited because of its resemblance to animal behavior and its disregard of li [propriety]. Lu Xun criticizes those pseudo-moralists, who on the one hand criticize immoral works in order to maintain social order and morality, but on the other hand never observe the moral rules themselves. Lu Xun also describes how people maltreat Nü Wa during her lifetime but later claim to be her only immediate descendants. This second part of the story contains a great deal of Lu Xun's characteristic satire and criticism. Lu Xun later criticized himself for transforming into flippancy his intention to use the Freudian theory of creativity in the story.[33] Yet this "flippancy" expresses pungent political criticism and brings the ancient legend into contact with the present time.

3.2 The Oedipus Complex

Through his self-analysis, which showed him his ambivalence toward his father and affection for his mother, as well as through analyzing his patients, Freud formulated his theory of the Oedipus complex--the infant's desire for the parent of the opposite sex and hatred of the rival parent. Based on his later observations he completed the idea of the Oedipus complex, which also included the infant's affectionate attitude to the parent of the same sex and the infant's corresponding jealousy and hostility towards the parent of the opposite sex. He believed that the two tendencies coexisted in dialectical relation to each other.[34]

---

33. Ibid., p. 449.
34. J. Laplanche and J.-B. Pontalis, *The Language of Psychoanalysis* (New York: Norton, 1973), pp. 283-284.

Why did Freud give such a complicated mental phenomenon the name of a figure in Greek tragedy? The association of the specific conflict of infancy with King Oedipus does not seem to correspond to any clearly formulated theoretical considerations. In his letters to his first disciples Freud more frequently used the term "Vatercomplex" than "Oedipus complex."[35] (This usage highlighted his focus on the standpoint of the son, as opposed to the other two members of the triangular relationship.) By giving the complex the name of a hero in Greek myth, Freud suggests that his theoretical edifice is deeply imbued with the Western cultural heritage. Using a literary legend to describe a universal psychic complex is bound to be controversial because the myth itself has embodied meanings other than those emphasized by Freud: for instance, the relationship between Oedipus and the Sphinx--a creator with his Muse--may suggest that Oedipus embodies the human search for knowledge.[36]

In Chinese literature, there is indeed an Oedipal story--a classic Chinese play, *At the Bend of Fen River* [Fenhe wan], also entitled *Xue Li's Return Home* [Xue Li huan jia].[37] Xue Li, or Xue Rengui, is a historical figure of the Tang Dynasty. He begins life as a poor tiller of the soil and later becomes a famous general who leaves home for the battlefield shortly before his wife gives birth to their son. The son lives with his mother alone in the mountains and, when he grows up, supports her by hunting. Eighteen years later, the father returns from war. At the Fen River, he meets a lad--his own son--shooting geese and spearing fish, and they engage in the following conversation:

> Xue (greeting the lad asks): How many geese could you bring down with one arrow?
>
> Boy: With one arrow I can bring down one goose.
>
> Xue: Why, that's nothing extraordinary! I can bring down two with a single shot.

---

35. Marthe Robert, *From Oedipus to Moses* (New York: Anchor Books, 1976), pp. 207-208.

36. See Michael J. O'Brien, *Twentieth-Century Interpretations of Oedipus Rex* (Englewood Cliffs N.J.: Prentice-Hall, 1968).

37. L. C. Arlington and Harold Acton, trans. and ed., *Famous Chinese Plays* (Beiping: Henri Vetch, 1937), pp. 217-225. This play is cited in Richard H. Solomon, *Mao's Revolution and the Chinese Political Culture* (Berkeley: University of California Press, 1971), and criticized in Leon Shaskolsky Sheleff, *Generations Apart: Adult Hostility to Youth* (New York: McGraw-Hill Book Company, 1981), pp. 37-38.

(The boy is incredulous but says he would be delighted to learn how to do it.)

Xue: Give me your bow and arrow and you shall see.

Boy: Here come the geese!

Xue: Thanks. (Aside, singing) Ah, he falls into the snare. His life is sped as swiftly as this arrow.

(He shoots; the boy falls, and is borne off by a tiger.)

Xue: I might have spared the lad, but it would never do for a soldier like me to let another live when he was so superior a marksman with the weapons I excel in.[38]

In the rivalry between the father and the son, the father wins by shooting the son. The paternal figure is presented as a powerful, treacherous, and jealous man who would do anything to prevent others--even his own son--from surpassing his powers. This passage also suggests a "father's reluctance to let the son grow to maturity; his unwillingness to be challenged by him."[39] The old man kills the young man whose marksmanship is better than his own without knowing that the boy is his own son. When he reaches his wife's house, he finds a man's shoes and becomes angry. In spite of his violence and tyranny, he is heartbroken and falls senseless as soon as he learns from his wife that the young man he has killed is his son. In the Greek tragedy, Oedipus kills his father at the crossroads when his father is on his way home. The Chinese Oedipus story also occurs when the father is on his way home, but despite the striking similarity of the setting in the two stories, the solutions are different, for in the Chinese Oedipus story it is the father who kills the son instead of the other way around. That is, instead of parricide, the Chinese Oedipal story ends in pedocide. In Freudian terms, the Chinese version focuses on the son's fear of castration by the father; the Greek version focuses on the son's murderous resentment in the face of the castration threat. In fact, in both cases, the killing is done when the people involved have no knowledge of their kinship. However, the Chinese Oedipus story is, arguably, more appropriate to the patriarchal structure of the Chinese family, in which the hierarchy does not allow for the growth of young children's individuality.

The theory of the Oedipus complex has been challenged ever since it came into being, partly because of its audacity in undermining the

---

38. Arlington and Acton, *Famous Chinese Plays*, p. 218.
39. Solomon, *Mao's Revolution and the Chinese Political Culture*, p. 35.

traditional view of the harmonious family relationship. The public grasp of his theory in those early years was frequently somewhat hazy, but the stimulus of Freudian hypotheses led to a serious reconsideration of family dynamics. Lu Xun referred to the Oedipus complex once when he was discussing the Freudian interpretation of dreams:

> He [Freud] told us that daughters usually love their fathers and sons usually love their mothers because of the attraction of the opposite sexes. But soon after a child is born, regardless of its gender, it protrudes its mouth and moves its head about. Does it want a kiss from an opposite sex? No, everyone knows it wants to eat.[40]

This paragraph is often quoted as evidence that Lu Xun opposed the Freudian theory of the Oedipus complex.[41] As we know, however, any remark should be seen in the context of its addressee, its setting, and its communicational modes (irony, sarcasm, or humor). A study of the context of Lu Xun's statement demonstrates that he was reacting to the abundance of popular stories of romance on the market at that time. "At present when people do not feel nausea about always talking about lovers and love letters, we should not find it forbidden to speak of eating as well."[42] He points out that eating, another essential aspect of human life, is neglected by writers. And if we look at the above quotation closely, we can see that the second and third sentences do not necessarily negate the first sentence; they are only observations. The period "soon after a child is born" is **before** the formation of the Oedipus complex which occurs between the ages of three and five years.[43] It seems that Lu Xun is not renouncing the Oedipus complex here but simply presenting a balanced view of two objects in human life: food and sex. We should also notice the jesting tone in his illustration "refuting" the Oedipus complex. For example, he also emphasizes the social significance of repression and criticizes Freud's

---

40. Lu Xun, "Ting shuo meng," in *The Complete Works of Lu Xun* (Beijing: People's Literature Press, 1973), Vol. 5, p. 63.

41. For instance: Bi Yan, "How 'Ting shuo meng' Criticized Freud" ["Ting shuo meng" shi zenyang piping Fuluoyide de] in *Studies on Lu Xun* [Lu Xun yanjiu] (Beijing: The Academy of Social Sciences Press, 1983), Vol. 5; Hu Shensheng and Lu Jian, "How Lu Xun Viewed the Freudian Theory" [Lu Xun shi zenyang kandai Fuluoyide xueshuo de] in *Studies on Lu Xun*, Vol. 9, 1985.

42. Lu Xun, "Ting shuo meng," p. 63.

43. Although Freud's theory of the Oedipus complex was modified by Melanie Klein, who considered that loving and hating impulses date from the early months of life (see Bice Benvenuto and Roger Kennedy, *The Works of Jacques Lacan*. New York: St. Martin's Press, 1986, p. 126), I doubt whether Lu Xun had that in mind.

bourgeois background: "Perhaps Freud has some money and is so well fed that he does not find eating a real problem. That may explain why he pays so much attention to sexuality."[44] This statement may indicate contempt for Freud's bourgeois origins, but it in no way renounces the study of sexuality, let alone that of infantile sexuality. Again, we should notice the ironical tone of the passage.

During the 1920s, it was a popular literary theme that parents did not prepare the nurtured child to seek alternative ways of living and behaving; on the contrary, they attempted to destroy the helpless child in order to prevent him/her from challenging them. Stories taking up this theme usually were written by the children, the younger generation; for instance, the average age of the May Fourth writers in the early 1920s was well under twenty-five. These writers focused on "exposing the defects on the familial system and the feudal ethical codes."[45] The same theme continued far into the 1930s and 1940s. From Ba Jin's *Family*, about a suffocating family environment which warps and destroys the younger members of the family, to Zhang Ailing's *The Golden Cangue*, in which the mother deliberately feeds her children opium to prevent them from leaving the household, this theme not only denounced patriarchal society, but also inspired a narrative mode. Of course, this quarrel with the patriarchy became possible only when the patriarchy was perceived to have weakened and become decadent.

The Freudian theory of the Oedipus complex has been used to explain the psychological origins of all conflicts between generations. Although Freud has been charged with ignoring the father's possible faults and concentrating on the guilt of the son in his Oedipus complex,[46] it is from the point of view of the sons and daughters, the new generation, that my inquiry is directed. The significance of the Oedipus complex is that it reflects the child's situation in a family triangle. In the Lacanian sense, it is produced by children's quarrel with the symbolic father, an agency that promulgates the law. The father's law is what binds people together in culture, and to break that law is to commit a crime. Hence, the consciousness of rebellion is born. Modern writings often deal with the

---

44. Lu Xun, "Ting shuo meng," p. 63.

45. Lu Xun, "Preface," in *Zhongguo xin wenxue daxi: xiaoshuo* (Shanghai: Liangyou, no date).

46. For instance, Marie Balmary, in her *Psychoanalyzing Psychoanalysis* (Baltimore: Johns Hopkins University Press, 1982), argues plausibly that Freud's emphasis upon Oedipus' incestuous desire is a repressive interpretation meant to conceal the real content of the Oedipus complex: the transmission of the faults of the father (Laius) to the son (Oedipus).

father in ways that echo Freud's theory of the Oedipus complex. The discourse of the father is, however, essentially one of absence, which can be traced to the father's symbolic authority. As a contemporary American literary critic says, "The father is that ambivalent shell; offering protection, his love allows the son to mature while, simultaneously, he presents a barrier which must be tested and, ultimately, overcome."[47] Like many modernist writers in the West, such as Kafka, who were at odds with their fathers, Chinese writers made their initial target the social order--the symbolic father--thereby undoing filial piety.

The symbolic father does not have to become an actual image in fiction: his law can permeate a representation, like the air people breathe. As often as not, in relevant modern Chinese writings the real father is absent from the picture. This, in fact, is a tradition in Chinese classical novels. For instance, Jia Zheng, Baoyu's father in *The Dream of the Red Chamber*, is almost nonexistent unless he appears to reprimand or punish the son. In most of Lu Xun's writings, the father is absent. In Guo Moruo's three volumes of memoirs, he never mentions his father, except to state that he was a landlord. Yu Dafu creates no father figures in most of his stories, and therefore many critics claim that his theme is mainly sexual love between young men and women. Bing Xin, one of the most prominent women writers of the century, praises only abstract maternal love and almost entirely omits the father from her early literary canon (except in "Alone, I Am Getting Withered"--Si ren du qiaocui). Yet all of these writers are arguing with the patriarchy or the symbolic father, including Bing Xin, who by her very conspicuous omission of the father figure in her prose fiction denounces the patriarchy. We can imagine such an absence, paradoxically, to enact the paternal function, which Lacan calls "the Name-of-the-Father." In Julia Kristeva's words, "the father is made a symbolic power--that is, ... he is dead, and thus elevated to the rank of a Name."[48] As a Name authorizing the compulsions and prohibitions of a social order, the symbolic father manifests a power far exceeding any individual father's power to oppress.

During his lifetime Lu Xun wrote a number of works in protest against the paternal rule, from the point of view of a son. He explored the question of how it is possible for people to endure the unjust patriarchal

---

47. Francesco Aristide Ancona, *Writing the Absence of the Father: Undoing Oedipal Structures in the Contemporary American Novel* (New York: University Press of America, 1986), p. 4.

48. Julia Kristeva, *About Chinese Women* (New York: Urizen Books, 1977), Anita Barrows, trans., p. 32.

order. The function of literature is, in his view, to awaken people to their deplorable situation and shake them into the realization that they are not only harming themselves but also causing the destruction of their future: the children. He hopes that once people become aware of the harshness of reality, they can try to cure it. Children who die young or are spiritually disfigured are among the most disheartening sights for Lu Xun. Therefore, in his story "Medicine," he symbolically arranges the graveyard meeting of the mothers of two dead children--one a revolutionary who has been beheaded, the other an ordinary country child dead in spite of taking bread soaked in the blood of the beheaded, a cure insisted upon by his father. Both dead sons are victims of patriarchal society. The two family names combine to form "hua xia," a reference to China as a nation. That Hua and Xia are deprived of their descendants is Lu Xun's great fear. It is worth noting that the feminine image -- the mothers in mourning -- is evoked in Lu Xun's quarrel with the symbolic order. Adopting a marginalized feminine position, he calls desperately on the society to save its children.

In some of Lu Xun's writings, the symbolic father is ever-present, whereas the real father is missing. Indeed, in his "Everlasting Light" [Chang ming deng] (1925),[49] the symbolic father is embodied in the absence of the real father. The story is considered to be the first portrayal of a revolutionary with full rebellious consciousness in the post-May Fourth era. Because the rebel is alone and cannot win the sympathy of the masses, he is defeated. Yet he will not easily surrender in his fight against the forces of tradition. His voice can still be heard through the bars of the dark room in which he is locked. This story is often taken as an example of Lu Xun's celebration of the spirit of revolutionary endurance [ren].[50]

It seems to me, however, that the discourse of the father may also account for the presence of persistent tradition in the story in the form of a lamp light in the temple of a village. The light in the temple is said to have been burning for more than a thousand years, and to commemorate it, the village is named "ji guang tun" [auspicious light village]. It is a symbol for the never-changing feudal social order and traditional ideas--in other words, the patriarchal order. A madman's threat to put out the everlasting oil light in the temple upsets the whole village. The light is believed to protect the village; if it were gone, the place would be flooded and people would be turned into cockroaches. In fact, few really take this

---

49. Lu Xun, "Chang ming deng," in *Lu Xun xiaoshuo ji* (Hong Kong: Jindai tushu, 1967).

50. See for instance, Bao Ji, "On the Historical Importance of 'Chang ming deng'" [Lun "Chang ming deng" de zhongyao lishi yiyi], in *Lu Xun yanjiu*, Vol. 5, 1981.

superstition seriously except when someone threatens to extinguish the light, and then suddenly people feel worried and alarmed. When the madman is stopped from putting out the light, he claims that he will set the temple on fire. In the end he is locked up in a dark room in the back yard of the temple. In the fight between the patriarchal society and the son, the son is defeated. The children's singing at the end of the story indicates that his fight is in vain and that the world outside his encagement goes on, indifferent to his plea. This story is permeated with Oedipal helplessness and frustration.

Like Oedipus himself, the sons in Lu Xun's stories are often wanderers and loners, or at least alienated from their native places. Lu Xun's story "The Loner" [Gu du zhe][51] portrays an intellectual who is an outcast in his society. Wei Lianyi, the protagonist, is isolated from his community. His distant family members in a remote village regard him as a stranger who behaves differently from themselves. Angered by the indifferent snobbishness of society and disillusioned with the younger generation, he takes his revenge, paradoxically by conforming to the society: he becomes an adviser to a military officer. He does what he formerly despised and opposed; he rejects what he used to worship and hold aloft. He is indeed defeated, yet he wins. He wins in that he can mock the system by working for it and by mocking himself.

His revenge against the society hastens his own death, though; his conscience tortures him for having made the compromise. He realizes that he is following the pattern of his grandmother, who leads a dull and monotonous life, always sitting at the window and knitting. By identifying with a mother figure and yet fighting against this identification, the son finds himself more alienated from the paternal society; yet his compromise with the society is the victory of his life instinct over the death instinct: "I have to live for a few days."[52] The compulsion to repeat the paternal pattern is a process of assimilation and dissimulation indeed. Lu Xun's image of a wounded wolf howling in the wild field aptly depicts the mental state of such a tortured loner. It captures the moment before its death when the wolf was, alone and in pain, howling not for help but to express its true suffering. Lu Xun's story suggests that in the modern Chinese version of the Oedipus conflict, the son is killed by the symbolic father--the family system and the society as a whole.

---

51. Lu Xun, "Gu du zhe," in *Lu Xun xiaoshuo ji* (Hong Kong: Jindai tushu, 1967).
52. Ibid., p. 325.

In twentieth-century Chinese fiction, few works about the family caught in the transition from the old to the new can surpass Ba Jin's trilogy, *The Torrent* [Ji liu]. Ba Jin's *Family* [Jia] (1931), the first and the best of the trilogy, is clearly about generational conflicts. Although the novel is about three generations of the Gao family, a family of the rich gentry-official class, it concentrates on the youngest generation--the grandchildren. Taking his stand with the young, Ba Jin aims his criticism at the old family system:

> I want to show how those families [typical families like those described in the trilogy] inevitably go down the road to ruin, how they dig their own graves with their own hands. I want to describe the inner struggles and tragedies inside those families...how lovable youths suffer there, how they struggle and finally do not escape destruction.... In those families we do not have much fresh air.[53]

The generation between the grandfather and the grandsons, that of the real father, is absent. This absence can be explained by a biographical similarity to Ba Jin's own family, a similarity that has already been investigated by many literary critics. In terms of the novel, the absence of the real father allows the confrontation between the generations to have a broader, less purely personal significance.

In this family, the archetypal tyrant is the grandfather, who dominates the family. Confronted by him, the rebellious third grandson ponders:

> He felt the person sitting in front of him was not his grandfather, but a representative of a whole generation. He knew that the grandfather's generation and the grandson's generation could not understand each other. But he wondered what was in this thin body that made them talk not like a grandfather to his granson, but like two enemies.[54]

Ba Jin clearly intends to make the grandfather a symbol of the decaying generation. Yet the grandfather is not presented as a caricature of the decaying society. An ambivalent feeling characterizes the relationship

---

53. Quoted in Olga Lang, *Pa Jin and His Writing* (Cambridge: Harvard University Press, 1967), p. 70.

54. Ba Jin, *Jia* (Hong Kong: Nanguo, 1968), p. 57.

between the grandfather and the grandsons, especially from the point of view of the younger generation.

Each of his three grandsons represents one type of relationship between a father and a son. Juexin, the oldest son, passively accedes to the demands of the grandfather. This passivity is itself a response to the tensions of the relationship. That is, the castration threat, the central event of the Oedipal crisis, is resolved by his passivity towards the grandfather's authority. He is, on one hand, a son, and on the other, the father of a young son and the head of his immediate family. By accepting his own passivity in relation to his father's "absence," he acts decisively to affirm the possibility of relationship with the grandfather. Yet his consequent failure to protect his own wife, who is forced to bear her child in very shabby conditions without proper help and who dies in childbirth as a result, indicates his incompetence as a patriarch.

Juemin, the second grandson, compromises with the patriarchal rule. Although he reads revolutionary pamphlets such as *New Youth* [Xin qingnian] and sympathizes with his younger brother's rebellious deeds, he does not take any action against patriarchal society until he faces the danger of perpetuating the unhappiness of the young--a marriage arranged for him by his grandfather. Unable to resist his grandfather head-on, he chooses to hide from his family. The third grandson, Juehui, is by far the most uncompromising rebel of the three. Yet even his rebellion is not without comprimise. In the world of *Family*, the final conflict is solved by universal humanitarian love, a compromise between the old and the young. The death scene of the grandfather is tenderly portrayed, and his reconciliation with his grandchildren somewhat bridges the gap between the generations. The grandsons' hatred for Grandfather Gao's tyranny is mixed with pity, love, and even respect. This ambivalence--the love and the hate for the grandfather who protects them yet blocks their path to maturity--is characteristic of the relationship between young men and patriarchy: only after the father is lost can the son assume the function of paternity. Death unites the generations. But death is also a marker between the possible and impossible; it leaves the gap forever open and yet closed. The father is thus elevated to the rank of a name.

The function of the symbolic father is often not confined within the family but extends to the clan as well because of the persistence of the traditional Chinese family system. Zhang Tianyi's story "The Backbone and the Breast" [Jiliang yu naizi] (1933)[55] shows the tension between the patriarchal family structure and young people. I choose this story because it is one of the early attempts by a Chinese writer to portray a daughter's daring and successful rebellion against the patriarchal family, especially against seduction by a patriarchal chief.

The plot is simple enough: the Ren family's daughter-in-law falls in love with a farmer in the nearby village. She lives with him and has a daughter by him. This is atrocious behavior in the eyes of traditional moralists, and the clan seeks to punish her. The significance of the story, however, is that the author portrays the punishment not as an act of righteousness, but as a product of the incestuous desire of the head of the Ren family, Eldest Grandfather [zhang taiye], for Sansao, the vivacious young wife of Ren San.

The old man's sexual desire for the young woman is described in great detail. After Sansao is brought back from the neighboring village, the clan chief orders a family gathering to punish her in front of the Ren Ancestral altar. All the Ren males have lustful thoughts at the sight of half-naked Sansao. In a remarkable demonstration of sexualized sadism, she is severely whipped before these men. But she does not beg for mercy, and each time she is asked whether she will give up her lover, she replies "No" and is beaten again until she loses consciousness.

The title, "The Backbone and the Breast," suggests the author's intention to portray a young woman who refuses to yield to the patriarchal pressure--who has a strong backbone--and who dauntlessly fights for her freedom and love. "The breast" refers to the patriarchal treatment of women as sexual objects. As seldom happens in these stories, the representative of the younger generation wins in this story. A resourceful woman, she outwits the old man. When she is sent by her husband to "serve" the old man, she knocks him down and runs back to the neighboring village. She and her lover leave the village that night in pursuit of their joint happiness. She breaks through the deadly Oedipal situation. Apparently, she feels no ambivalence--maybe because a woman does not have the option of becoming one of the fathers who holds power herself.

In the fictional world, the young people win by running away from the suffocating system, as in the case of Sansao and Juehui. Is it possible to escape the Law of the Father? Lu Xun posits this question in his article "What Happens After Nora Has Left Home?" in which he sees only one

---

55. Zhang Tianyi, "Jiliang yu naizi," in *Twenty-One and Others* [Ershiyi he qita] (Jiangxi: People's Publishing House, 1981).

choice for the heroine of Ibsen's *A Doll's House* --either to die of cold and starvation or to return to her cage if she does not obtain economic independence.[56]

According to Freud, incestuous desire originates from the pressure exerted by the Oedipus complex.[57] The taboo against sexual relations within the nuclear family is strong and almost universally observed. Discussions of incestuous deeds and even incestuous desires have been almost as taboo as the act of incest itself in most known cultures. But a preoccupation with incest was not uncommon in Chinese literature, even in serious historical literature such as *The Record of History*. I use the term "family romance" not in Freud's sense--which presumes the desire to denigrate the parents from one angle while exalting them from another, wishes for grandeur, and attempts to circumvent the incest barrier[58]--but as a descriptive term for the theme of incestuous desire in literary works.

I would like to suggest that the introduction of Freudian theory changed certain perceptions of incest in Chinese literary works. Writers began to treat this theme from a Freudian point of view, as some literary critics have noticed. For instance, as early as 1928, a famous literary historian discussed the use of the Oedipus complex among Chinese writers.[59] His list covers only the time before 1928, and after that period writers continued to use Oedipal materials. As we know, all readings involve rereading and reinterpretation. Some classic Chinese stories attracted the imaginations of modern writers, who gave them new interpretations that assimilated current forms of knowledge. Yuan Changying's rewriting of a classical theme is an example of this rediscovery. It transposes the original discourse, a love story, into a new dimension, the Oedipal situation.

Yuan Changying, the author of the play *The Peacock Flies Southeast*, received her Ph.D. from Edinburgh University in the 1930s. She was a specialist in French literature as well as a playwright. Originally, *The Peacock Flies Southeast* was a long lyric poem about ancient times. It describes the triangular relationship between a mother, her son, and her daughter-in-law. A widowed mother is not happy with her daughter-in-law, even though the young woman is almost faultless in her

56. Lu Xun, "Nala zou hou zenyang," in *The Complete Works of Lu Xun*, Vol. 1, p. 145.

57. Laplanche and Pontalis, *The Language of Psycho-Analysis*, p. 160.

58. Ibid., p. 160.

59. Zhao Jingshen, "New Chinese Literature and Abnormal Sexuality" [Zhongguo xin wenyi yu biantai xingyu], in *Yiban*, Vol. 4, No. 1, January 5, 1928, pp. 204-208.

attentive service to the mother. As a result, the mother forces her son, who loves his wife but fears his mother, to divorce his wife. Back at her own home after the divorce, the young woman drowns herself after realizing there is no chance for her to return to her husband. In great despair, the son hangs himself from a tree. It is a Chinese Romeo-and-Juliet story. After their deaths, the two families bury them together and on each side plant a pine tree and a Chinese parasol tree. The two trees later grow intertwined, and upon the trees two birds sit chirping all the time. This is the origin of a Chinese saying about the desire for everlasting love: "In the sky, we wish to be the birds always flying together; on the earth, we wish to be the two trees whose trunks are intertwined."

Yuan Changying thought that the theme of this ancient poem was good material for a tragic play, but she hesitated to start writing it. One night, after reading the poem over and over again, she fell asleep. Her sleep was troubled, and she awoke from her dream suddenly. Sitting up in bed, she asked herself the key question: why did Mother Jiao dismiss Lanzhi, her daughter-in-law?

> Of course, from ancient time on, mothers-in-law in China have had absolute authority over their daughters-in-law. Mother Jiao's dismissing Lanzhi could be nothing more than an assertion of such authority. But such answers could not satisfy me. I knew that there were psychological factors in human relations. Mother Jiao's dislike of Lanzhi was natural from the psychological perspective. My own experience and my observation of others told me that the reason why female in-laws could not get along well with each other is jealousy.[60]

Yuan used the term "chicu" for jealousy, a term that refers only to sexual jealousy. Yuan suggested that a sexual tension existed between the mother-in-law and daughter-in-law. She acknowledged the implication of her usage but hastened to explain that by sexual tension she did not mean to imply that an actually incestuous relationship existed between the mother and her son but that their relationship was emotionally incestuous. She specified that by sexual tension she meant that after a mother had taken all the pain and trouble to raise her son, an outsider--a daughter-in-law--came to replace her as the man's caretaker, so that the mother naturally felt left out and therefore indignant. Women who were old and had mild tempers could

---

60. Yuan Changying, Preface to "The Peacock Flies Southeast," in *The Peacock Flies Southeast and Other One-Act Plays* [Kongque dong nan fei ji qita dumuju] (Changsha: The Commercial Press, October 1930), p. 1.

bury such pain inside themselves. But those who were widowed young and had hot tempers could not put up with the intrusion of an outsider. Therefore, a tragedy like Lanzhi's was likely to ensue.

Once Yuan came to a Freudian interpretation of the ancient story, her writing of the play flew. She was aware of the Oedipus legend and cited it in her preface. But her explanation followed a traditional interpretation of the tragedy: she saw the tragedy of Oedipus as a struggle between man and his fate. Although she did not consider the Oedipal situation to be archetypal for the human psyche, the Freudian concept of the Oedipus complex clearly influenced her writing.

Yuan's play brings a new understanding to the role of the mother. In the past, the mother's motivation was either left unquestioned or portrayed as incomprehensible and cruel. In her play, Yuan creates elaborately affectionate scenes between the mother and the son: the mother aggressive and passionate, and the son passive and docile. The mother's possessive love surfaces in her praise for her son's dark, smooth hair and her wish that he should stay at her side forever and not take any job. Confined within the household and left with no role but to raise her children, Mother Jiao's fate is in fact pathetic. Apparently, she transfers her sexual love for her husband to her children, a boy and a girl, but especially to the boy. After the arrival of her daughter-in-law, she is filled with sexual jealousy. For instance, she becomes extremely annoyed at discovering an embroidered pair of underwear that her daughter-in-law has sewed for her son. The incident leads to a fight between her and Lanzhi, because she feels she, not the young woman, should take care of the man. By displaying such details, the play produces a strong psychological effect on its audience.

The name "Mother Jiao" has become a common way of designating widowed women who are jealous of their daughters-in-law. The mother in *The Peacock Flies Southeast* is Mother Jiao, and the mother in another modern play, *The Wilderness* [Yuan ye] (1937), is also named Jiao.

Cao Yu's *The Wilderness* is a play of revenge: Chou Hu escapes from prison after eight years and returns to his village to take revenge on Jiao Yanwang, who has framed Chou's family and killed all of them. The subtheme, which adds to the complexity of the relationship among the characters, is that of a double triangle: (1) Mother Jiao, Daxin (the son), and Jinzi (the daughter-in-law); (2) Mother/son, Jinzi, and Chou Hu (Jinzi's lover). In both cases, the son Daxin is the victim.

Daxin's dilemma lies in his inability to choose between his mother and his wife. His wife, Jinzi, unlike the pale and obedient Lanzhi in *The Peacock Flies Southeast*, is aggressive and seductive. Mother Jiao, though blind, is vicious and cunning. One critic identifies Mother Jiao as "a remnant of the cultural past and present, an exemplar of Chinese superstition and backwardness."[61] In contrast to his mother, Daxin is weak and feeble-minded. Caught in the fights between his mother and his wife, he can satisfy neither. The fight between the two women for Daxin's affection is fierce because both are strong. Jinzi, the daughter-in-law, becomes a thorn in Mother Jiao's side. She even puts a witchcraft curse on Jinzi, using a cloth-made figure resembling Jinzi and covered with needles. Her love for her son is possessive; she unabashedly declares that he is her property, hers alone.[62] Jinzi is no less aggressive, but her tactic is to manipulate Daxin to fight against his mother. Daxin, bound in the conflict, cannot find a resolution and so desires death. When Chou Hu comes back to kill the Jiao family and take away his lover Jinzi, Daxin does not put up any fight to save his own life. According to Chou Hu, Daxin even welcomes his own death:

> I grabbed him and suddenly he woke up--the way he looked at me as though he wanted to say something; he stared right at me. I know he was sad in his heart, so sad he couldn't tell anybody. I raised the knife and then he knew he had only a moment left; he was suddenly very afraid. He looked at me, but he was laughing in his throat, laughing so square-like; he pointed at his heart, and then he nodded to me.... And then I stabbed him! He didn't make any cry; he just closed his eyes.[63]

Daxin welcomes his death because he cannot solve the emotional Oedipus complex. A tragic death ends his conflict; in the fictional world, just as in the real world, family romance often has a fatal side.

During the 1940s, a writer who conscientiously employed Freudian psychology was Zhang Ailing, a popular short-story writer. Her fictional work, "Xin jing" (The heart sutra), is a meticulously constructed piece about the Oedipus complex. Without any evasion, the story presents the incestuous love between a father and his daughter and their attempt to overcome this "abnormal sensual" instinct. Twenty-year-old Xiao Han has an unusual attachment to her father, and her mother fades into the background. Xiao Han wishes never to grow up, so that she can stay with

---

61. Christopher C. Rand, "Introduction" in *The Wilderness [Yuan ye] by Cao Yu* (Hong Kong: Hong Kong University Press, 1980), pp. xxxiv-xxxv.

62. Ibid., p. 88.

63. Ibid., p. 142.

her father forever. The father unconsciously resents having to give up his daughter to another man, not wishing to part with her himself; the daughter rejects other men's pursuit and concentrates her love on her father. Her attachment to her father is unconscious until one particular scene in which they discuss the mother:

Xiao Han said, "She's old, but you are still young--how can you blame this on me?"

Fengyi replied in a low voice: "If you were not here to be her rival, to make her feel that she is inferior to you in every way, she wouldn't have become old so soon."

Xiao Han turned to Fengyi and smiled: "Ho, you are not being reasonable. She's become aged because I've made her look aged and she is more aged. This is a bit illogical. Anyway, you are mad at me today. If you want to blame me, please do so."

Fengyi leaned against the arm of the sofa, his hands in his pockets, his voice became calm and tired, "I don't blame you. I blame nobody. I am to blame because I am just so muddle-headed."

Xiao Han said, "You sound as if you blame yourself for falling into my traps, as if I intentionally wanted to make trouble for Mother, to separate the love between you two."

Fengyi replied, "I have not said this. I don't know how things started. It's been over seven or eight years--you were so small ... unconsciously ..."[64]

As an attempt to solve the psychological conflict, the father starts dating Xiao Han's classmate, who resembles Xiao Han in appearance and who is in need of financial security. He plays the "fort-da" game of trying to control an inevitable loss, as described by Freud from his observation of his grandson's "child's play."[65] He finds it necessary to create a substitute for a relationship because of the inaccessibility of his real sexual object. Active control, rivalry, and the desire to make himself master of the situation prompt him to give up his daughter. The process of sublimation redirects him toward new objects.

---

64. Zhang Ailing, "Xin jing," in *The Golden Cangue* [Jin suo ji] (Hong Kong: Nüshen Publishing House, 1983), pp. 101-102.

65. Samuel Weber, *The Legend of Freud* (Minneapolis: University of Minneapolis Press, 1982), p. 95.

To resolve the Oedipal triangle, one member of the triangle has to withdraw from the scene. The story ends with Xiao Han leaving home in the hope that her parents can resume their harmonious marital relationship. The action is arranged deliberately to fit the pattern of the Oedipus complex. It indeed takes a Freudian mind to write the following observation, in a scene which shows the neglected mother talking to her daughter after her husband starts dating Xiao Han's surrogate:

> After I was over thirty, you would laugh at me whenever I wore colorful clothes or showed some affection to your father. ... He laughed together with you. How could I blame you--you were just a naive kid. ... Now, I know you meant it."[66]

All the family's sexual tensions have come to the surface, so there is no need to remain silent. The knowledge is horrifying and shattering for the mother. But once she confronts it, the daughter's wish becomes conscious to her, and shows hideously in the daughter's eyes.

3.3 The Interpretation of Dreams

Freud's interpretation of dreams is a study of the workings of the mind, rather than just a therapeutic method. It is usually understood that Freud viewed dreams as wish-fulfillments, but this is only one aspect of his explanatory model. In fact, his actual analysis of "dream-work" mechanisms is a more important and useful contribution to the human understanding of dreams. His mechanisms of condensation, displacement, representation, and symbolization constitute the core of his interpretation of dreams, as he himself suggests:

> At bottom, dreams are nothing other than a particular form of thinking, made possible by the conditions of the state of sleep. It is the dream-work which creates that form, and it alone is the essence of dreaming--the explanation of its peculiar nature.[67]

Literature has often explored the workings of dreams, and changes in the literary treatment of dreams reflect changes in the historical and social understanding of dreams. In classical Chinese literature, dreams are

---

66. Zhang Ailing, "Xin Jing," p. 118.
67. *TCPWOSF*, Vol.V, pp. 506-7, n. 2.

sometimes revelations from spirits. It is generally believed that dreams can foretell the future, either by transmitting direct prophecies or by previewing some future events. In *The Dream of the Red Chamber*, for example, Baoyu has a dream in which the goddesses reveal to him the fate of the twelve women. Dreams are also forums in which the dead come back to bid farewell to the living or to ask the living to avenge them. Two famous cases are *The Sorrow of Dou E*, in which Dou E's spirit appears in her father's dream and begs him to avenge her, and *Water Margin*, in which the ghost of Wu Song's dwarf brother cries out his grievances in Wu Song's sleep in the mourning hall. In the realm of dream interpretation, the influence of Buddhism--which sees the world as a dream--was also prevalent; an example of that influence is *The Mirror of Flowers*, which treats a whole trip abroad as a dream.[68] Occasionally, also, dreams represented wish-fulfillment, as we shall see below.

In twentieth-century China, a significant shift in cultural and artistic values can be seen in changing attitudes toward dreams in fiction. Influenced by Lin Shu's translation of foreign novels, the most popular novels in the teens started giving longer descriptions of their protagonists' inner world by using either the form of nocturnal dreams or that of daydreams, although their dream content often followed the old patterns.[69] In the 20s and 30s, however, the literary method of depicting dreams largely changed, and many classic features in the literary use of dreams disappeared. Instead of portraying dreams as prophecies, revelations from spirits, or messages from the dead, the writers concentrated on revealing their protagonists' psychology through dreams.

Did the introduction of Western psychology affect people's understanding of dreams and their creative process? A positive answer has to be given for the role of Western psychology in redirecting the interpretations of dreams. Dream interpreters among Western psychologists ranged from Bergson to Wundt and the American behaviorist school.[70] But none were as powerful and influential as the Freudian interpretation of dreams. In order to examine the Freudian influence on dream scenes in early twentieth-century Chinese literature, we should first look briefly at how the Freudian theory of

---

68. For details about the pre-modern Chinese treatment of dreams, please see Roberto K. Ong, *The Interpretation of Dreams in Ancient China* (Bochum: Studienverlag Brockmeyer, 1985).

69. For instance, Kuang Jie, "Ti juan xie," in *Xiaoshuo shi bao*, No. 10, May 1911, p. 2; and Bu Ning, "Yi zhu tong," in *Xiaoshuo shi bao*, No. 23, September 1914, pp. 1-2.

70. O. Briére, *Fifty Years of Chinese Philosophy 1898-1948* (New York: Frederick A. Praeger, 1965), pp. 136-139.

dream interpretation was understood and discussed by Chinese intellectuals so as to recreate the atmosphere which generated literary interest in Freud's dream theory.

Although Freud first published his *The Interpretation of Dreams* in 1900 and subsequently revised it in later editions, it was not until 1932 that this book was finally translated into Chinese.[71] But before 1930, or as early as the first introduction of Freudian dream theory to China by Zhu Guangqian in 1920, almost all the articles and books about Freud discussed his interpretation of dreams and considered that to be the key point in Freud's theory. Freud was considered to be the first person to try to offer a scientific explanation for dreams.[72] Freud's way of interpreting dreams was the best known part of his theory and drew a great deal of attention from Chinese intellectuals.

As in the West, Chinese reactions to the Freudian interpretation of dreams were varied. In particular, there was wide disagreement about the extent to which Freud's interpretation of dreams privileged sexual content. The sexual symbolism of dreams commonly accepted in the West was challenged time and again in Chinese responses to the Freudian interpretation of dreams. The following assertion by Freud was most frequently cited as an example of the Freudian theory's absurdity:

> All elongated objects, such as sticks, tree-trunks and umbrellas (the opening of these last being comparable to an erection) may stand for the male organ--as well as all long, sharp weapons, such as knives, daggers and pikes. ... Boxes, cases, chests, cupboards and ovens represent the uterus, and also hollow objects, ships, and vessels of all kinds.[73]

Gao Juefu exaggerated this sexual association: "According to Freud, we are surrounded by sexual symbols: a writer picks up his pen to write; a woman sews her clothes with a needle; a doctor inserts medicine into his patient's arm with an injection needle; things like trees and electricity posts

71. Zhang Jingshen, trans., "Meng de fenxi" [Freud, *The Interpretation of Dreams*], in *Dushu zazhi*, Vol. 1, No. 6, 1932.

72. Zhao Qinwu, "A Critique of Psychoanalysis and Sigmund Freud" [Guanyu xinli fenxi ji Fuluoyite zhi piping], in *Zhongfa daxue yuekan*, Vol. 5, No. 2, May 1, 1934, p. 93.

73. Freud, *TIOD*, p. 389.

are all phallic symbols."[74] Gao questioned the validity of such interpretations. Zhang Jingsheng's selected translation of Freud's *The Interpretation of Dreams* devoted only one paragraph to Freud's interpretation of dream symbols. But Zhang, in the midst of translating Freud's text, could not help inserting his own doubt about the assertion: "This explanation of dream symbol is quite baffling. Without careful examination, no one dares to agree with it."[75] Considering that Zhang had written a *History of Sexuality* [Xing shi], a book-length volume which concentrated on the development of bedroom technique, it was certainly not for reasons of prudery that he did not translate Freud's interpretation of sexual symbols. Zhang's bafflement stems from the difference between Chinese and Western cultures. Freud's insistence on sexual interpretations sometimes caused embarrassment even to those who attempted to use psychoanalysis to cure patients. Qian Pin, a psychology student, stopped short of interpreting the symbols in the dreams of her young female patient sexually--symbols such as a vase, a snake, and sticks.[76] Other people, however, accepted Freud's interpretation of dreams and stressed the fact that it was through *The Interpretation of Dreams* that Freud developed his theory of the unconscious. But even in their arguments for Freud, they did not attempt to justify his insistence on sexual meanings in dreams; they shied away from it. For instance, Chen Silie in his "Freudian Psychoanalysis of Dreams" explained that although sexual meanings could occur in dreams, other kinds of desires also prompted dreams. He argued that Freud had claimed, after all, that dreams were the fulfillments of desires or wishes, and not just of sexual wishes. Chen tried to refute those who charged Freud with reductively sexual interpretations of dreams:

> In the whole system of Freudian theory of psychoanalysis, the dream occupies an important position. At the same time, his theory of dream interpretation has met the most severe attack. Among these attacks, however, many are based on ignorance or misunderstanding of the theory. For instance, sexual desire is a vital element in his theory, but aside from sexual desire, Freud acknowledges that there

---

74. Gao Juefu, "A Critique of Freud and His Psychoanalysis" [Fuluoyite jiqi jingshen fenxi de pipan], in *Education Magazine* [Jiaoyu zazhi], Vol. 23, No. 3, March 1931, p. 9.

75. Zhang Jingshen, trans., Freud, *The Interpreation of Dreams*, in *Dushu zazhi*, Vol. 1, No. 6, 1932, pp. 49-50.

76. Qian Pin, "A Case-study of a Melancholy Child," p. 10.

exist other desires as well. He only says that dreams are wish-fulfillments, which includes fulfillment of sexual desires.[77]

It would be easy to claim that all who deny the sexual contents of dreams are sexually "repressed" human beings, but such a claim would be arbitrary and forced if it did not take the cultural aspect of symbols into consideration. Freud himself acknowledges that dream-symbols derive from fairy tales, myths, epics, and jokes which are culturally specific.[78] It has been observed that in China the sexual data in dreams so prominent in modern Western reports is noticeably lacking.[79] The argument about whether Freud's interpretation of dreams is exclusively sexual depends on people's interpretation of his theory. Given the controversial responses to Freud's dream theory among people who introduced the theory to China, one can expect a similar splash in the literary community.

In several of his articles about creative writers, particularly in "The Unconscious and Day Dreaming," Freud suggests that writers are on his side when they cause the people created by their imagination to dream. Yet one doubt remains: if actual dreams are considered to be unrestrained and irregular phenomena, the status of such free literary re-creations of dreams can be problematic. Freud believes that dreams have meaning and can be interpreted, but he does not take into account the manipulation of writers in the literary dreams he considers. He studies literary dreams as manifestations of symptoms and suggests two methods for such investigation into literary dreams: to delve into a special case, or to bring together and compare all the examples of the use of dreams which are found in the works of different story-tellers. Although he himself is not prepared to use the second method, he thinks the second way is by far the more effective, "perhaps the only justifiable one," because it offers profound insight into psychic life.[80] Rather than tracing the psychic life through one particular case of literary dreams, I wish to employ the second method to examine the Freudian influence through a collection of literary dream scenes by Guo Moruo and Lu Xun.

---

77. Chen Silie, "Freud's Theory of Dream Psychology" [Fuluode de meng de xinli], in *Culture and Education Biweekly* [Wenhua yu jiaoyu], No. 44, January 1935, p. 16.

78. Gao Juefu, "A Critique of Freud and His Psychoanalysis" [Fuluoyite jiqi jingshen fenxi de pipan], in *Education Magazine* [Jiaoyu zazhi], Vol. 23, No. 3, March 1931, p. 10.

79. Carolyn T. Brown, ed., *Psycho-Sinology: The Universe of Dreams in Chinese Culture* (Washington D.C.: Woodrow Wilson International Center for Scholars, 1987), p. 3.

80. Freud, *Delusion and Dream* (Boston: Beacon Press, 1956), pp. 27-28.

In estimating Freudian influences on literary dream scenes, two alternatives have to be considered: whether the author consciously uses a psychoanalytic approach in his or her creative writings, or whether it is the reader or critic who discerns such a Freudian tendency in the writings and claims either a Freudian influence or an independent depiction of phenomena that lend themselves to Freudian interpretation. Ideally, one would like to find the stated intentions of writers who use dreams in their writings. It is not, however, the case that writers always state outright what they intend in their writings. Indeed, writers' records of their intentions might make the critic's task uninteresting. Moreover, writers' accounts of their own creative processes might well be intentionally or unintentionally misleading. Such statements nevertheless often offer a rare chance for us to compare the writers' stated intentions with the impact of their literary works.

There is an essential difference between a real dream and a literary dream. The cause of a real dream is yet to be determined or interpreted. A nocturnal dream cannot come and go at the dreamer's behest; whereas a fabricated dream is a conscious, willed attempt at conveying something in relation to the whole design and plot of a text. The Freudians do not believe that dreams have complete, well-organized plots like those of stories. The difference between real dreams and literary dreams is that the latter have by their nature already undergone what Freud calls "secondary revision": that is, a literary dream is meticulously presented, whereas a real dream is not meant for interpersonal communication and undergoes secondary revision only when it is told or recorded. Guo Moruo points out that

> Depicting dreams is a common practice which literary people use in their stories. Real dreams are usually associated with previous events and have a coherence of their own. If a literary person makes up a dream scene, he has to carefully arrange his plot before the dream scene. Otherwise he would not sound convincing, or, to put it another way, the dream would look unnatural. To map out the dream scenario means to prepare the dream process or the latent content of the dream before writing, to arrange the biological and psychological material in such a way as to focus on the central element in the dream-work. A dream should not suddenly appear in the story without foreshadowing and arrangement beforehand. Literary people who are dreaming in their writings should preserve such an intent.[81]

---

81. Guo Moruo, *Moruo wenji* (Beijing: People's Publishing House, 1959), Vol. 10, p. 115.

Guo Moruo refers to the manipulation and the craftsmanship of writers, distinguishing between real dreams and manufactured dreams, dreams which belong to the literary genre. In literary works, few things presented are accidental or are there simply because they happen to be. Even the most apparently disordered "stream-of-consciousness" fiction is arranged deliberately by the author with artistry. Dreams in literary writing also serve literary purposes, just as literary works presented as diaries or private journals are not really personal outpourings. Guo differentiates talented writers from mediocre writers in their use of dreams:

> A writer of genius with superior talent does not have to make such a conscious preparation and can unconsciously make his works intelligible. For instance, the last dream in *The West Chamber Story* flows very naturally.[82] But we, who have limited talent, have to prepare our material according to our knowledge of the science.[83]

This passage is important because Guo seems to have made a distinction between the use of dreams before and after the "enlightenment" of Western psychology. Before achieving a theoretical understanding of dreams, the ancients were "talents" and made their discovery of dreams "unconsciously." After the "enlightenment," writers must address the dominant theories about dreams. By the "knowledge of the science" here, Guo Muoro was referring to the Freudian theory of dreams.[84]

Guo Moruo is a writer who openly claimed to have applied a psychoanalytic approach to dreams. He tended to offer interpretive introductions to his own literary works for fear that his readers might not understand points hidden in his metaphors and imageries. This practice is deeply embedded in his belief that a writer has the most immediate intimacy with his own works, even closer than the parent-child relationship. In his view, a qualified critic should have more sympathy, sensibility, and knowledge than the creative writer before the critic can successfully carry out the task of criticism and be worthy of the trust of readers. But such critics, he sighed, were hard to find. (The question we face today is, what is the

---

82. In classical Chinese literature, there are excellent scenes in which dreams are described, not as being caused by superstition but as being the result of daily thoughts and stimuli. Guo's citation is such a dream. In Book Four of *The West Chamber Story*, Zhang Sheng, who has to leave the woman with whom he is madly in love to attend imperial examinations, stops in an inn on the way and at night dreams that his dear Yingying has followed him all the way and finally found him in the inn.

83. Guo Moruo, *Moruo wenji*, Vol. 10, p. 115.

84. Ibid., p. 115.

function of a literary critic--is it to discover the intentions of the writers? But of course, we cannot expect our questions to have preoccupied an earlier generation.)

At the time of the publication of his story "Late Spring" [Can chun] (1922), most of the reviewers did not understand what he intended to convey through the story. One of the critics commented that this story was "plain and lacking a climax."[85] Guo felt exasperated with the critic and argued that his story did have a climax and that it was the critic's fault not to have noticed it. He stressed that his "climax" lay in the psychological depiction rather than in the progression of events:

> When composing the story, I had a luxurious wish to show a stream
> from the unconscious. Indeed, if one evaluates my story with a
> factual yardstick, he will not find any climax there at all. But if my
> story is read by a person with some knowledge of psychoanalysis or
> dream psychology, he will have no difficulty in detecting my
> intention and offering valuable criticism of the story.[86]

Guo recounted the event which prompted him to write out his motivation for composing the story. When he talked to Yu Dafu, another writer, about his plan for the story, Yu predicted that if Guo did not speak out about his intention, no one would understand the story in the way that Guo intended. Following his friend's advice, Guo proceeded with a psychoanalysis of his own story, "Late Spring." Because this is one of the most unambiguous cases in which Freudian dream theory has been applied to a literary work, we shall look at the story in some depth.

Before we go on to his story, which he claimed was influenced by the Freudian theory of dream interpretation, it is necessary to consider how well Guo understood Freud's theory. Guo's understanding of the Freudian interpretation of dreams is as follows:

> In summary, psychoanalytic scholars interpret dreams as "emotional
> complexes which are repressed during the day and come alive in a
> disguised form in the state of sleep when the censorship is loose."
> To say it in common language, ..."what affects our minds during the
> day is dreamed at night" [ri you suo si, ye you suo meng]. This

---

85. Guo Moruo, "Criticism and Dream," in *Moruo wenji*, Vol. 10, p. 113.
86. Ibid., pp. 113-114.

saying has comprehended all the principles of Freudian interpretation of dreams.[87]

It may appear that Guo holds that external stimuli cause dreams at night. This saying, however, does not represent Freud's view well because Freud also believed that dreams draw on long-buried memories harking back to childhood. Yet we may also argue that since Chinese words are usually allusive and have multiple meanings, the word "si" (think) might also include the unconscious part of the mind; "what occurs during the day" may also include what occurs in the mind but is repressed into the unconscious.

Guo's story, mainly faithful to Freud, suggests that dreams represent expressions of deep-seated instinctual (that is, biologically based) yearnings, mostly of a sexual nature, which are largely unsatisfied and remain repressed from conscious experience. The title of the story, "Late Spring," suggests a sexual meaning for the story. Universally, "Spring" is a metaphor for youth, a stage full of bursting energy and growing sexual desires; but "late Spring" suggests a decline from the peak of vitality and sexuality.

Like many of Guo's stories, "Late Spring" uses a first-person narrator resembling Guo himself: a Chinese medical student who lives with his Japanese wife and two children in Japan. (Guo studied medicine in Japan and married a Japanese woman who bore him two sons.) At first glance, the story does not appear to have any climax; indeed, everything is narrated in a monotonous and, at times, bored, voice. Aimu leaves his wife and children to visit one of his friends who is hospitalized in another city. There he happens to encounter, briefly, a beautiful yet consumptive young nurse. That very night he falls asleep amid his roommates' chattering gossip about the nurse. Suddenly, the narrative shifts to sharp imagery: a steep and piercing hill and a bright moon form the upside-down image of an exclamation point. Like two ghosts, he and the nurse walk to the top of the hill in silence. There the young woman bares her breasts and asks him to give her a medical check-up. Before his hand touches her body, his friend rushes toward them and urges him to go home because his wife is said to have killed his two sons during his absence. Like an arrow, he flees back home and sees his two sons bleeding, dying. His wife, enraged and hysterical, accuses of him of killing them. Eventually, his wife hurls a knife at him and he drops dead on the ground. Then he wakes up with a

---

87. Ibid., p. 114.

start. After the dream scene, everything resumes its normal pace: the narrative becomes flat and uneventful again; soon it ends.

This dream, however, is odd in that although the narrator did not even touch the nurse, he was punished by his wife for having a slight attraction to her. It shows how the sleeping psyche stirs under the stimuli which have remained active in it from waking life. After he wakes up, he associates his dream with the legend of Medea, a Greek sorceress who kills her children when her husband Jason deserts her to marry another woman. In his dream, his wife is even more vindictive than Medea, for she kills not only the children but also her husband. It is clear that Guo writes about the guilt of a married man who has some sexual attraction to a virgin beauty. (Many stories at that time emphasized the importance of virginity.) His attraction to the nurse is unconscious when he is awake; but during his sleep, when the censorship is loosened, his sexual desire emerges in the dream. However, that desire does not have the approval of his conscience: he dreams that his wife resorts to a drastic method of reprimand. An impatient writer, Guo gives away his intention in the story: "When I told my wife about my dream, she laughed and said that I felt guilty and therefore had that dream. I could not deny her criticism."[88]

To a Western reader, the psychological implications of the dream are quite obvious, so much so that the protagonist's unconscious impulse seems hardly to have been disguised at all. But this is clearly not the case in the context of China during the 1920s, since critics evidently misunderstood the story. It is worth pointing out that what distinguishes the Freudian dream theory from others is not the assumption that dreams reveal a person's character, but instead Freud's ideas about the dreamwork processes. In this story, Guo specifically wants to show that the dreamwork has produced the dream and that the emotional complex is represented "in a disguised form."

If we say that his story "Late Spring" was a deliberate attempt to use a Freudian theory of dreams in fiction, another story of Guo's may well fit in the same category. "Donna Carméla" [Ka'ermeiluo guniang] (1925)[89] has a similar motif: a young married man is strangely attracted to a candy shop girl who has lovely eyelashes. Like "Late Spring," "Donna Carméla" adopts a first-person narrative. The protagonist's unexpected encounter with a beautiful girl during the day triggers a dream in which he fulfills his sexual desire: they meet on the verge of a cliff and become intimate with

88. *Moruo wenji*, Vol. 9, p. 34.
89. Guo Moruo, "Ka'ermeiluo guniang" (Donna Carméla), in *Dongfang zazhi*, Vol. 22, No. 4, February 25, 1925.

each other. Enhancing the girl's desirability, the protagonist dreams that she was born to an unmarried aristocratic woman and was given away when she was very young. However, censorship functions clearly in the dream: his self-reproach for not being loyal to his wife is expressed through the girl's apologies before she finally kisses him. Moreover, the woman ends her first love experience by jumping off the cliff, in a Freudian displacement: her death represents his guilt. The irony of the story surfaces when he suddenly wakes up from his nightmare and finds he is holding his own wife closely. This last detail reminds us of the dream scene in *The West Chamber Story* : when Zhang Sheng suddenly wakes up from his dream in which he meets his lover, he finds he is holding his lute-bearer.

This literary allusion to *The West Chamber Story* is not accidental, for in one of his essays, Guo praises the last dream of *The West Chamber Story* as a creation of a genius who had no knowledge of modern psychology but used dream psychology intuitively.[90] Having been fortified by Freud's interpretation of dreams, Guo's use of dreams is much more deliberate and contemplated than the genius's.

Guo Moruo constantly peppers his fiction with Western words that indicate the source of his knowledge. Many references in the story are exotic: the protagonist asserts his right as a common human being to have sexual desires, unlike "Jesus of Nazareth," or "Asöka of ancient India." The candies he buys from the woman are "manna"--bread from Heaven; her shop becomes the holy ground of Jerusalem and he the pilgrim, etc. Although this biblical emphasis has its roots in romanticism, the story--particularly the dream--is not derived from romantic tradition, but from more recent forms of psychological interpretation.

"Donna Carméla" is more sophisticated than "Late Spring." It is full of word play and free association: for example, the protagonist's imagination roams from matches to a burning heart. Like many of his characters, this "I" is well versed in Western literature. Whenever he reads an "M" in his English book, he thinks of his Madonna, and similarly "A" signifies Aphrodite. These two associations, attached to his beloved, pose a tension: as Madonna, she is a virginal mother eliciting almost spiritual devotion, but as Aphrodite, she is powerfully erotic. These two fundamental images of women promulgated by Western culture apparently contradict each other, but in conjunction dramatize an ambivalent male fantasy about women's capacity both to transcend sexuality and to embody it. The eyes of "Madonna" or "Aphrodite" are glittering everywhere in all

---

90. *Moruo wenji*, Vol. 10, p. 115.

the books he reads. Throughout the story, the "I" is obsessed with irresistible desire for the woman. Her love for him, however, remains a mystery because they almost never exchange any words except about buying candies. The story demonstrates that he merely imagines the girl's attraction to him: "It was more groundless than a dream."[91] The narrator even accuses himself of being "a sex-obsessed person" [seqing kuang], "a drop-out," and "a person of dual personality." The highlight of this story--the fulfillment of his sexual desire--emphasizes once more the contrast between "pure" and "sensuous" women. Instead of the nameless girl, whom he secretly calls "Donna Carméla" and whom he often perceives as the Madonna, an experienced, seductive woman embodying the allure of Aphrodite offers herself to him. Significantly, he turns her down.

On the surface, his obsession with that woman is not so much sexual as aesthetic: love for a beauty. Yet this is what Freud would term a sublimated form of sexuality. This sublimation is a common feature of classical literature. For example, Feng Youlan in his *A Brief History of Chinese Philosophy* states that the traditional romantic works in China often express more of an aesthetic than a carnal interest in the opposite sex. This story falls into that category, except for the dream scene, which is clearly full of sexual desires and not at all sublimated. This effect is achieved through the literary use of dreamwork which contributes to the understanding of a common male complex.

Lu Xun is another writer who expressed interest in the Freudian interpretation of dreams and used it in his fiction. His translation of foreign theories, such as Kuriyagawa Hakuson's *The Symbol of Angst*, helped familiarize him with the Freudian interpretation of dreams. A great lover of books, he also read Freud's works and related works.[92] Lu Xun uses Freudian theory both in his interpretation of dreams and in his literary works. But he objects to those social dreamers who seem to have taken refuge in a premature metaphysics of dreams, instead of forcing themselves to confront their everyday and sometimes sordid reality.[93] Lu Xun's use of dreams, however, reflects a general tendency during his day, when the general understanding of dreams changed in important ways.

---

91. Guo Moruo, "Ka'ermeiluo guniang," p. 116.

92. Lu Xun recorded having some of Freud's works in his own library: *Introductory Lectures on Psychoanalysis, Jokes and Their Relation to the Unconscious, Three Essays on the Theory of Sexuality*, and *Studies on Hysteria*. Some related books in his collection are Reuben Osborn, *Freud and Marx*, and Albert Mordell, *The Erotic Motive in Literature*.

93. Lu Xun, "Ting shuo meng," in *The Complete Works of Lu Xun*, Vol. 5, p. 62.

Lu Xun understands the mechanisms of dream work, but he is more concerned with examining the conscious, intentional uses that people make of what they have dreamed: "One is free when dreaming, but when he attempts to talk about dreams, he is not free. Dreaming may be real; talking about dreams is unavoidably lying."[94] In this way he draws a division between dreaming itself and the literary and political use of dreams, pointing out that a dream, once written or told, is no longer the property of a single author but enters into a network of social relations. He is concerned with the part consciousness plays in creative processes and the effects of ideology on reading and writing.

Interestingly enough, Lu Xun drew the above-quoted distinction as a response to a special New Year's issue of *Eastern Miscellany* [Dongfang zazhi] in which more than 400 readers replied to questions from the magazine about their "dreams" for the new year of 1933.[95] The editor, comparing the readers' expectations and hopes to genuine nocturnal dreams, in his afterword divides dreams into two categories according to Zhou Zuoren's division of literature: dreams conveying a didactic message [zaidao] and dreams of self-expression [yanzhi]. Inverting the political categories one might expect, the editor concludes that dreams that convey the "dao" are heterodox--exceptional--whereas dreams that reflect self-expression are orthodox--the norm, because dreams belong to individuals rather than to the society. The author cites Freud to support his argument:

> According to the Freudian interpretation, dreams are the consciousness repressed during the day, which is liberated in sleep at night. During the day time, our thoughts are monitored by various censorships (Freud's term), but when we go to sleep at night, the thoughts of "order," "law," and "moral obligation" characteristic of censorship are dismissed; they do not find expression in our dreams. Dreams represent the private part of consciousness. Therefore, preaching, teaching, doing propaganda, and putting up slogans are not normal dreams. At best, these are daydreams rather than night dreams and should not be called "orthodox" dreams.[96]

But Lu Xun, also citing the Freudian theory of dreams, argues against this division. He stresses Freud's central theory of repression in dream work and pushes the question further to give the apparently personal experience of

---

94. Ibid., p. 60.
95. *Eastern Miscellany* [Dongfang zazhi], Vol. 30, No. 1, 1933.
96. Ibid., p. 82.

individuals a collective meaning: "Why are human beings repressed? This has to do with social systems and customs." This dispute over the framework in which dreams should be interpreted echoes a continuing debate between two different views about the purpose of literature: one that interprets literature as the product of individual experience and emotion, and another that interprets literature as an index of the social realities amid which it was produced.

Although the dream has long been a metaphor for art, and especially lends itself to figuring lyricism and imagistic modes, the modern interest in dream theory has not informed poetry as much as might be supposed. Lu Xun once tried to employ the image of a dream in a work of experimental free verse:

"Dream"

Many a dream makes riot in the dusk.
One dream ousts the dream before, then is driven off by the next.
The ousted dream is black as ink: so is the one that stays.
Both seem to say, "See what a fine color I am."
Fine they may be, but in the dark you cannot tell.
Nor can you know in the dark which one is talking.
In the dark you cannot tell, with your fever and headache.
Come, clear dream, come.[97]

This seemingly simple poem has baffled and perplexed its readers. Su Xuelin, a well-known literary critic, comments that this poem is characteristic of Lu Xun, as "stark and cold" as his fiction and essays, but she refuses to analyze it.[98] However, we must assume that this poem was intended to be meaningful to the person who wrote it as well as to readers. Its initial place of publication offers a context that might be important for its explication: it was published in *The New Youth* [Xin qingnian], a political magazine influential at the time. Moreover, it was composed in Beiping in 1918, the same year Lu Xun published his first novella, "A Madman's Diary," and at a critical juncture between the Russion October Revolution and the May Fourth Movement. These circumstances are worth

---

97. W. J. F. Jenner, trans., *Lu Xun: Selected Poems* (Beijing: Foreign Languages Press, 1982), p. 97.

98. Su Xuelin, *Chinese Writers in the 20s and 30s* [Zhongguo er san shi niandai zuojia] (Taibei: Chun wenxue chubanshe, 1983), p. 65.

bearing in mind as we examine the work of this poem about dreams more closely.

Lu Xun sees the importance of dreams and deliberately delineates the mind through its own raw materials. His poem poses an opposition between allegorical and literal meanings. The first stanza refers to the natural phenomenon that dreams occur at night. Dreams are usually disjointed, disregarding temporal or spatial consistency, and thus can "make riot" [qi hong]. But because dream content is disguised and censored, it is hard to see through to its real meaning. A closed world, a dream posits a certain distance from reality, devoid of physical sensations. Just as language can address its own processes as well as comment on extralinguistic reality, Lu Xun's poem about dreams not only dramatizes and reflects upon the working of dreams but also has political implications. The poem is about both dreams and politics: we need not privilege one content over the other. Only with this understanding can we discuss Lu Xun's intention to speak of something else besides the first object of the utterance. As the poem's reference to a cycle of ousting suggests, Lu Xun uses evening dreams to refer to the confusing political situation after the 1911 revolution: within a few years, state power changed hands from one politician to another, who have "emperor dreams," "restoration dreams," "president dreams," and other dreams of political ambition. The word "riot" indicates politicians' chaotic fights with one another. Their power struggles are all as "black as ink," even though they each boast about their own programs. Not losing his hope for the future, Lu Xun aspires for a "clear dream," the arrival of a new world.[99] His final line, though not a prophecy, certainly expresses hope about the future of the country; he cares less about the futures of these dreamers.

One common literary use of dreams is to reveal the inner world of a protagonist. Lu Xun, in his story "Brothers" [Dixiong],[100] depicts such a dream that reveals an inner world. In the story, two brothers are known to have an exemplary relationship with each other, until one brother falls ill. He is suspected of having contracted scarlet fever, though it is later diagnosed as measles--a less serious disease. The elder, Shijun, relieved of his anxieties, has a nocturnal dream that his brother has died and that, because he has treated his brother's children badly, Shijun himself is condemned by the spirit of his brother and others at his ancestral temple.

---

99.   Zheng Xinling has done an excellent sociological study of this poem in *An Analysis of Lu Xun's Poems* [Lu Xun shi qian xi] (Hebei: Hua Shan Literary Publishing House, 1985), pp. 52-56.

100. *Collected Stories of Lu Xun* (Hong Kong: Jindai tushu, 1967), pp. 367-383.

His dream expresses impulses which are denied during the day but which have been able to find release during the night. Let us not assume that Shijun is a hypocrite, but rather that he is a person trying hard to behave according to conventional expectations. Still, his foreshadowing dream has the haunting quality of real nightmare and reveals to him the side he himself does not want to know. All his efforts to rescue his brother, elaborately described in the story, are deflated by this single dream with a satiric sting. Lu Xun labors over this scenario only to wait for the right moment to turn it upside down: for example, the dream depicts Shijun's palm, growing grotesquely large--three or four times larger than normal--to strike his nephew's face like iron, over and over. The scene graphically illustrates the potential in himself that Shijun finds horrifying. We are privy to Shijun's unconscious thought and find his situation pathetic. Even in his dream, he cannot escape his deepest fear: doing bad things without being punished. The dream unmasks both the protagonist's mind and the social and familial expectations and obligations he confronts by making two figures embody the conflict in the protagonist over his dual role--as a biological being and a social being. Such conflict between desire and reality creates the need for the work of the dream. Interestingly, although this is Lu Xun's most explicit use of dreams in fiction, he shows reluctance to step in and depict what his protagonist dreams; the dream is recalled by Shijun after he suddenly wakes up from his nightmare rather than narrated as it happens. In keeping with Lu Xun's emphasis on the uses people make of what they have dreamed, it is a distinctive characteristic of his writing that he avoids representing dream experiences directly.

For Lu Xun, dreams do not function to comfort the waking and do not come as people wish. In the short story "Tomorrow" [Mingtian],[101] after the death of her son, Fourth Shan's Wife hopes to meet him again in her dream, but all she hears is "her own hard breath through the silence, the vastness, and emptiness of the night." Lu Xun deliberately fails to say whether she meets her son in her dream, refusing to make the dream a cheap fulfillment of the protagonist's desire. However, neither is he stone-hearted enough to disappoint his reader by unequivocally denying such a poor woman, whose single joy in life has been taken away, some illusion to comfort her. He explains elsewhere that he is unwilling to impart his own miserable loneliness to his young readers, who still have fine dreams.[102] He conscientiously avoids making dreams places of refuge, and yet in exchange,

---

101. *The Complete Works of Lu Xun*, Vol. 1, p. 311-320.
102. *The Complete Works of Lu Xun*, Vol. 1, p. 275.

to soothe his young readers, he leaves the dream unconcluded and therefore open-ended.

Similarly, in "Mending the Sky" [Bu tian],[103] Lu Xun captures the moment when Nü Wa, the goddess, suddenly wakes up from her dream. ("Mending the Sky" and the Nü Wa legend are discussed in Section 3.1 above.) She cannot recall the content of her dream, but feels a touch of regret, a nameless, superfluous energy and an urge to create. This story is Lu Xun's open attempt to apply Freudian theory to creative writing. His reticence about the dream's actual content is once again characteristic of his emphasis on people's waking use of their previous dreams, but it is also faithful to one claim of Freud's: that we cannot remember and relate our dreams without forcing them into some kind of narrative continuity (however slight) that distorts them. Unwilling to efface this transformation with a representational "lie," Lu Xun explores the untamed realm of dreams, while at the same time respecting their elusiveness, in line with the strict principles of empiricism so important to Chinese and Western thinkers at this time.

Daydreams, though often betraying an interplay of wishes and their censorship similar to that which structures nocturnal dreams, are waking fantasies whose content is less elusive. In "The True Story of Ah Q,"[104] Ah Q meditates and dreams in a deserted and shattered temple; he imagines that he successfully defeats those who have insulted him. Lu Xun never depicts the dreams Ah Q has while asleep, but tells of at least five of his wakeful night fantasies. These fantasies of self-aggrandizement both fend off and reveal his anxieties about his questionable ancestry and means of survival. Through Ah Q's dreaming, Lu Xun again presents an uncanny world with both individual and collective significance. In fact, many critics have pointed out that Ah Q serves as the allegory of a China caught in a life-and-death cultural struggle in which its spiritual vision of self-justification was inadequate and ludicrous.

Lu Xun's use of dreams in fiction, poetry and essays shows his profound awareness of psychology, as well as his keen interest in dreams' ability to express the predicaments of individuals while also figuring the complexities of political life. His conscientious avoidance of the direct presentation of dream content evidences his great commitment to the world of fact. This commitment also, in some sense, explains why he later turned

---

103. *The Complete Works of Lu Xun*, Vol. 2, pp. 345-356.
104. *The Complete Works of Lu Xun*, Vol. 1, pp. 359-416.

to writing essays, preferring to be involved directly in the outer world of day rather than to linger in the myriad worlds within.

3.4 Conclusion

It is unquestionable that Kuriyagawa Hakuson's theory of creative angst influenced most Chinese writers' interpretation and use of the Freudian theory of creativity. Social unrest caused anxiety and anguish for many, and the personal experience of many writers whose lives were miserable led them to accept both general and individual pain as an impetus to literary creativity. Clearly, creativity, a complex psychological process, should not be understood entirely in terms of drives and the forces that direct or block them. Commenting on a psychological interpretation of Edgar Allan Poe, Freud stated that "investigations such as this do not claim to explain creative genius, but they do reveal the factors which awaken it and the sort of subject matter it is destined to choose."[105] The popularity of the Freudian notion of creativity among Chinese writers lay to no small degree in its vagueness, which rendered it open to various interpretations.

Another facet of Freudian theory, the Oedipal theme, proved useful for Chinese writers who focused on problems of identity, individual growth and freedom, and the dissolution of the family unit. Thus, a great variety of fictional works deployed the Oedipal pattern in literal and symbolic modes of representation. It is important to realize that the writers I have discussed were working in a transitional era, caught between declining literary and social systems and the new systems yet to be created. Writing about the absence of the father was one way of representing this situation. It also provided a way to organize depictions of the family, whose dynamics increasingly came to preoccupy modern Chinese writers. The introduction of the Freudian theory of the Oedipus complex apparently stimulated some writers' imaginations and lent them certain insights into the complicated psychological makeup of human beings. Consequently, their deliberate use of Oedipal situations in a family is sometimes impressively revealing.

Overall, Freud's radically innovative understanding of dreams had powerful effects on Chinese literature. Freudian dream theory reinforced two assumptions of the Chinese tradition: that dreams meaningfully reflect

---

105. Freud, Preface to Marie Bonaparte's *The Life and Words of Edgar Allan Poe: A Psychoanalytic Interpretation* (London: Imago, 1949), p. xi.

important aspects of human experience, and that dreams can be interpreted.[106] Chinese writers also experimented with Freud's specific model of the wishes, repressions, and distortions that produce dream contents. Thus, Freudian dream theory on the one hand helped give shape to explorations of subjectivity: it is interesting to note that diary literature flourished in the late 1920s and early 1930s.[107] Starting with famous works such as Ding Ling's "Diary of Miss Sophia" and Yu Dafu's "Nine Diaries," twentieth-century writers further developed this subjective literary form. And in private forms, that is, in diaries and letters, dreams appeared even more frequently than in other forms, usually as the recorded personal dreams of the narrator. This emphasis on subjective experience is, of course, the consequence of advances in psychology. On the other hand, though, Freudian dream theory also influenced new efforts to interrelate individual and social realities, as the work of Lu Xun especially demonstrates. Chinese writers' knowledge of psychology during the era I am considering resulted in the melding of fantasy and realistic fiction that characterized their use of dreams.

106. See Roberto K. Ong, *The Interpretation of Dreams in Ancient China* (Bochum: Studienverlag Brockmeyer, 1985).

107. Jaroslav Průšek, *The Lyrical and the Epic* (Bloomington: Indiana University Press, 1980), pp. 18-19.

Chapter 4

MODERNIST WRITERS[1]

Freud's name is closely linked with modernism in both East and West, but the term "modernism" has different meanings in the two cultural arenas. In the West, modernism is a label for the dominant tendency of twentieth-century literature and art, as opposed to romanticism, realism, or neo-classicism. Although such a characterization is simplistic, it is generally acknowledged that modernist literature and art embody certain beliefs and styles which are distinct from other trends in the twentieth century. In China, though, literary modernism diverges from other isms but does not exclude them, since a modern Chinese writer can write realistic, romantic and modernistic stories in the same period. The intersection of these modes represents, as Fredric Jameson says, "a cultural struggle that is itself a reflexion of the economic situation of such areas [regions] in their penetration by various stages of capital, or as it is sometimes euphemistically termed, of modernization."[2]

To be "modern" means to be equipped with "new sensibilities," to present different--if not new--views, and more importantly to legitimize such practices. It is commonly assumed that the modernization of Chinese literature is a process assimilated from the West. For instance, the Chinese written literary form grafts western machineries of representation, such as punctuation and westernized syntax, onto traditional Chinese writing practices. The issue of "Europeanized" [ou hua] language in literature has been controversial throughout the twentieth century in China. We can say

---

1.   This chapter benefits a great deal from the anthology *Selected Works of the School of New Sensibilities* [Xin ganjue pai xiaoshuo xuan], (Beijing: People's Literature Press, 1985), compiled by Yan Jiayan, Professor of Chinese Literature at Beijing University. This book helped me avoid much strenuous research for primary materials on the topic.

2.   Fredric Jameson, "Third-World Literature in the Era of Multinational Capitalism," in *Social Text*, No. 15, Fall 1986, p. 68.

that, to some extent, modern Chinese literature is itself essentially a search for a proper method of representation, a way, in other words, of "modernizing" Chinese literature. And Chinese literary modernization was catalyzed by the introduction of Freudian theories.

As the Appendix listing Chinese publications on Freud shows, between the late 1920s and mid-1930s the dissemination of Freudian theory reached its height. During this era, a very distinctive group of literary writers emerged who deliberately used Freudian theory in their creative writing and whose common goal was to create a new way to write fiction. This group is sometimes called "xin ganjue pai" (the School of New Sensibilities), a literary term taken directly from the Japanese term "Shinkankaku Ha,"[3] since both Japanese and Chinese share the same hanzi [kanji] writing system. Some literary critics call this Chinese group "xinli fenxi xiaoshuo pai" (the school of psychoanalytic novelists).[4] Regardless of its different names, this group's shared goal was to explore the psychological process of the mind through the medium of language, or, to use Virginia Woolf's somewhat impressionistic phrase, "to trace the pattern, however disconnected and incoherent in appearance, which each sight or incident scores upon the consciousness."[5] To do so, they learned from the experiments of Western Europe and Japan, experiments ranging from the use of stream of consciousness and expressionism to the use of psychoanalysis. They therefore can be best understood as kin to the modernism that emerged in the West and in Japan.

According to Professor Yan Jiayan, the prelude to the emergence of this school was the circulation of a bi-weekly magazine *Trackless Trolley* [Wugui lieche] in 1928. Among other things, it published a special issue on the occasion of French writer Paul Morand's visit to China. At his best a mediocre popular writer, Morand was nevertheless hailed as a forerunner of

---

3.   The Shinkankaku Ha was a modernist literary group of the mid-1920s in Japan. Among the 19 young writers who were members of the group at one time or another during the three or four years of its existence were Yokomitsu Riichi, Kawabata Yasunari, Kataoka Teppei and Nakagawa Yoichi. These writers published the coterie magazine *Bungei jidai* (Literary Age) from October 1924 to May 1927. The Shinkankaku writers, who saw it as their mission to provide an art-centered alternative to the drab confessional fiction of so-called Japanese naturalism, on the one hand, and to the politically oriented writings of the Japanese proletarian literature movement, on the other, were strongly attracted to such post-World War I European artistic movements as futurism, cubism, expressionism, and dadaism. See *Kodansha Encyclopedia of Japan* (Tokyo: Kodansha International Ltd., 1983), Vol. 7, p. 116.

4.   Zhao Jiabi, "A Memory of My First Edited Series of Books" [Huiyi wo bian de di yi bu cheng tao shi], in *Xin wenxue shiliao*, No. 3, 1983.

5.   Virginia Woolf, "Modern Fiction," in *The Comon Reader* (London: The Hogarth Press, 1929), p. 190.

a new-wave world literature by the *Trackless Trolley*. But after eight issues, the magazine was banned by the government for its "indecency." Soon afterwards, its writers got together and created another magazine called *New Arts and Literature* [Xin wenyi], which was also banned by the authorities in 1930.

The publication of *Xiandai*, with a French title, *Les Contemporains*, marked the writers' coming-of-age in 1932 as an important literary school.[6] Although the editor's column of the first issue stated that the magazine did not intend to create any literary trends, isms, or factional parties,[7] it clearly gave preference to Western modernist writers such as James Joyce, William Faulkner, the Russian imagist poet Sergei Essenin, the Austrian novelist Arthur Schnitzler, the Japanese writer Yokomitsu Riichi, and the French writer Paul Vaillant-Couturier. In every issue there was a column reporting on current literary events in Europe and North America.

Although identifying authors by their allegiances to literary schools is problematic because it inevitably excludes many other writers who do similar work but without the institutional affiliation, we can identify major members of each literary school. There are four psychoanalytic writers who are identified most closely with the School of New Sensibilities: Shi Zhecun, Liu Na'ou, Mu Shiying, and Ye Lingfeng,[8] all of whom, in one way or another, conscientiously incorporated Freudian concepts into their stories. All of them contributed to the magazine *Les Contemporains*. Among the four writers, Liu Na'ou was the pioneer of the Chinese school of New Sensibilities because he grew up in Japan and received a B.A. degree in literature there. However, his literary achievement, apart from a diligent borrowing from the Shinkankaku School in Japan, is overshadowed by the works of the other three writers, and he was the least

---

6.   For details, see Yan Jiayan, Preface to *Selected Stories of the School of New Sensibilities* (Beijing: People's Literature Press, 1985), pp. 3-6.

7.   *Les Contemporains* [Xiandai], Vol. 1, No. 1, 1932, p. 1.

8.   Ye Lingfeng was an artist and designed the covers for many of the modernist publications. Some literary critics are reluctant to include him as a major writer of the psychoanalytic school, not solely because of the obsessive focus on sexual desire in his writings, but also because of his political stand and personality--even Shi Zhecun mentions that Ye was not popular among the literary writers of that time ("Shi Zhecun tan Xiandai zazhi ji qita," in *Lu Xun yanjiu ziliao*, Vol. 9, 1982, p. 231). And Yan Jiayan includes only one story by Ye in his anthology. In fact, that story is not representative of Ye's writings because it describes an unfulfilled romance in language that is sentimental rather than sexual. But I believe that, judging from Ye's attempts to expand the range of literary language and subject-matter on the basis of psychological explorations, he is undoubtedly a psychoanalytic writer whose works have an important position in Chinese psychoanalytic literature.

prolific writer of the four, with only one story collection, *Urban Scenery Lines* [Dushi fengjing xian], published in 1929.

In what follows, I shall discuss three aspects of these Chinese modernist writings: their explorations of urban life, their psychological dimensions, and their depictions of sexuality. In fact, the division among these three aspects is tenuous because they are so much intertwined. But for analytic purposes, I prefer to treat them separately.

4.1 Exploration of Urban Life

Urban experience is an important focus for Chinese modernist writers. The city is both an increasingly conspicuous fact and a universally recognized symbol of modernity. It constitutes and amplifies the modern predicament: that of being a person in a crowd, anonymous and rootless, anxious and insecure, cut off from one's past and from the network of human relations in which one formerly existed, and enslaved by a fast-changing way of life. Urban life for these writers was Shanghai, the biggest commercial city in Asia in the 1930s, the city once called "the Oriental paradise" for Western adventurers. Shanghai was subjected to a vast invasion of Western culture, Western goods, and Western colonial concessions. This peculiar fusion of Chinese urban culture with international influences (due especially to the presence of the French Concession and the International Concession) contrasted radically with the agrarian life of the rest of the country. Shanghai therefore epitomized urban life and modernity for all Chinese.

Although there were some novels and short stories about Shanghai in the teens, it was not until the late 1920s that urban literature in China came into its own.[9] Psychoanalytic writings also reflected the urban scene, contributing to the emergence of an urban literature in Chinese literary history.[10] Of course, we should not confuse the imaginary Shanghai in their fiction with the real Shanghai. The imaginary Shanghai was the product of a representational process which reproduced, not colonial Shanghai itself, but certain of colonial Shanghai's ways of signifying itself. For these modern writers, the line between literal and symbolic Shanghai was tenuous. Often they used the Shanghai setting to invoke a certain type of

---

9. Yan Jiayan, ed., *Selected Stories of the School of New Sensibilities*, p. 16.

10. There were of course other Chinese writers, including many major writers, who wrote about urban culture. But my present concern is with these four writers as especially illuminating representatives of this trend in conjunction with psychoanalytic influences.

people in the society--the petty bourgeoisie or the "pierrots" who "have fallen from life, been squashed, or pushed outside."[11]

A metaphorical anecdote of Mu Shiying's exemplifies this new modernist sensibility:

> Last year, I was suddenly thrown on to the railway. Turning back to see the approaching train rushing at 50 miles an hour, I ran forward to save my life with unsure footsteps. All the spiritual support built in the past twenty-three years collapsed; I lost all concerns and all beliefs. All standards, laws, and values blurred before my eyes ...[12]

Mu Shiying apprehends modern society as a victim of multiple crises. This idea is not new; Yeats describes the same thing: "Things fall apart; the center cannot hold."[13] Terms such as "blurry," "falling apart," and "decentering" are, of course, metaphors, descriptive but somewhat imprecise. However, modernism was not just an "imagination of disaster," as Henry James proclaimed,[14] since not only radical erosions of traditional authority but also equally radical attempts at creating new authorities characterized modernist thought. Although the sense of crisis in the West was different from that in China because of the differences between the two cultures, this sense of crisis and alienation heralded the birth of new literature in both East and West early in the twentieth century.

As Professor Yan Jiayan has noticed, the sense of crisis fostered a kind of sad pessimism among cultural observers.[15] Amid the hustle and bustle of metropolitan life, there was a sense that the individual was lost and left alone, a sentiment that was a predictable by-product of capitalist industrialization and commercialism. As Mu Shiying describes it, "Everyone has a kind of unresolvable solitude; everyone is either partially or entirely misunderstood by others and spiritually separated from others."[16] Here, romantic love had no place, and sentiments were superfluous. "We all are fallen people" [Tong shi tian ya lun luo ren]. Liu Na'ou's "Two People Who Have Not Grasped the Concept of Time" [Liang ge shijian de bu gan

---

11. Mu Shiying, Preface to *Public Cemetery* [Gong mu] (Shanghai: Xiandai, 1933), p. 4.

12. Yan, p. 14.

13. W. B. Yeats, "The Second Coming" in *The Collected Poems of W. B. Yeats* (London: MacMillan, 1963), p. 211.

14. Richard Ellman, ed., *The Modern Tradition* (New York: Oxford University Press, 1965), p. vi.

15. Yan, p. 3.

16. Mu Shiying, Preface to *Public Cemetery* [Gong mu], pp. 1-2.

zheng zhe], Mu Shiying's "The Night" [Ye], Shi Zhecun's "The Business of Sixizi" [Sixizi de shengyi], and Ye Lingfeng's "The Influenza" [Liuxing xing ganmao] reflect this acute disillusionment. In particular, Mu Shiying's writings contain a certain metaphysical distaste for life, a renunciation of the illusions of love. Most of his characters wear a sad mask; they are tired of the hurdles of life, but they nevertheless seek happiness desperately and in vain. For instance, in his story "Five People at the Nightclub" [Yezonghui li de wu ge ren] each of the five knows that his or her life is based on a fraud. Yet they refuse to repent, but aimlessly and crazily keep pursuing sensual pleasures. The only apparently sober person is Jijie, who is obsessed with various editions of Shakespeare's *Hamlet* that, in his hallucination, open their mouths and keep asking him unanswerable philosophical questions: "What are you? What am I? You are what? I am what?" In the night club when everybody else is trying to forget unhappy events and renew social contacts, Jijie sits silently and looks on with "his eyes as dark as night, bearing a mystery of depth and content."[17] Yet the depth of Jijie's thought is farcical: calculating that he can break one match stick into eight pieces in four seconds, he breaks six boxes of matches before he finally decides to leave the night club. It is the silence in the story which creates the tension, and that silence is broken only by the gunshot of one of the five who commits suicide in the end. What is the meaning of life? No one offers an answer, and our attention is returned to the enigmatic urban environment in which they come together to pay their last tribute to the dead. In front of them is "a far-away city and a far-away journey."[18]

Terry Eagleton points out that anxiety, fear of persecution, and the fragmentation of the self can be found throughout recorded history, but what is peculiar to the twentieth century is that such experiences become constituted in a new way by a systematic field of knowledge known as psychoanalysis.[19] The pressure of modernity prompts Chinese writers to realize that realist methods cannot grasp the fast-changing world that they wish to present. They have to look for new methods to convey their acute feelings and carry the spirit of the time. And they find psychoanalysis useful for sharpening their perception of the world.

---

17. Yan, p. 218.

18. Ibid., p. 227.

19. Terry Eagleton, *Literary Theory: An Introduction* (Minneapolis: University of Minnesota Press, 1983), p. 151.

4.2 Psychological Dimension(s)

Freud demystifies psychological reality. His discovery of the unconscious suggests that human reality is not fundamentally rational, and that all the conventionally institutionalized beliefs and ideas of culture and civilization are just historical constructs. His studies on parapraxes, be they slips of the tongue, jokes or dreams, show that these are not simply accidental, but actually result from mechanisms of repression. After Freud, we have a much deeper appreciation of the ways in which each person lives in a world of his/her own, and of the depth of the epistemological uncertainty in our knowledge, especially our self-knowledge. One literary consequence of his theory is that it makes writers think more about the relationship of their linguistic medium to the world it attempts to recreate.

Western twentieth-century modernist novels show an increasing inwardness of vision, a progressive narrowing and sharpening of plot and subject matter, and an intensification of the focus of narrative attention. "It is the practice of the Western twentieth-century novelist to restrict his or her attention to the consciousness of his main character and build the scaffolding with the conventional devices expected of fiction, but with far less scene setting and stage directing," one critic explains.[20] This practice is also characteristic of Chinese modernist writings, although there are exceptions, such as "The Shanghai Fox Trot," "Five People at the Night Club," and "Street Scenes," stories which attempt to grasp the pulse of the whole symbolic Shanghai by drawing portraits of people from all walks of life. But most of the stories in *Selected Stories of the School of New Sensibilities*, restricting settings and events, share an inward-turning tendency to convey the flow of mental experience and have been called "psychological" or "psychoanalytic novels" [xinli xiaoshuo].

These writers of psychoanalytic experiment rejected the assumption that fiction can be a mimetic representation of reality and offered an alternative to realism, the then-dominant mode of fiction in China. They often exhibited a playfulness in their writings, which was criticised by a serious-minded critic in the 1930s:

> From hyperbolism there comes what we can least tolerate, that is, they (the modernist writers) treat their characters with playfulness. They depict people whom they do not clearly understand and whose lives they do not know much. They tend to exaggerate and to put in

---

20.   Melvin Friedman, *Stream of Consciousness: a Study in Literary Method* (New Haven: Yale University Press, 1955), p. 23.

a great deal of technical "spice" in order to present a vivid picture of their characters.[21]

Indeed, these modernists paid a great deal of attention to the work of literature as an artifact, but we should also point out that this playfulness enabled these writers to get away from the dominant realistic writing mode. It yielded a sort of aesthetic freedom from the usual rules and regulations.

Among the psychoanalytic novelists, Shi Zhecun is recognized as a vanguard figure who has a solid foundation in classical Chinese literature. Shi Zhecun's stories are about the declining feudalist families and make use of historical events and figures. His fiction covers a wide range of settings--from rural to urban--and themes--from psychological exploration to social investigation. His most representative works, in which he shows much Freudian influence, are three collections of short stories, *The General's Head* [Jiangjun de tou], *A Rainy Evening* [Meiyu zhi xi] and *Kind Women's Ways* [Shan nüren xingpin]. Here I shall examine two of his stories, paying special attention to their endings.

Shi Zhecun's story "Jiangjun de tou" (the general's head) was recognized as the product of Freudian influences soon after its publication. Critics such as Qian Xingcun, Su Xuelin, and, more recently, C. T. Hsia,[22] have stressed the parallel conflicts in the story: between the national and racial, between the personal and the communal, and between the sexual and the political, all embodied in one character. Shi Zhecun himself unambiguously states that he intends to pave a new path in the writing of fiction through his collection *The General's Head*.[23] Unsurprisingly, then, the reader finds the title story startling and hard to grasp. Here, I shall offer a tentative interpretation of the story in terms of a simple and yet neglected aspect of the story: the conflicts between the body and the desires.

The title most obviously refers to the story's gothic ending, in which a general loses his head in battle, but his body runs back to the girl he loves. On the surface, the piece seems conventional: it starts with a narrator giving an account of the time and location of the story and describes the physical appearance of the protagonist Hua Jinding. Even the plot is

---

21. You Zhiwu, "Some Tendencies in Modern Chinese Novels" [Xiandai Zhongguo xiaoshuo zhong ji zhong qingxiang], in *Zhongshan wenhua jiaoyu guan jikan*, Vol. 3, No. 3, 1936, p. 1088.

22. C. T. Hsia, *A History of Modern Chinese Fiction 1917-1957* (New Haven: Yale University, 1961), p. 135.

23. Shi Zhecun, *The General's Head* [Jiangjun de tou] (Shanghai: Xin Zhongguo, 1933), p. 1.

conventional: the romance between a hero and a beauty. Hua Jinding, one of whose ancestors is Tibetan [tufan], grows up in Chengdu and becomes well known for his military bravery and ability. He is sent off to combat the Tibetan invaders on the border. Along the way he keeps debating with himself whether to fight the Tibetans or join them, since in his veins Tibetan blood flows. To complicate his plans further, he falls in love with a Han woman in the village where he is stationed. This last factor induces him to fight the Tibetans, symbolically on her behalf. But during the battle, as soon as his thoughts turn to the girl, his head is cut off by the enemy chief and he in turn cuts off the chief's head. Veering off from this unlikely but still realistically described event, the ending of the story transgresses the conventional and realistic mode even further:

> The headless General Hua was carried by his horse along a stream. Because it was deep in the forest, the government guards on the other side of the stream did not see him. Suddenly, the general felt very hot and stuffy. Why can I not see anything in front of me? I have been to many battles, but never had such an experience. The general felt he was smeared all over with blood. How can I go see that beautiful and gentle young girl? So thinking, the general felt it necessary to find a place to wash himself.

> The general got off the horse and walked towards the stream. He wondered, why is the river so muddy so that I can not even see my own reflection on it? At that time, the girl, of whom the general was thinking, was washing her dishes at the stairs. When she raised her head by accident, she suddenly saw that a headless warrior holding a head in his hand was standing at the other side of the stream. Taken aback, she stopped washing and kept looking at the warrior. But when she saw that the general squatted down to touch the water in an attempt to wash his hands, she could not help laughing:

> "Hi, have you lost the battle? Even your head has been cut off, what's the use of washing your hands? Why don't you die quickly? What do you want? A headless devil like you still wants to be a human being? Yuck!"

> The general's heart could tell whose voice this was. For a moment, he recalled her prophecy--a headless suitor was easy to handle--and suddenly felt weak and empty when he perceived her indifferent attitudes toward him. Waving his hands wildly in the air, he soon collapsed on the ground.

At this time, a smile appeared on the face of the Tibetan chief's head in Hua's hand.

At the same time, far away, the tears rolled down from the eyes of the General's severed head, which was held by the Tibetan chief on the ground.

The intensity of the story culminates in this bizarre picture, which is perfectly intelligible--though impossible--on a literal level, but which eludes easy interpretation. There is clearly a playfulness in the sudden shift from General Hua's psychological conflicts in battle to a fantastic joke. For anyone who is familiar with classical Chinese novels, the image of a headless man on horseback evokes another image in a classical Chinese novel, *Romance of the Three Kingdoms* by Luo Guanzhong (1330-1400), in which Guan Yunchang, a famous general, is defeated in a battle and beheaded. His spirit does not dissipate into space, but rather wanders through a void and shouts "Give back my head; give back my head" until it comes to a hill. On the hill lives a venerable Buddhist priest who enlightens Guan and persuades him to be content with his death.[24] For anyone who is familiar with American literature, the headless horseman may recall Washington Irving's short story "The Legend of Sleepy Hollow," the legend being that a headless Hessian trooper from the Revolutionary War is often seen by the country folks, riding a horse in the gloom of night.[25]

Both examples may show that the image of a headless man in Shi Zhecun's "The General's Head" has transcultural relevance. Significantly, in the Irving story Brom Bones is a sexual rival of Ichabod Crane's. By playing the headless Hessian trooper, Brom threatens Crane with castration: headlessness. The headless horseman in all three cases represents the uselessness of the head to the functioning of the body. "The General's Head" thus carries a philosophical message about the separation of the body from the mind. Although the mind-body problem is an age-old philosophical inquiry, the presentation of the issue here is specifically modernist because psychoanalysis teaches people that the body has a life of its own but is unable to express itself well through the tropes and figures of language. Here, in an uncanny moment, the dead returns, a mere body, which has literally lost its head. Hua becomes impersonal, a mechanical "it"--the body. This body is mute, unlike Guan Yunchang's body in

---

24. Luo Guanzhong, *Romance of the Three Kingdoms* [San guo yanyi] (Hong Kong: Youlan, 1961), Vol. 2, pp. 607-608.

25. Washington Irving, "The Legend of Sleepy Hollow," in *Stories of the Hudson* (New York: Harbor Hill Books, 1984), p. 69.

Romance of the Three Kingdoms, which can still chant for the return of the head. Hua's body cannot see--"all is dark"--but it is driven by a never-dying desire. As a Freudian allegory, the story dramatizes the sometimes alarming independence of the body from the mind's conscious control. The ending only figures luridly what the rest of the story implies: from the very start, the narration sets up the stresses that begin to sever Hua's head from his body. Wrestling with so many conflicts--national, racial, sexual, personal--inevitably results in a division figured by the physical severing of head from body.

Shi Zhecun also uses dreams with Freudian overtones in the story to show Hua Jinding's psychological makeup: after he orders one of his soldiers to be killed for attempting to rape a village girl (this also hints at the threat of castration as punishment for desire), in his dream Hua Jinding reviews the whole scene of the soldier's pursuit of the girl in the courtyard, but this time it is he himself rather than the soldier performing the act. His dream spells out to the general his own potential for violent desire. Hua's dream shows a possible way to explore the unconscious side of the human mind.

Shi Zhecun prides himself on being a writer good at depicting abnormal psychology, a practice which began in modern China with Lu Xun's "A Madman's Diary" and continued among the modernists. Shi Zhecun's "The Magic Track" [Mo dao] belongs to this category. The narrating "I" has delusions about being followed by an old ugly woman. Otherwise, he is intelligent and able to function well in his daily affairs. Lu Xun's epic story is a political allegory about a madman who one day discovers the cannibalism of Chinese tradition, but Shi's "The Magic Track" does not contain any social criticism. To put it simply, Shi's story is an exercise in envisioning how the mind at the paranoid stage works. It may also be Shi's parody of Henry James' *The Turn of the Screw*.

The Turn of the Screw has generated many interpretations and controversies. One influential interpretation holds that it is not a ghost story, but a madness story, a study of a case of psychosis. In *The Turn of the Screw*, neither the narrator nor the other characters refer explicitly to psychology; indeed, the novella was written before Freud's first publications. The ambiguity and suggestiveness of the text give rise to the many controversies. But "The Magic Track" clearly refers to psychology. The textual clues show the protagonist falling under a "magic power" by reading books about sorcery, Le Fanu's gothic novels ("Le Fanu" is the original name used in the text), Persian religious hymns, reports of sexual crimes, and copies of *Psychology Journal* [Xinlixue zazhi].

The plot of the story is very simple: a Shanghai clerk is invited by his friend and the friend's wife to spend a weekend with them in the countryside. He imagines that he is followed by an old ugly woman all the way, and his strange behavior alarms his friend. But if we simply conclude that the narrator is psychopathological, we cannot explain why in the end he gets a telegram saying that his three-year-old daughter has suddenly died, in confirmation of his fear and suspicion. This point is where Professor Yan Jiayan ends his interpretation, and there is indeed no way to stretch the analysis further within a realistic evaluation of the story.[26] But this is clearly not a realistic story. It is a mixture of the real and the fantastic, mediated by its constant references to psychology. It is a deliberate attempt by Shi to juggle literature and psychology.

Unlike the Madman in Lu Xun's "A Madman's Diary," who is literate but has a limited range of knowledge, the urban clerk (the narrator) in "The Magic Track" is very learned as a result of extensive readings. He associates Western folklore about witches flying on broomsticks to catch children, as well as the Chinese legend about a dry-faced old fox-woman spitting magic water outside the window under the moonlight in *Strange Tales of Liaozhai* [Liaozhai zhi yi], by Pu Songling (1640-1715), with the image of an old woman sitting opposite him on a train. He is terribly self-conscious and even tries to diagnose his own symptoms:

> My memory is bad indeed. I am afraid that I might have a nervous breakdown, palpitation. ... It's useless. If I continue to live like this, taking drugs cannot prevent me from attracting such illness. Polytamin does not help me even after I have taken three bottles of it. What is fated cannot be avoided. Ha, ha, I've become a determinist. Which school does this thought belong to? Schopenhauer's? Yah, just as sorcery can exert magic on people, no one can escape determinism. Sorcery? Why do I use this as a metaphor?[27]

Here, many signifiers crisscross: from Western medical knowledge, "nervous breakdown" [shenjing shuairuo]; the Western drug "polytamin" (his own English word); the Chinese traditional diagnosis "palpitation"; Schopenhauer's determinism; and sorcery. The text is terribly self-analytical: each sentence negates or modifies the previous one, producing accumulations of uncertainty. For example, the three sentences

---

26. Yan Jiayan, ed., *Selected Stories of the School of New Sensibilities*, p. 11
27. Yan, p. 111.

"My memory is bad indeed," "I am afraid that I might have a nervous breakdown, palpitation....," and "It's useless" all refer to the fact that the narrator cannot remember things well. The first sentence states the fact; the second tries to explain the statement; the third surrenders to the futile effort of speculation. This textual strategy resembles the narrative in Dostoievsky's *Notes from Underground*, which is hesitant and self-contradictory, alternating between narrative self-debasement and self-aggrandizement. What is signified is the modern sensibility--the embrace of a "blooming buzzing confusion" (William James's phrase to describe the stream of consciousness) and at the same time a hopeless search for order.

How then shall we understand the ending of the story? In "The Magic Track," we know in advance that the behavior of the narrator is considered to be mad--delusional paranoia. What we are concerned to know (and it is at this point that our hesitation comes) is whether or not the clerk's madness alone accounts for all the confusion of the story. Shi Zhecun does not even try to concoct a credible ending--if the story is only an hallucination of the narrator, why is there an ending which confirms his hallucination and suspicion? It seems that this writing falls into the category of the "fantastic" provided by Tzvetan Todorov:

> The fantastic refers to an ambiguous perception shared by the reader and one of the characters. Within this genre of the fantastic, it is **probable** that "fantastic" reactions will occur.[28]

This ambiguity which mixes the real and the imaginary suggests a collapse of the limits between matter and mind. The supernatural event is perceived against the background of what is considered normal and natural. Both of Shi's stories are characterized by surprises at the end. If we take seriously the Chinese critic of the 1930s who found the playfulness of modernists so disturbing, it is possible for us to imagine that their deliberate ambiguity produces an effect which is similar to jokes as Freud describes it:

> [T]he very nature of surprising someone or taking him unawares implies that it cannot succeed a second time. When a joke is

---

28. Tzvetan Todorov, *The Fantastic: A Structural Approach to a Literary Genre* (Ithaca: Cornell University Press, 1975), p. 46.

repeated, the attention is led back to the first occasion of hearing it as the memory of it arises.[29]

The endings of the stories overthrow their previous equilibria and bypass distinctions between the real and the imaginary. This effect of Shi's rhetorical skill leads to an interpretive ambiguity or richness rather than to a clear invocation of the supernatural. In fact, both endings show an epistemological concern with different ways of exploring the shifting relations between self and world.

Another writer who is concerned with the effect of the fantastic is Ye Lingfeng. Although Ye tries to be a popular writer by doggedly insisting on sexual themes--particularly female sexual psychology--in his stories, he personally prefers the fantastic and considers his best stories to be those which use the strange, abnormal, and unscientific as themes. He also differentiates his stories from the popular practice of rewriting historical figures and events, and stresses that the function of his fantastic fiction is to weave the present and the past together, thus "creating the effect of psychological complexes."[30]

"Jiulümei" is just such a fantastic story: a Chinese novelist, by chance, is given a miniaturized reproduction of a skull of a Persian princess. Somehow he becomes the incarnation of the princess's lover, who was her private tutor, in his night dreams about their love affairs. During the day, the novelist behaves normally and continues his social contacts, but at night in his dream he reenacts the role of the tutor. The central symbol of the story is the miniature head. Every night when he goes to bed with the skull, he can continue the dream; if he does not hold the head when he sleeps, the dream does not come that night and on the next the princess will reproach him for failing to meet her. The head--it is worth noting that it is a miniaturized reproduction of the "real thing"--proves to be located at the crossroads of several cultures: Chinese, French (the "real" skull was allegedly on display in the French national museum and its reproduction was given by a Frenchman to an overseas Chinese student as a parting present), and Persian. Yet it is also an empty signifier that escapes all the "depths" of worlds. "As a novelist, he is used to the mixture of reality and phantasy."[31] The metaphor of the skull also furnishes the mirage effect of a mirror: it evokes the scene in *The Dream of the Red Chamber* in which Jia

29. Sigmund Freud, *Jokes and Their Relation to the Unconscious* (New York: Norton, 1963), p. 154.

30. Ye Lingfeng, *Lingfeng xiaoshuo ji* (Shanghai: Xiandai, 1931), p. 3.

31. Ye Lingfeng, "Jiulümei," in *Lingfeng xiaoshuo ji*, p. 194.

Rui is given a magic mirror by a Taoist and is told to look only at one side of the mirror if he wants to cure his illness. On that side, he sees a frightening death's head and he instantly feels better and gains strength to fight against his pathological symptoms--his will to live triumphs. But when he turns the mirror, against the advice of the Taoist, he sees the image of the woman he desires waving at him. Gazing at the desirable side of the mirror, he manages to get into the mirror and fulfill his sexual urges, but finally he dies of exhaustion.[32] These two texts both feature objects that give access to fantasy worlds--the mirror and the skeleton head. However, the objects do not serve the same function: the mirror finally draws Jia Rui into its mirage and wraps him up in the same way as a mirage lures desert travellers to destruction, but the skeleton head is crushed when the novelist falls from the bed to the floor. He wakes up and thereafter his life goes on. The difference between the two stories resembles the distinction made by Freud between a pathological patient and a creative writer: the artist can find a way of returning from the world of fantasy back to reality, whereas a neurotic, unable to recreate the world which can make his life bearable, turns into a madman.

Although Mu Shiying's "The Black Peony" [Hei mudan] is not as fantastic as the previous three stories I have mentioned, it depicts seemingly impossible worlds and events. It sets up a contrast between urban life with its perpetual worry and anxiety, and the fantasized quiet, rustic, and wealthy leisure of rural life. Life in the city is dreamlike: it is made up of "jazz, foxtrot, mixed drinks, popular Spring colors, cars of eight cylinders, and Egyptian cigars."[33] In spite of the materialist affluence displayed, the essence of urban life is that "our generation is the slave of the stomach and the body... smashed by Life."[34] The ideal life for city dwellers is in the countryside, where one can "drink a cup of coffee, smoke two cigarettes, sit on the balcony, and read at leisure some novels, or books on gardening, and in the evenings, listen to the radio."[35] (This ideal life is certainly not the common Chinese country life of the 1930s; signifiers like "coffee," "cigarettes," "books on gardening" and "the radio" clearly suggest a Westernized way of life. Here we see how deeply the Chinese modernist imagination was affected by "Westernization.")These two worlds of the city and the countryside are incompatible in the text, but somehow linked by a "Black Peony Spirit"--a dancer in a ballroom for the city dweller and the

---

32. Cao Xueqin, *Hong lou meng*, Vol. 1, Chapter 12.
33. Yan, p. 196.
34. Ibid., p. 196.
35. Ibid., p. 198.

spirit of a black peony for the country hermit. The story offers several alternative accounts of the same events. One is the Gothic reading of the event from the viewpoint of the country hermit, who thinks the woman visitor found in his garden at night is the spirit of a black peony bush there and who therefore marries her within a month. Another is the viewpoint of the Black Peony, a dancer who states that she was fleeing from a drunken customer nearby and happened to run into the garden. Later, when she saw that the hermit was pleasant, she decided to act out his fantasy and be the incarnation of the black peony. The third version is that of the city dweller "I" who meets the dancer in the city and is introduced to her again by his friend the country hermit. The entire drama is based on the intersection between the hermit's delusion, the dancer's willful deceit, and the city-dweller's perception that spans both other versions. There is yet another reading of the story, though, that of the reader, who knows that the observer knows the whole thing is a deceit but does not agree with the observer's version of the event--it is not true that "one more person in this world is relieved of the burden of life,"[36] that the Black Peony is rescued and can live a happy life ever after.

The Black Peony's constant worry about how to continue the deception of the country hermit by no means offers her relief from the burden of life. One cannot help but admire the technical virtuosity of Mu Shiying, particularly when the story produces the effect of exceeding both the understanding and the control of the narrator who is subjected to it. The enigma of the Black Peony therefore is not just a matter of individual psychological projections, but the product of four functional positions in a structure which, determining four different viewpoints, embodies four different relations to the act of observation and forms a hermeneutic circle. Everyone is in the know except the hermit, who is represented as astonishingly innocent and naive. Yet "the naivety which we come across can either be in the nature of a joke... or in the nature of smut."[37] And hence we go full circle and start reading for clues in the text again.

4.3 Sexual Desire

In a lecture given at Harvard University, Douwe W. Fokkema pointed out the importance of sexuality to the modernists in general:

---

36. Ibid., p. 204.
37. Sigmund Freud, *Jokes and Their Relation to the Unconscious*, p. 186.

Modernism has introduced a number of topics which were rarely or never treated in Realist or Symbolist texts. The semantic field of sexuality (including homosexuality) is a Modernist acquisition. The semantic fields of psychology, science and technology were expanded.[38]

By the 1930's the general idea of an unconscious mind had become a commonplace in Chinese literary circles. Writers of "new sensibilities" [xin ganjue] characteristically explored this most impalpable aspect of psychic life. They took an interest in the unconscious and recognized its fundamental role in love and sexuality. They not only explored the "normal" forms of sexuality, but also the "abnormal" forms. Their approach to sexuality was different from that of traditional erotic literature, such as *The Golden Lotus* and *Rou pu tuan*, which concentrated on displaying sexual acts in detail. Rather, the modernist writers explored the contradictions, hesitations, and conflicts within the minds of their protagonists.

Shi Zhecun's "Shi Xiu" is generally viewed as a Freudian story, "an attempt to depict sexual psychology"--indeed, the author himself overtly signals a Freudian interpretation of it.[39] It is a deliberately psychoanalytic interpretation of an episode in the historical novel *Water Margin* by Shi Nai'an. *Water Margin* is about a rebellion during the Song Dynasty (Hui Zong 1101-1126). In one episode the protagonist Shi Xiu, while staying with his sworn brother Yang Xiong, finds that Yang's wife, Pan Qiaoyun, is having an affair with a monk. He then incites Yang Xiong to dismember Pan Qiaoyun--to cut her to pieces--in an act of capital punishment.[40] There is no explanation for Shi Xiu's being so unduly inquisitive into other people's business. Capital punishment is indeed excessive for such an "offense." Shi Zhecun puzzles over the event, finally comes up with a Freudian interpretation of Shi Xiu's cruelty, and presents it as the story of "Shi Xiu."

In Shi Zhecun's version of the story, Shi Xiu is a grown man who has never had any sexual relationship with a woman and is therefore greatly attracted to Pan Qiaoyun, the vivacious wife of his sworn brother Yang Xiong. At night he dreams of telling her that he loves her, but during the

---

38. Douwe W. Fokkema, *Literary History, Modernism, and Postmodernism (The Harvard University Erasmus Lectures, Spring 1983)* (Amsterdam/Philadelphia: John Benjamin, 1984), p. 35.

39. Shi Zhecun, Preface to *The General's Head* (Shanghai: New China Press, 1932), p. 1.

40. *Shui hu zhuan* (Water Margin), Chapter 45.

day he dares not even look at her. He tries to suppress his desire for Pan Qiaoyun and resist her flirtation because he feels he has a moral obligation to his sworn brother. Although at first Pan Qiaoyun flirts with him, after she sees it is impossible to tempt him she turns her love to a monk. Shi Xiu is jealous of their love affair and imagines the pleasure of witnessing her death: "This sharp knife pierces into Pan Qiaoyun's naked body. Red blood flows down from her soft and white skin. Her beautiful head twists around in pain. Her black hair spreads down to her breasts. Her lips are tight against clenched teeth. Her limbs shiver in rhythm. Just to imagine this, isn't it exceptionally beautiful?"[41] This love-become-hatred causes Shi Xiu to incite Yang Xiong to kill Pan Qiaoyun. The killing scene in the story is grotesquely portrayed.

We can restate the story in a Freudian vocabulary, since a Freudian interpretation of Shi Xiu's psychological motivation is clear from the text: the killing resulted from Shi's sexual repression. Shi Zhecun concentrates on Shi Xiu's sadism and masochism, which are the most common and the most significant of all the perversions--the desire to inflict pain upon the sexual object, and its reverse. At first he passively receives Pan's flirtation, suffering mental pain at the hands of his sexual object. His pain causes him to feel disgust and shame that nonetheless gratify his libido. Finally, his masochism is transformed into aggressive sadism. The paragraph about Shi Xiu's imagination--"This sharp knife pierces into Pan Qiaoyun's naked body...."--is actually a penetration metaphor showing a transformed sexual desire. Shi Xiu wishes to obtain mastery and revenge for his unfulfilled sexual drives by watching the death of Pan. His pleasure in looking [scopophilia] is a perversion as well.

This Shi Xiu, however, exists only in the text. The Shi Xiu in *Water Margin* is different from the modern Shi Xiu. Shi Xiu is transformed by being rewritten. How does Shi Zhecun evoke a psychoanalytic interpretation from the events of the older novel? Rather than describing what Shi Xiu does, the modern text focuses on what he dreams, in the territory between consciousness and the unconscious.

The first of the five chapters gives an account of his night dreams, which demonstrate displacement and condensation. When he hears some hushed sounds outside his door, he imagines seeing Pan Qiaoyun holding a lamp on her way to her bedroom. As she steps over the threshold, one of her shoes drops. She uses her bare foot to hook the shoe, instead of taking it with her hand. Shi Xiu imagines this movement as a dancing posture: "Her

---

41. Yan, p. 101.

body leans forward, her left hand holding the lamp and her right hand stretching ahead to maintain the balance."[42] This dream is a displacement from a previous scene in which he saw a young woman carrying firewood. Following the always-present authorial voice, we see how Shi Xiu is trapped in his attraction, repulsion, hesitation, and intellectualization. The first three chapters exhibit the same psychological structure: attraction and then repression, each time more inexorable and obvious than in the previous chapter. The fourth chapter represents a turning point in Shi Xiu's psychological life because of his discovery of the adultery, and the fifth chapter recounts his plot to kill Pan. "Shi Xiu" is in many ways carefully arranged as a conventional narrative, in terms of its time sequence, its gradual build-up of intensity, and its authorial control. But in spite of its realist technique, "Shi Xiu" is a modernist story because it bears many calculated moments, which are deliberately set as psychoanalytic.

Mu Shiying's "A Female Silver Statue" [Baijin de nü ti suxiang] is about the awakening of sexual desire in a middle-aged man at the sight of his naked female patient. It is an ironic exploration of male sexuality set in a typically convenient place: a clinic where a male Christian doctor treats an anonymous female patient. A clinic is a place from which sexuality is usually believed to be excluded, but it is also a place which evokes people's sexual imagination. In a single word-string running through the mind of the doctor--"Sexually over-active, weak, irregular menstruation, early consumptive stage, an enigma"--collide clinical terms mixed with his personal judgments about the Female as an enigma. Taking advantage of his authoritative position as a doctor, the man indulges his sexual imagination by freely asking the woman intrusive questions about her married life. The woman is described as "mystical" and impenetrable. Under the male gaze, she becomes "a female silver statue without shame, without any sense of morality and human desires. An inorganic statue."[43] In fact, the anonymous woman patient is a male-projected female figure who incarnates the doctor's ambivalence toward both female sexuality and his own sexuality. The man's psychological transformation from piety to violent sexual overtures is triggered by the sight of this naked "silver statue." Not without irony, the text states that in the end Doctor Xie solves the problem of his irresistible sexual urges by getting married to a widow--a socially acceptable solution. The doctor is traditionally a figure of reason and rational control; the fact that this doctor is "infected" with desire is a

---

42.   Yan, p. 73.

43.   Yan, p. 262.

characteristically modernist way to say that the intellect is subject to being influenced by libidinal energies.

Women are objectified in other modernist texts as well. Ye Lingfeng's "The Influenza" [Liuxing xing ganmao][44] starts with:

> Streamlined body
> V-type water tank
> Foam rubber seat
> Hydraulic damper
> Five-gear transmission
>
> She, a new car of 1933, breathing the orange air of May, along a bituminous road, was gliding through crowds like a fish.[45]

This is not a description of a new car, but of a woman as seen by the protagonist. Within the story, the image of a car recurs often and becomes the "flu," which torments the narrator because he finds woman contemptible but cannot do without her.

Ye Lingfeng often accommodates his fiction to the needs of common readers; that is, he often treats sexuality according to the conventions of popular literature. He is fully aware of their needs:

> I know that ordinary readers require me to produce stories like "Bathing" [Yu] and "Lang tao sha" which contain strong erotic stimulation or extremely melancholic romances.[46]

His writing is not usually about Platonic love but about the psychology of sexuality. Ye is particularly known for his ability to probe the psychology of female sexuality. He even adorns the cover of his story collection with a picture of a naked woman, supposedly Eve, in a garden full of apples.[47] In spite of his avowed desire to curry favor with his readers, however, Ye transgresses literary conventions and touches taboo topics such as incest, the sexual experiences of puberty, and the seduction by older married women of

---

44. Ye Lingfeng, "The Influenza" [Liuxing xing ganmao], in *Les Contemporains*, Vol. 3, No. 4, September 1, 1933.

45. Ibid., p. 653.

46. Ye Lingfeng, *Lingfeng xiaoshuo ji*, p. 3.

47. Ye Lingfeng, *Lingfeng xiaoshuo ji*.

younger men.[48] He investigates the concepts of shame and duty in relation to sexual desire.

His "National Hatred" [Guo chou][49] is a satirical story about the intersection between national causes and individual sexual desires. Xitian, a Chinese student in Japan, is lonely and sexually frustrated. He becomes attracted to a Japanese housemaid who cleans his room every day. When he finally plucks up enough courage to go to her room at night, in his nervousness he happens to knock over a cupboard in the corridor and disturbs the whole house. Under the electric light, both he and the landlady are startled to find the housemaid with the naked landlord. The next day, he moves away from the house and explains to his friends that he cannot endure the Japanese anymore because they have invaded China: his "national hatred" does not permit him to live there anymore. Xitian passes off the adventure of his lust and his subsequent departure as nationalist indignation.

An important predecessor of "National Hatred" is Yu Dafu's "Sinking" [Chen lun]. Both in part describe the masturbation, sexual fantasies, and pathological behavior of lonely male Chinese students in Japan at the time. Both end by associating sexuality with political missions: "He" in "Sinking" shouts "My motherland, my motherland, you cause my death!" while leaping into the sea to drown himself, and Xitian in "National Hatred" attributes his embarrassment to his national identity rather than his sexual humiliation. Both stories suggest that political identities are merely cloaks for personal, sexual identities. Both are examples of an "Ah Q complex," characterized by the lack of self-reflection.[50] Yu Dafu's story is written in a sympathetic and touching tone, and some of the experiences in it are autobiographical. But in Ye Lingfeng's story, the narrative seems insincere and unreliable--it even seems to parody Yu Dafu's influential story in a jocular manner.

---

48. For instance: "Nü Wa's Offspring" [Nü Wa Shi zhi yi nie], "Inner Regret" [Nei jiu], "On the Night of His Sister's Wedding" [Jie jia zhi ye], and "Forbidden Place" [Jin di]. All are included in *Lingfeng xiaoshuo ji*.

49. Ye Lingfeng, *Lingfeng xiaoshuo ji*.

50. "Ah Q jingshen" is usually called "Ah Q spirit," but I prefer to refer to it as "Ah Q complex" or "Ah Q syndrome." Ah Q is a character in Lu Xun's story "The True Story of Ah Q," which I discussed in Chapter 3. Zhou Zuoren wrote in 1922 about the Ah Q complex: "This man Ah Q is a synthesis of all the 'roles' a man may play in Chinese society. He is a man with no will of his own: his consciousness consists of the accumulated customs handed down by society from one generation unto another. For that reason, Ah Q cannot be said really to exist in contemporary society, and yet he exists everywhere at once." See Zhou Qiming (Zhou Zuoren), *Lu Xun de qingnian shidai* [The period of Lu Xun's youth] (Beijing: Chinese Youth Press, 1957), p. 114.

4.4 The Decline of the Modernist Writers

The modernist claim to be searching for more psychological literary methods was directed against the popular trend of critical realism borrowed from the Soviet Union in the 1930s. The Leftist writers exerted tremendous pressure on writers who wrote "non-political" fiction. The leading modernist, Shi Zhecun, had direct confrontations with the leading critical realist, Lu Xun, on several issues.[51] There was vigorous debate among writers in Shanghai about the "third type of people," those who opposed the use of literature for immediate political ends and who hoped to find a compromise between largely political and largely psychological literary modes. The modernist writers were usually on the side of depoliticizing literature. When the wave of proletarian literature was dominant, for example, Shi Zhecun decided that he could not write proletarian fiction,

> Not because I did not sympathize with the movement for a proletarian literature, but because I felt that my life along this line would be without any prospects; at a certain time it even seemed to me that I could not even make a realistic story of my life, from my pen. But since all readers of Chinese literature demand such realistic worlds, I have no choice but to lay my pen aside, if not then to write as it suits me.[52]

His last sentence was a response to the Leftist claim that Chinese readers demanded realist literature. Mu Shiying, in a way reminiscent of Yu Dafu, offered a similar justification:

> I don't have one sentence that I cannot say to the public [an expression to show his honest attitude toward writing as a career], and I don't want to imitate many of my contemporaries who cover themselves with protective coloration and live a hypocritical life and shout hypocritical slogans. On the other hand, they make use of mass psychology, political strategy, self-propaganda to justify their past positions or to raise their present status. I think this is dirty business which I don't want to do myself. I can be accused of falling behind, of being an opportunist, or a turnip whose red skin has been

---

51. C. T. Hsia, *A History of Modern Chinese Fiction 1917-1957* (New Haven: Yale University Press, 1961), p. 612.

52. Shi Zhecun, "Wo de chuangzuo shenghuo zhi licheng" [My creative life], in *Chuangzuo de jingyan* [Creative experience] (Shanghai, 1935), p. 71.

peeled [a Chinese expression for someone who has changed his position from the Left to the Right--from "red" to "white"] and so on. At least, I can stand on the roof of the world and cry, "I am loyal to myself and to my friends."[53]

But such a gesture is a political action, even though it takes the form of a denial of dogmatic political propaganda. It is not true that the modernists did not make moral judgments in their stories, as many people have alleged. The protagonists in Mu Shiying's stories may be crazy, immoral, and decadent, but the authorial voice is always there, judging by its tone and emphasis. For example, "Shanghai's Fox-Trot" starts and ends with the same sentence: "Shanghai. A paradise built on hell!" Afraid that readers may fail to see his political stand, Mu puts a more definitive statement of it in parentheses: "Lincoln Street. (Here, morality is trodden under foot and crimes are held high above the head.)"[54]

Social analysis is never entirely absent from these modernist writings. In Mu Shiying's "The Breadbaker who Stole a Loaf of Bread" [Tou mianbao de mianbao shi](1932), the breadbaker's honesty and timidity come to a crisis when he decides to steal a loaf of "foreign bread" from his own shop for his mother's birthday because his whole family has been thinking of tasting the bread for years. He cannot afford to buy even one loaf of bread because it costs him half a month's salary. His is an economic and ethical problem: he is a dutiful son and a loving husband and father, but even though he works long hours every day, his earnings are not enough to satisfy his family's small wish. The best part of the story is a minute, vivid description of how he feels when he commits the "theft" and when he is caught, and of how he has to hide his worry in front of his family and refrain from telling them the bad news before they finish eating the bread. The last sentence of the story makes the story's moral clear: after hearing that his father has been expelled because of taking the bread from the shop, the son wonders why one cannot take what one makes. The collision between ethical codes and economic circumstances which induce the breadbaker to steal is clear and acute.

Most of Shi Zhecun's stories have social significance because they depict the daily psychological life of ordinary people. Two of his story collections, *A Rainy Evening* and *Kind Women's Ways*, are attempts to "depict a psychological process."[55] Like "The Breadbaker who Stole a Loaf

53. Mu Shiying, Preface to *Public Cemetery* [Gong mu], pp. 1-2.
54. Ibid., p. 160.
55. Shi Zhecun, *A Rainy Evening*, p. 1.

of Bread," these stories are told by third-person narrators and have traditional narrative arrangements.

Both external and internal pressure led to the discontinuation of these writers' experimental writings. The Chinese political environment did not encourage writers to live in their own ivory towers. As the Japanese intensified their invasion of China in the 1930s, national survival became a priority for many writers. Shi Zhecun quit his general editor's job at the magazine *Les Contemporains* in 1934; the other writers in his group also began to take different paths in their lives. Liu Na'ou went to Japan in 1932, came back with the Japanese to occupied Shanghai to organize a collaborators' newspaper, and was killed in 1939; Shi Zhecun turned to teaching classic Chinese literature and basically stopped his experiments in literary presentation; Mu Shiying collaborated with the Japanese and was mysteriously assassinated in 1940; and Ye Lingfeng, although he kept writing love stories, resumed painting as a profession. Two writers left the literary field for political reasons and the other two changed their technique and artistic mode to forms that were not clearly connected to the political situation. Their aspirations for an apolitical literature were unrealized. But none of them abandoned his interest in psychology entirely. In particular, in Shi Zhecun's later writings, there are still clear traces of psychoanalysis.

The early 1930s were an experimental phase for both Chinese and Japanese modernists. The Japanese Shinkankaku Ha writers, by the time that *Bungei jidai* (Literary Age), their major magazine, ceased publication, had begun to drift away to other movements and styles better suited to their individual talents. Even Yokomitsu Riichi, the chief writer of the Shinkankaku style, began to explore a completely different approach to fiction after 1931.[56]

---

56.   Yokomitsu once described the many phases of his creative career.   His experience illustrates the path that many Chinese writers travelled.   For that and for his delightful irony, I feel compelled to quote his description in full:

I first began by writing poems, then plays, then symbolist novels, then novels of pure description. I then worked on ways of heightening the sense of reality in my writings, then I went back to symbolism again which was my "Shinkankakuha Period."   And now I'm back to realism again, where I want to settle down for a bit.

Implicit in this was a changing way of looking at the world, at things. At first objects were seen in a fantasy world, and then I concerned myself with attempting to see them in the normal, everyday way. I gradually lost interest in that, and attempted to see things in personal terms, using the viewpoint of the self as the basis for description. However, that also became uninteresting, so I concentrated on the ways the sensations take in the world. While attempting this I got an

This "new tradition" of psychoanalytic novels was carried on individually by people like Zhang Ailing and Qian Zhongshu in the early 1940s.[57] But as a literary group, the psychoanalytic writers ceased to exist.

4.5 Conclusion

Put simply, Western modernism as a forceful voice in literary history began in or about 1910, the year Virginia Woolf proposed as the moment when human character changed.[58] However, this periodization is of course problematic for non-Western literatures. The frequent coexistence and often sudden disappearance of different avant-garde movements in twentieth-century Chinese literature in fact preclude easy historical categorization. Although psychoanalysis left its imprint on a large proportion of the fiction being produced, it would be an error to draw the boundaries between the various literary currents too sharply. All the isms and trends introduced, although apparently so far apart, had very real affinities with each other. Virginia Woolf speaks of the impossibility of categorizing literary works securely:

> Directly we speak of tendencies or movements we commit ourselves to the belief that there is some force, influence, outer pressure which is strong enough to stamp itself upon a whole group of different writers so that all their writings have a certain common likeness. But let us always remember--influences are infinitely numerous; writers are infinitely sensitive; each writer has a different sensibility. That is why literature is always changing, like the weather, like the clouds in the sky.[59]

---

obsession with structure, with seeing things as a whole, as a form. Yet recently I've got rather tired of that too.

(Yokomitsu Riichi, *Yokomitsu Riichi: Modernist*. Dennis Keene, trans. New York: Columbia University Press, 1980, p. 1.)

57. See chapters on Qian Zhongshu and Zhang Ailing in C. T. Hsia, *A History of Modern Chinese Fiction 1917-1957* (New Haven: Yale University Press, 1961).

58. Virginia Woolf, "Mr. Bennett and Mrs. Brown," in *The Captain's Death Bed and Other Essays* (New York: Harcourt, 1950), p. 96.

59. Virginia Woolf, "The Leaning Tower," in *Collected Essays* (London: The Hogarth Press, 1966), p. 13.

Nevertheless, I agree with the literary critic Su Xuelin's judgment that Mu Shiying is the most successful exponent of the New Sensibilities.[60] Mu Shiying brings concentrated intelligence to bear upon chaos and reveals the infinite range and complexity of human sensibility. His works, brief and fragmentary, have some sense of the vastness of fiction. In a sense he is close to Freud in his view of writing and in his self-consciousness. He finds vulgar Freudian interpretation of texts distasteful. In "Pierrot" he ironically portrays the gathering of a group of Chinese intellectuals. Their conversations go from one subject to another at random. Each offers as his own opinion what is in fact that of an intellectual school. There are a modernist, a Freudian, a behaviorist, and a Marxist. The Freudian critic is hideous and views everything in reductively sexual terms. His dogmatic Freudian interpretation is, like the other forms of criticism, ridiculed in the text. After hearing their different interpretations of his novel, Pan, the author of the novel they are discussing, feels as if he has "swallowed iron nails," and thinks:

> Why do they see themes in my work which I myself have not realized? Why do they see thought in my work different from what I know about my own work? The same thing can be turned into a thousand, even ten thousand entirely different things. They do not hear what I have said, but hear what is not said by me. Why? Why? Is it the failure of my techniques? But how then does my work move so many readers and make them sigh with me?... Many people read my work, praise it, and shed tears with it. But they do not shed tears at the ideas, sentences, and places I want them to, but rather shed tears at places where I do not understand why they should shed tears.[61]

This is a particularly modern worry about the breakdown of communication among author, text, reader, and critics. It suggests that any text, once made public, is the property not only of the author, but of everyone. Interpretations and misunderstandings become inevitable, in spite of the wishes of the author.

The short-lived literary prosperity of Chinese modernism in general and of psychoanalytic methods in particular is sometimes regarded as proof that Western literary techniques are not suitable for the Chinese national character or the Chinese environment. Any discussion of the Chinese

---

60. Su Xuelin, *1500 Modern Chinese Novels and Plays* (Hong Kong: Lung Men Bookstore, 1966), p. xx.

61. Yan, p. 296.

character is too complex for this study to tackle, but it is possible to comment intelligently about the historical phenomena of the 1930s. As we know, literature is sensitive to its national and cultural circumstances. When a society is at a critical stage and social attitudes remain conservative, literary innovation is hard to sustain. Shi Zhecun has said that he "found there was no room for development in literary themes, forms, and techniques."[62] By "room," he meant conceptual room, an environment favorable to the growth of new literature. Yet in the shadow of the War of Resistance against Japan, the literary ivory tower began to lean.

---

62.   Shi Zhecun, Preface to *A Rainy Evening*.

Chapter 5

PSYCHOANALYTIC CRITICISM

What is psychoanalytic criticism? Does it mean to look at a piece of work with a Freudian eye? But what is a Freudian eye? Freud initiated discursive practices and introduced some important transformations into science that made possible a certain number of divergences even within psychoanalytic discourse itself. As Michel Foucault points out, psychoanalysis opens itself to a variety of possible applications and transformations,[1] and (we may add) misapplications and deformations. The phrase "psychoanalytic criticism in China" implies that there was a real movement or serious attempt to "apply" psychoanalysis to literary criticism in China like that in the United States, and that there were committed disciples of Freud like Otto Rank or Marie Bonaparte (although even these disciples limited, rejected, and transformed some of Freud's concepts). On the contrary, there was hardly a "movement" toward psychoanalysis in Chinese literary criticism, but still there were people who were interested in psychoanalytic criticism and used it in their literary practice on occasion. This chapter will therefore examine psychoanalytic literary criticism in China practiced by both psychologists and literary critics.

It is not an exaggeration to say that the introduction of Freudian theory has changed and enriched people's vocabulary and perceptions in both the East and the West. But compared with Freudian criticism in the West, Freudian criticism in China was by and large less single-minded and was usually inflected with social criticism.

Psychoanalytic literary criticism embodies a variety of practices, and it is useful to be able to distinguish between them. Terry Eagleton broadly divides the genre into four subvarieties on the basis of its object of

---

1. Michel Foucault, "What is an Author?" in Paul Rabinow, ed., *The Foucault Reader* (New York: Pantheon Books, 1984), p. 116.

attention: the author, the work's contents, its formal construction, or the reader. As Eagleton points out, most psychoanalytic criticism has been of the first two kinds.[2] Indeed, some important Freudian analyses done by Ernest Jones, Herbert Read, D. H. Lawrence, and particularly by Freud himself resulted from the early struggles between psychoanalytic theory and literature and pointed to the first two critical approaches outlined by Eagleton. Even though these two kinds were often limited and reductive, for a long time they dominated the whole scene of psychoanalytic criticism. The obvious reason for this is that psychoanalysis focuses on the analysis of personality, which is the main goal of literary criticism focused either on the author's biography or on the characters in a work of fiction. And even non-psychoanalytic criticism at that time was interested in the personality or moral character of the author. More adventurous literary applications of psychoanalysis became possible only when literary criticism itself became more adventurous.

Psychoanalysis and literature are each concerned to understand individual people, each make free employment of the imagination, and each stresses the importance of multple and unexpected levels of significance. It is therefore only natural that psychoanalysts would take an interest in literature and literary people in psychoanalysis. Just as Freud was influenced and inspired by Dostoevsky, Shakespeare and other great literary figures, many twentieth-century writers such as James Joyce, Thomas Mann, and Eugene O'Neill have drawn on Freud's insights in creating their works. The mutual interest of psychoanalysts and literary writers in each other during the twentieth century plays an important role in the interdisciplinary study of literature and psychoanalysis.

5.1 Literary Use of Psychoanalytic Criticism by Chinese Psychologists

As in the West, where psychologists ever since Freud and Jung have shown an enormous interest in literature, in China many psychologists attempted to use psychoanalysis to analyze literature and literary figures. Their works are, in Edward Said's words, "a bold interventionary movement across lines of specialization."[3] I shall discuss three exemplary

---

2. Terry Eagleton, *Literary Theory: An Introduction* (Minneapolis: University of Minnesota Press, 1983), p. 179.

3. Edward W. Said, *The World, the Text, and the Critic* (Cambridge: Harvard University Press, 1983), p. 3.

psychologists whose interest in literary criticism was combined with Freudian theory.

Among the Chinese theoretical monographs on the relationship between literature and psychoanalysis, one remarkable piece about the literary application of psychoanalysis is "How to Use Freudianism in Literature" [Fuluoyite zhuyi zenyang yingyong zai wenxue shang] by Gao Juefu.[4] As I discussed in Chapter 1, Gao Juefu was a psychologist and a professional educator who translated two books by Freud. His work pays special attention to the Freudian theory of sublimation, a process postulated by Freud to account for human activities which have no apparent connection with sexuality but which are assumed to be motivated by libidinous instincts. Displaying a wide knowledge of Freudian theory, Gao notices its failure to distinguish between different kinds of sublimated activities. He contends that sublimation cannot account for all literary activities, although it seems to explain some cases in Chinese literature. For instance, the sublimation theory can throw light on some sexually motivated classical love poems which were mistakenly interpreted to express loyalty for rulers.[5] But the poem "Officials from the Stone Ditch" [Shi hao li] and the novel *The Scholars* [Ru lin wai shi] do not have a conspicuous sexual motivation and so cannot plausibly be interpreted as results of sublimation. Some political, social, and satirical books also bear no relation to sexual themes. He disagrees with what he sees as the tendency of psychoanalysis to focus on a search for sexual meaning, and deems Freudian theory a crude overgeneralization if "after all the twists and turns it (psychoanalytic interpretation) comes down eventually to sexual motivation."[6]

Gao believes that the usefulness of Freudian theory for literature is not Freud's theory of sexual themes, but that of the transformation of psychological conflicts into parapraxes and jokes. He suggests that anyone intending to apply Freudian theory to literature should pay special attention to Freud's works in these areas showing how repression and resistance function in the unconscious. Both jokes and parapraxes direct attention to the social interaction between speaker and listener. In this way, Gao shifts the emphasis from the psychosexual apparatus of psychoanalysis to its semiotic and sociological interface: the study of how unresolved and

---

4. Zheng Zhenduo, ed., *Wenxue bai ti* (Shanghai: Shenghuo, 1935), pp. 327-331.

5. Wang Tongzhao makes this point clearly in his excellent critique of an interpretatin of the Mao Heng version of the *Book of Odes* : "Reading *Mao shi fugu lu,* " in *Literary Quarterly* [Wenxue xun kan], No. 63-67, 1923.

6. Ibid., p. 328.

134

internalized conflicts are rechanneled into socially accepted forms of behavior and purposeful labor through verbal and written expressions. Gao's insight into psychoanalytic criticism avoids reductive accounts of human motivation and makes possible the fruitful exploration of both literary studies and psychoanalysis.[7] Although Gao himself did not extensively practice psychoanalytic criticism in literature, his suggestion was followed by some literary critics, such as Su Xuelin, whose works I shall later discuss.

The study of writers' lives to explain their works and the study of their works to explain writers' minds were the dominant modes of psychoanalytic criticism in the first half of the twentieth century. An example is Pan Guangdan's psychobiographical study of the woman poet Xiaoqing, *An Analysis of Xiaoqing* [Xiaoqing zhi fenxi].[8] Xiaoqing (1595-1612) was sold as a concubine to a rich man whose jealous wife forced her to live in a separate house and forbade her to meet the husband. So miserable was Xiaoqing that she died at the age of seventeen, leaving behind some scattered poems. Because she was a talented beauty who died young, many literary men have written eulogistic poems to express their sorrow for her early death. Her tomb became a favorite tourist spot in Hangzhou, the so-called "paradise on earth." (It was a familiar practice in China to persecute a woman to death and then elevate her to the status of a semi-legendary heroine.)

Assuming that his readers know little about psychoanalysis, Pan takes pains to explain the theory before he proceeds with his analysis of Xiaoqing. He unambiguously favors psychoanalysis over other frameworks for literary study, because he believes that, even aside from the medical value of Freudian theory, psychoanalysis illuminates literature.

Pan begins his study with Xiaoqing's life-story, which he gives in considerable detail. Drawing his material from the historical records available, he attempts to offer a new view of Xiaoqing as a person. He argues that Xiaoqing was narcissistic on the basis of her poems and her

7. It is regrettable that recent Chinese articles criticizing Freudian psychoanalysis have generally ignored Gao's insightful comments and concentrated on the alleged pan-sexualism of Freudian theory.

8. Pan Guangdan, *An Analysis of Xiaoqing* [Xiaoqing zhi fenxi] (Shanghai: Xinyue, 1927). Pan Guangdan completed the initial draft of his study on Xiaoqing in 1922 and published his research as "On Feng Xiaozing" [Feng Xiaoqing kao] in the *Women's Magazine* Funü zazhi]. In 1927, Pan revised this article and published it under the title of *An Analysis of Xiaoqing* [Xiaoqing zhi fenxi] and in 1929 with some additional materials as *Feng Xiaoqing: A Study of Narcissism* [Feng Xiaoqing: yi jian yinglian zhi yanjiu].

biography. Pan finds narcissistic significance in her stylistic nuances. He particularly pays attention to the recurrence of words, such as "often" [shishi] and "talking at length" [xu xu dao dao], when Xiaoqing looks at her reflection by a pond and in a mirror while talking to herself. In one of her poems, she compares herself with lotus flowers, an image that coincides with the Greek legend of Narcissus. Pan's study of Xiaoqing's poems is embedded in an analysis of her biography. He notes that before her death, Xiaoqing called in an artist to draw a portrait of her. She afterwards sighed and wept over her portrait before breathing her last breath. And this, for Pan, is significant enough to indicate that Xiaoqing mourned for her lover--her self, considered as the Other--and wished her image, not herself, to live forever. Pan sees a displaced master-slave dynamic in which Xiaoqing as a slave submits to the law that she is to satisfy the desire and enjoyment of the Other, and this narcissistic mode of relationship to the Other reveals an inverted image of the self.

Not satisfied with his conclusion that Xiaoqing dies of her narcissism like Narcissus, Pan further investigates the extent to which Xiaoqing was aware of her abnormal sexual fixation. Pan bases his argument on the following facts: although Xiaoqing's friends advised her to marry another man, she refused, not because she loved the man who rarely came to visit her in fear of his jealous wife, nor because she had to take social formality into consideration--since as a concubine she was socially allowed to remarry, nor because she could not find a man who wanted to marry her--since her beauty and talent were widely known to her contemporaries. Her written reply to her friends, in which she compared herself to "the soft willow catkin braving the wind," expressed her doubt that she was fated for another marriage. Nor did she want to become a nun, a solution many women chose to avoid the pains of marriage. From these facts, Pan speculates that Xiaoqing knew what she had chosen: to be different from ordinary people, for whom emotional love for other people was an essential part of life, and also from Buddhists, who attempted to live a life devoid of sensual and emotional love. She lived a life full of emotional love and yet did not have to depend on others for it. Considering the psychoanalytic tenet that the completeness of a patient's recovery depends on his or her awareness of the causes of the illness, Pan speculates that because her sickness eventually killed her Xiaoqing must have been only half aware of her state of mind. Pan examines Xiaoqing's family background in accordance with the methods of medical psychiatry. It would be tempting for a psychologist to trace the poet's psychosis back to her childhood, but Pan could find very little material about Xiaoqing's family background and her life before the age of ten, except that intellectually she matured very early. Of course, like a stereotypical Romantic woman, Xiaoqing had tuberculosis. At the age of sixteen, she was forced to undertake sexual relations with a mature man whose sexual desire was abundant. Before she married, she was a lively girl whom everyone liked, but after her marriage she often sat alone, staring vacantly into space. Pan diagnoses in Xiaoqing a homosexual tendency and mother-fixation. He also sees tendencies toward paranoia, self-aggrandizement, jealousy, and suspicion in her.

The book is, however, not designed to condemn Xiaoqing morally, Pan stresses. He criticizes the traditional denigration of women and opposes women's subjugated status. Indeed, he traces Xiaoqing's frustrated sexual life to social causes. Women are not offered fulfillment in society, and they do not know how to adjust their energy. Therefore, they contract psychological diseases, and many women, especially among the intelligentsia, become depressed [jingshen yujie]. From the medical point of view, Pan believes it is bad that women are forbidden to talk about their sexual desires and problems. As a result, many women die without even voicing their sufferings. Pan advocates sex education, coeducational schools, and public occasions for people of different genders to associate with each other. He also proposes that such measures can prevent the growth of homosexuality.

As in the early attempts in the West to apply psychoanalysis to literature, attempts for which Freud himself set a precedent, Pan has certain hypotheses about Xiaoqing's pathological symptoms. Pan's combination of sociological and psychological analysis, which aims at recreating an image of a woman distorted and ultimately destroyed by a patriarchal society, is invaluable. This innovation compensates for his limitation in failing to explain how Xiaoqing as a poet, and not as a psychotic, can be addressed by Pan's psychoanalytic criticism, and in exploring the relationship between psychoanalysis and aesthetics.

In an appendix to the book, "Women's Writings and Psychological Depression" [nüzi zuopin yu jingshen yujie], Pan makes a statistical study of women poets' choice of words. He summarizes four types of words that reflect women poets' sensitive response to their environment and to the stimuli which induce their depression. Pan gathers his evidence from a book entitled *Heartbroken* [Xiao hun ji], a collection of poems by woman poets in the late Qing period. In 230 poems, negative words to express a psychological sense of enclosure appear over 1,600 times. Phrases such as "locking doors" and "putting down curtains," and verbs such as "weep," "cry," and "worry," indicate the psychological state of those women poets--constant melancholy. Pan assumes that this represents the general social norm and attributes this, not surprisingly, to sexual repression.

Many psychologists did not confine themselves simply to applying Freudian theory to psychobiographic studies. With psychoanalytic insights, they also tried to account for the psychological nature of common phenomena in literary rhetoric. Zhang Yaoxiang, a psychologist, not only introduced Freudian theories into China but also wrote articles using psychological methods to analyze literary works and writers. For example, in "The Imagination of Literary Writers" [Wenxuejia zhi xiangxiang][9] he examines the creative process, and in "A Study of Abnormal Behavior of Famous People in Chinese History" [Zhongguo lidai ming ren biantai xingwei kao][10] he produces brief psychobiographies of famous people. In one article called "New Poets' Sentiments" [Xin shiren zhi qingxu],[11] he examines the use of exclamation marks in modern free-verse poems. Because it is difficult to test people's emotions clinically, Zhang uses the theory of repetition to deal with the recurrence of punctuation on the assumption that the compulsion to repeat is an ungovernable process originating in the unconscious. Zhang uses the concept of repetition freely and symbolically in his attempt to understand a peculiar yet common literary device. He notices that modern Chinese poets like to use many exclamation points in every poem they write. He presents this situation in the following doggerel:

> To look up at them [exclamation points],
> They are like spring rain falling down.
> To look down at them,
> They are like seedlings in a rice field.
> To look at them with a telescope,
> They are like bacteria;
> With a microscope,
> Many rows of bullets.

---

9. Zhang Yaoxiang, "The Imagination of Literary Writers" [Wenxuejia zhi xiangxiang], in *Psychology* [Xinli], Vol. 1, No. 3, July 1922.

10. Zhang Yaoxiang, "A Study of Abnormal Behavior of Famous People in Chinese History" [Zhongguo lidai ming ren biantai xingwei kao], in *Dongfang zazhi zazhi*, Vol. 31, No. 1, January 1934.

11. Zhang Yaoxiang, "New Poets' Sentiments" [Xin shiren zhi qingxu], in *Psychology* [Xinli], Vol. 3, No. 2, April 1924.

Zhang holds that it is common knowledge that poems express the poets' sentiments, even without the help of exclamation marks. The subtle difference between the meaning of an exclamation point in English and in Chinese is that in English, it indicates forceful utterance or strong feeling, whereas in Chinese, it is "gan tan," which suggests a "sigh with feeling" and may express melancholy.

Zhang examines nine collections of poems--over one thousand poems and ten thousand lines--and discovers that on the average there is a "!" in every four lines. Because it is impossible to compare the modern use of exclamation points with that in classical Chinese poems,[12] Zhang turns to English examples and cites Shakespeare's sonnets, Milton's *Paradise Lost*, Browning's *The Ring and the Book*, and a popular poetry collection called *The Golden Treasury*, from all of which he finds that the average use of "!" is one in every twenty-five lines. Zhang mockingly concludes that the Chinese poets are six times as easily excited as these foreign poets. It seems to me that the immature use of punctuation by Chinese poets in experimental free-verse poems may simply show a tendency to try to inject into their poetry more meaning than could be conveyed by the words themselves, but it also shows the energy and enthusiasm with which young Chinese intellectuals approached their writing. The average age of Chinese poets at the time was well under twenty-five, whereas the English poets, including Browning, wrote those poems long after they had reached the age of "establishment."[13]

J. Hillis Miller's *Fiction and Repetition* (1980) studies certain forms of repetition: words, figures of speech, shapes, gestures, or covert repetitions that act like metaphors. It is interesting to see that fifty years before, in China, a psychologist also paid attention to the issue of repetition. Zhang does not explicitly discuss the Freudian concept of repetition compulsion. However, he treats the repetition of "!" as a psychopathological phenomenon in a way that clearly draws on Freud's ideas. Because repetition belongs to the realm of the unconscious, the poets

---

12. Classical Chinese texts do not contain punctuation. The end of a sentence is discerned by context and grammatical particles. With the translation of foreign works into Chinese from 1840 on, punctuation was introduced, but it was not until the May Fourth Movement that punctuation became popular. See *Encyclopedic Knowledge* [Baike zhishi], No. 12, 1987.

13. Confucius said, "At fifteen I was bent on study; at thirty my mind was firmly established; at forty I had no doubts; at fifty I understood the ways of heaven; at sixty my ear was attuned; and at seventy the wishes of my heart passed not the proper limits" (*Lunyu: wei zheng*). Hence, "establishment" [er li] usually refers to a person's thirties.

have no idea that they are repeating what others have done or what they themselves have been doing, but rather "unconsciously" (Zhang's own word) choose to express their emotions by using the same technique. There is, of course, another interpretation of repetition: lack of originality. But Zhang does not rely on this common interpretation of repetition. Since Freud links the repetition compulsion to the death drive, it is appropriate to view the repeated "!"s as melancholy rather than enthusiastic.

The value of Zhang's analysis is not derived from a direct or rigid application of psychoanalysis to literary texts. Rather, he carefully studies the texts and applies somewhat general psychoanalytical ideas to them in a creative, insightful way.

5.2 Literary Critics

After the end of World War I, literary criticism was a young field in China, and there was no systemized literary theory at that time. Practical literary criticism usually consisted of book reviews, literary journalism, appreciation, explanation, and, in addition, as Liang Shiqiu put it in 1930, "introductory criticism"[jieshao de piping], a term that he believed did not exist in Western literary terminology.[14] "Introductory criticism" was the means by which Western literature was imported into China. Liang Shiqiu, who received his literary training at Harvard, summed up this particular phenomenon in China: "'Introductory criticism' is a brief biography of a writer, a detailed list of his works, and an introduction to his major works."[15]

As my previous chapters have shown, writers paid considerable attention to Freudian theory. Zhu Guangqian's contribution to the discussion of the relationship between psychoanalysis and literature still remains one of the best testaments to Chinese scholars' view of Freudian aesthetics. Some psychological terms overflowed into literary criticism. Zhao Jingshen, a literary historian, noted in 1928 that the New Literature was filled with descriptions of homosexuality--male and especially female--sadism and masochism, autoeroticism, the Oedipus complex, the Electra complex, and sexual dreams.[16] He used such terms as "zi wo lian"

---

14. Guo Fengshen, ed., *Xiandai wenxue piping ji* (Shanghai: Shijie, 1930), pp. 3-4.

15. Ibid., p. 4.

16. Zhao Jingshen, "Zhongguo xin wenyi yu biantai xingyu," in *Yiban*, Vol. 4, No. 1, 1928.

(autoeroticism), "tong xing lian" (homosexuality), "nüe dai kuang" (Sadism), and "shou nüe dai kuang" (masochism) so fluently and easily that it seems that these terms had already become a familiar vocabulary for literary critics. But his closing sentence--"It is interesting for me to be able to speak so freely"--discloses his ambivalent feelings about such a transgressive approach to literary criticism. The relationship between psychoanalysis and literature was heatedly discussed during the early part of the twentieth century and even, apparently, turned into university students' graduation theses.[17]

Modern Chinese literary criticism drew much of its insight from foreign theories. For example, psychoanalytic critics constantly referred to the translations of Mordell's *The Erotic Motive in Literature*, Kuriyagawa's *The Symbol of Angst*, Fritche's "Psychoanalysis and Literature," and other translations. For the present study, I wish to stress these three translations, which were representative of the incoming flow of foreign views of Freud from United States, Japan, and the Soviet Union, because they help us understand the kind of literary criticism done by Chinese critics. In general, they represent the early application of Freudian theory to literature: Mordell explored, in a fashion typical of the early Freudian critics, the sexual aspects of works by literary figures such as Keats, Shelley, Schiller, and Poe; Kuriyagawa abandoned this concentration on sexuality and viewed literature as an expression of dissatisfaction and anguish; Fritche made a simplified and dogmatic critique of Freudian theory. Earlier in this study, I have mentioned Kuriyagawa and Fritche, but not Mordell. Yet Mordell's book was often discussed by the Chinese critics and therefore deserves attention here.

Mordell's *The Erotic Motive in Literature* was received seriously at the time of its publication and was chosen as the "book of the month" by *The North American Review* in 1919. Freud himself read the book with "great interest" and ranked it highly, together with Otto Rank's book on the incest motive. However, just as Freud had some reservations about Marie Bonaparte's analysis of Edgar Allan Poe,[18] he also must have had enough qualms about Mordell's work to send him a sympathetic warning "not to

---

17.   Professor C. T. Hsia mentions that his late brother T. A. Hsia wrote his B.A. thesis on the relationship between Freudian psychoanalysis and literature in the 1940s. See C. T. Hsia, *Xia Ji'an xiansheng jinian ji* (Hong Kong: Chuangzuo shushe, no date).

18.   Shoshana Felman, *Jacques Lacan and the Adventure of Insight* (Cambridge: Harvard University Press, 1987), pp. 38-39.

take so hard the attacks and unfavorable criticism."[19] By the 1950s, Mordell's book was judged as "the epitome of all that is bad in psychoanalytic criticism."[20]

Mordell's book traces a writer's works back to the outward and inner events of his life, revealing his unconscious, or "that part of his psychic life of which he is unaware."[21] He believes that an author's unconscious can be discovered by an application of "a few well-tested and infallible psychoanalytic principles."[22] He regards the term "unconscious" as almost synonymous with "erotic" and contends that a literary work can be better appreciated after the facts about an author's sexual life are revealed to the readers. This reductive use of Freud's theories is an example of the danger of the "easy acceptance" of psychoanalysis, and particularly of its erotic aspects, that Freud feared.

Mordell's book was translated into Chinese in 1931. But long before 1931, his book both in English and in Japanese was available in China. This book drew considerable attention from Chinese literary critics. Among them was Zhou Zuoren, who cited examples from the book in the early 1920s. The Japanese scholar Matsumura Takeo's *Literature and Erotic Love* [Bungaku to seiai] was also translated into Chinese in 1927. However, because its selection of psychoanalytic examples from Western literature and its basic arguments are similar to Mordell's,[23] I shall not go into detail about this book. Instead, I shall discuss two professional literary critics' use of psychoanalysis in their criticism of modern Chinese literature to highlight the kind of issues they addressed through psychoanalytic criticism.

Undoubtedly the first Chinese critic to take sexual psychology and behavior seriously was Zhou Zuoren, Lu Xun's younger brother.[24] Zhou was indisputably one of the pioneering literary critics of the May Fourth

---

19.   Ernest Jones, *The Life and Work of Sigmund Freud* (New York: Basic Books, 1957), Vol. 3, p. 442.

20.   Claudia C. Morrison, *Freud and the Critic* (Chapel Hill: The University of North Carolina Press, 1958), p. 71.

21.   Albert Mordell, *The Erotic Motive in Literature* (New York: Boni & Liveright, 1919), p. 1.

22.   Ibid., p. 1.

23.   Matsumura Takeo, *Literature and Erotic Love*, trans. Xie Liuyi (Shanghai: Xinyue, 1927).

24.   See Ching-mao Cheng, "The Impact of Japanese Literary Trends on Modern Chinese Writers," in Merle Goldman, ed., *Modern Chinese Literature in the May Fourth Era* (Cambridge: Harvard University Press, 1977), p. 83.

Movement, even though his reputation suffered badly from his later collaboration with the Japanese during the War of Resistance. He often includes psychoanalytic theory in his essays and comments. The author he admires most is Havelock Ellis, whose works Freud also liked. Zhou recalls in his memoirs that his greatest enlightenment had come from Ellis's writings on sexuality. Zhou sees his function, like that of Ellis, to be that of a light-bearer:

> In the moral world we are ourselves the light-bearers, and the cosmic process is in us made flesh. For a brief space it is granted to us, if we will, to enlighten the darkness that surrounds our path. As in the ancient torch-race, which seemed to Lucretius to be the symbol of all life, we press forward torch in hand along the course. Soon from behind comes the runner who will outpace us. All our skill lies in giving into his hand the living touch, bright and unflickering, as we ourselves disappear in the darkness.[25]

Zhou's major contribution to modern Chinese literary criticism was to establish a more liberal literary morality and to clear room for the growth of new literature. Qian Xingcun, an influential literary critic, regards Zhou Zuoren's collection of essays, *My Own Garden*, as the foundation of new Chinese literary criticism and as a forceful argument against the dominant feudal thinking of the time.[26] Two of the important essays are accounts of modern Chinese literature: "On 'Sinking'" and "On 'Love Poems'." Both essays, interestingly enough, make use of the Freudian concept of sexuality.

"Sinking" [Chen lun] is a representative work by Yu Dafu, a vanguard writer of the May Fourth Movement. At the time of its publication in the early 1920s, the story was condemned as immoral and decadent because it depicts a lonely and sexually frustrated male Chinese student in Japan who commits suicide. Zhou Zuoren wrote "On 'Sinking'" to justify the story and embarked on a fundamental discussion of moral standards in literature. Claiming to base his argument on Mordell's book *The Erotic Motive in Literature*, he asserts that there are three types of literature which are called "immoral": the first undermines tradition and has nothing to do with eroticism, but is the literature of new morality or that of

25. Zhou Zuoren, "Ailisi de shidai" in *Ku cha sui bi* (Shanghai: Bei xin, 1935), p. 279. The Enlish text is from Havelock Ellis, *Studies in the Psychology of Sex* (New York: Random House, 1910), Vol. 2, p. 642.

26. Li Jingbin, *On Zhou Zuoren* [Zhou Zuoren ping xi] (Xi'an: Shanxi People's Publishing House, 1986), p. 74.

revolution; the second is a natural expression of sexual desires which does not evoke pornographic feelings in the readers; the third is deliberately erotic and designed to promote criminal prostitution. In Zhou's view, the first two classes of literature are acceptable, even admirable; only the final kind is genuinely immoral.

Zhou Zuoren holds that "Sinking" belongs to the second category, the "unconsciously improper": although it contains some sexual scenes, it is not immoral because these scenes form a natural part of the story, not something forced upon it. The story, as Zhou points out, is about the conflict between flesh and soul, between ideals and reality, and reflects the distress of the modern youth. He explains the origin of such literature in terms of psychoanalysis:

> According to psychoanalysis, all spiritual activities in the world are focused on a loosely defined term called sexuality. Human beings have sadistic, masochistic, exhibitionistic, and voyeuristic instincts, which, once satisfied, can create the foundation of a happy sexual life, but if repressed can become diseased sexual desire, that is, erotic; and if expressed through literature, it becomes either beautiful poems or "improper" stories.[27]

The value of the story, Zhou insists, lies in the fact that it is unconsciously exhibiting itself, artistically depicting the sublimated eroticism, and therefore the so-called immoral part does not ruin the literary value.

"On 'Love Poems'" [Qing shi] is another example of Zhou's use of psychoanalytic knowledge to support the growth of new literature. The occasion for the essay was the severe critical reception given to the love poems of Wang Jingzhi, a young poet. Zhou, just as in "On 'Sinking,'" does not directly analyze the literary text itself, but uses it as a starting point for a discussion that differentiates among emotion, love, and eroticism. Historically speaking, this general discussion was probably even more important than a textual analysis would have been at that time because it helped to establish the premises for a fruitful exploration of the literary qualities of texts. Zhou takes an affirmative attitude toward sex and sees it as a natural part of human life: "As the knowledge of modern sciences about human sex has increased, the value of sex and love has grown."[28] Poems are

---

27. Zhou Zuoren, *A Garden of My Own* [Ziji de yuandi] (Shanghai: Bei xin, 1923), pp. 76-77.

28. *A Garden of My Own*, p. 66.

the voice of human emotion, and therefore the theme of love occupies a major position in poetry. He repudiates the popular conception that love and sex are leisure-time luxuries for the patriarchal elders, and bitterly argues on behalf of young people:

> If young people show their instinctive desire through literature, they are regarded as having violated the moral law. Old people are liable to be sexually abnormal and the old social opinion made by them is unhealthy. A society governed by the old is rotten from the inside and deservingly faces a death sentence. What is regarded as immoral by the old morality is precisely the moral spirit of love poems.[29]

Zhou warmly praises the young poet for his daring exploration of his emotion and sees his act as a means to alter "non-human literature," which obliterates human emotions and whitewashes them for the patriarchal rulers. Psychoanalysis is for Zhou a liberating force in establishing a new morality.

Su Xuelin, one of the most famous and prolific Chinese women critics in the twentieth century, constantly refers to Freudian theories not only in her analyses of literary texts, but also in her creative writings.[30] Compared with her critical enterprise, her fiction is less psychoanalytic although she often uses psychological terms like "split personality," "dual personality," and "abnormal psychology" either for narrative comment on her protagonists or in characters' dialogue.

As a critic, she was one of the first commentators to notice the Freudian elements in Shi Zhecun's fiction. "On Shi Zhecun's 'The General's Head' and Other Stories"[31] is a fine example of her attempts at psychoanalytic criticism. She pays a great deal of attention to psychological conflicts: between flesh and soul and between nationalism and love. Her excellent analyses fulfill Gao Juefu's prescription about the usefulness of psychoanalysis for literary studies. She concentrates on three aspects of Freudian analysis: double personality (her own English term), abnormal sexual emotions such as sadism and masochism, and the use of dreams. Although her psychoanalytic criticism largely falls into the first

---

29. Ibid., pp. 66-67.

30. For instance, her short story "When I Am Depressed," [Fanmen de shihou], in Bing Xin, ed., *Women Writers* [Nü zuojia] (Shanghai: no publishing company or date).

31. Su Xuelin, "On Shi Zhexun's 'The General's Head' and Other Stories" [Ping Shi Zhecun "jiangjun de tou" ji qita], published in 1936 and collected in *Su Xuelin xuanji* (Taibei: Xinlu, 1961).

and the second categories provided by Eagleton, she does not neglect the stylistic aspect of the writing, particularly since Shi is well known for being a "stylistic" writer [wenti zuojia]. Shi's writing, first of all, is a work of artistic fiction. A trained literary critic, Su discusses many aspects of Shi's stories in terms of literary concepts such as plot, theme, character, setting, symbolism, and point of view. She surpasses earlier Freudian readings, which distilled hidden monolithic meanings and general authorial motivations without attending closely to literary effects.

Rather than applying a strict Freudian analysis, Su tends to rely on commonsensical psychology in evaluating what seems believable in the story. For instance, when reviewing "Shi Xiu," she comments that the author is so over-anxious to put Freudian material in his story that the ancient Chinese warrior sounds like a twentieth-century young man with an awareness of Freudian theory. The episode she cites occurs when Shi Xiu tells Pan Qiaoyun, whom he is about to kill, that he loves her more than anybody else does and that his killing her is a result of his passion for her. Su Xuelin argues matter-of-factly that although Shi Xiu is driven by his sadistic personality and the circumstances to play the role of a tragic hero, there is no way that Shi Xiu can be aware of his role because it was impossible for a warrior in the Song Dynasty to know Freudian theory and be able to understand himself in these terms.

Freudian psychology was sometimes seen as depth or dynamic psychology. This view enabled Su Xuelin to justify the young writers' attempts to break away from the Chinese literary tradition. She once wrote an essay on Shen Congwen, another famous "stylistic" writer in the 1920s and 1930s. The essay is generally appreciative of Shen Congwen's works but also critical of certain stylistic defects. Su notices the European influence on the dialogues in Shen's stories. A large number of these stories treat the Miao tribes in Hunan, but the images of Miao heroes and heroines remind readers of Greek mythological figures, like Apollo and Diana, and the plots resemble either ancient legends or Western romantic movies set in Australia and Africa. It is quite a spectacle to see this combination of Western and Chinese mythological idealization in the Miao people. Why does Shen do it? Su Xuelin, a critic with no less imagination and insight herself, points out Shen's intention in such borrowing, even though "Shen himself may not be aware of it":

What is Shen Congwen's motivation? I think he wants to use linguistic power to inject the barbarians' blood into the old and decaying body of China so as to make China regain its youth and ability to fight for its right of survival with other nations.[32]

Echoing many May Fourth writers' beliefs, Su holds that Chinese culture is growing too old and "like stagnant water has too much sediment." Figuratively speaking, it is a pond of "sewage" which drowns many brave young people who want to bring reform to the country. Compared with Chinese civilization, Western cultures are seen to be as full of vitality as tigers and lions. She recalls a Japanese scholar's remark that there is less animality on a Chinese face than on a Japanese or Western one. Comparatively speaking, the Miao nationality is less "civilized" than the Han and therefore full of youth. Su believes that Shen establishes a parallel between his fiction and the mythology. Shen gets his inspiration from the Greek gods and borrows their images to describe his "ideal" people--the Miaos--living in primitivism. It was a common nineteenth-century belief that primitive culture was freer, a source of some vitality that civilization wanted to tap. It is also a Freudian concept that civilization is seen as requiring instinctual repression. Su's analysis of Shen's intentions is shrewd and pointed, especially if we take Shen's own confession into consideration: during an interview in the 1980s, Shen retrospectively recalled that "having read books such as Zhang Dongsun, *The ABCs of Psychoanalysis* in 1929, [his] whole approach to fiction changed."[33] In her criticism of other literary works, Su also uses Freudian theory: for instance, in "On Gui Youguang's Essays" and "Li He's Poetry,"[34] she reconstructs psychobiographies of the authors. She emphasizes their psychopathological side, diagnosing them to have "mélancolie malsaine" (her own phrase--unhealthy melancholy). Although confining her Freudian analyses to authors' motivations and their psychobiography, Su is sensitive to literary nuances and cultural elements in the texts.

Psychoanalytic criticism became so popular that even pro-left critics, those from the League of Left-Wing Writers, used it in their literary critiques. In fact, very few literary critics did not use some psychoanalytic terms--at the very least, the phrase "abnormal sexuality." Zheng Zhenduo published a series in a literary magazine introducing psychoanalytic

---

32. Su Xuelin, *Su Xuelin xuanji* (Taibei: Xinlu, 1961), p. 133.

33. Jeffrey G. Kinkley, "Shen Congwen and the Use of Regionalism in Modern Chinese Literature," in *Modern Chinese Literature*, Vol. 1, No. 2, Spring 1985, p. 168.

34. Su Xuelin, "Li He's Poetry" and "On Gui Youguang's Essays," in *Su Xuelin xuanji* (Taibei: Xinlu, 1961).

criticism.[35] Han Shiheng, a member of the Leftist Literary Association, wrote extensively on the works of his contemporaries and used Freudian notions to judge them.[36] One of the objects of his study was Zhang Ziping, a popular novelist whose books had a single theme: triangular love. In addition to criticizing the decadent elements in Zhang's novels, Han charges that Zhang's language is "sick" and shows Zhang's own diseased mind. Han believes that "books are their authors" [shu shi ren] and holds that every book reflects its author in every page and every line.[37] He asserts that from Zhang's works one can see that Zhang is sexually abnormal: an overly masculine and cruel person. Indeed, he questions how Zhang could be otherwise, having fathered so many abnormal characters in his fictions. Such criticism may seem crude and laughable, but it is based on common sense: if a writer consistently produces mono-thematic novels, readers will tend to suspect that the theme represents a personal obsession. But for Han, the "knowledge" of psychoanalysis becomes merely a convenient tool against his opponent, producing a tautological criticism. If Zhang is mentally sick, his novels must be valueless, and if his novels are full of sickness, the author must be a diseased person. This is an example of how badly psychoanalytic criticism can be abused.

5.3 Conclusion

The early use of Freudian theory by literary critics was limited in that it aimed at discovering the deeply buried psychobiographical side of authors or of protagonists. Lacan directed the study of psychoanalysis along a different path: he enriched psychoanalysis with twentieth-century theories about language and subjectivity. The best psychoanalytic criticism is not that based on the dogmatic assertion that the sexual repression of authors appears in their literary works, but rather the creative use of psychoanalysis in combination with literary analysis. Freud himself saw that psychoanalytic explanations must be combined with others (for

---

35.   Xi Di (Zheng Zhenduo), "Psychoanalysis and Literature" [Jingshen fenxi yu wenxue] , in *Literary Quarterly* [Wenxue xun kan], February 1923.

36.   Shiheng, *A Collection of Literary Criticism* [Wenxue pinglun ji] (Shanghai: Xiandai, 1934).

37.   Shiheng, p. 79.

example, economic, historical, and sociological) to offer a complete picture.[38]

Chinese approaches to Freud are varied and thus coincide with what Felman says about the impossibility of "application" of psychoanalysis:

> One can use theories only as enabling metaphorical devices, not as extrapolated, preconceived items of knowledge. In much the same way that one cannot simply "apply" Freud's concepts to a patient, one cannot apply Freud (or Lacan) to a literary text. The practice of psychoanalysis (as well as the experience of a practical reading) is a process, not a set of doctrines. In the process, one can **implicate** the doctrines; one can perhaps imply them, not apply them.[39]

My brief survey shows that literary people of different political allegiances borrowed Freudian theories for their criticism. Freudian theory served as a tool, rather than a dominating theory. This tool usually served a progressive function in the critics' arguments for social reform and literary liberalization, and its implications were enormous.

It is significant that certain elements in Freudian theory were singled out to be emphasized in China but not in the West. For instance, the notion of conflict was believed to be the essence of Freudian psychoanalytic criticism among the Chinese, whereas in the West repression was perceived to be the dominant concept. Nevertheless, both Chinese and Western literary critics at that time emphasized the analysis of authors and their characters. It was sometimes problematic for these critics to treat the authors and their fictive characters as patients and the text as manifestation of their psychological symptoms.

Through this examination, or rather, this sampling of psychoanalytic criticism in China, I have tried to uncover the usefulness of psychoanalytic criticism in a different cultural setting. It is true that there is no powerful tradition of psychoanalytic criticism in China, unlike in the West. But through the few cases examined here, we can see some common features in the use of psychoanalysis in literary studies during the early days. There have been debates about how deeply the Chinese critics absorbed foreign literary theories, including Freudian theory, and especially about whether their absorption remained only on a superficial level. Many

---

38. Reuben Fine, *A History of Psychoanalysis* (New York: Columbia University Press, 1979), p. 466.

39. Felman, p. 11.

contemporary critics seem to think that the critics of the pre-1949 period borrowed only the Freudian terms without fully exploring their meanings. But the point they fail to consider is that new words necessarily register important changes in thought, because language monitors and governs people's thinking. The use of psychoanalytic criticism by the Chinese intellectuals demonstrates their creativity in accommodating their cultural traditions to a new set of ideas and vice versa.

EPILOGUE

One of the remarkable things about the twentieth century is that it is hard for any one nation to remain totally isolated from the rest of the world. Almost always, events and trends in one country find echoes or parallels in other countries. Psychoanalysis has become one of the most influential intellectual developments of our age, not just in the West, but in the East as well. A review of the history of the psychoanalytic movement shows that the curve of interest in Freudian psychoanalysis in China coincides with that in the rest of the world. For instance, after the First World War, a new spirit of optimism and intellectual inquiry became noticeable in the European psychoanalytical movement, especially in the years from 1925 to 1933.[1] In Russia, a sizable group was formed before the First World War and continued after the October Revolution until 1928, when Stalin dissolved it.[2] In Japan, psychoanalysis was introduced by the 1920s, though it did not have much impact on the Japanese population, especially with Japan's rising commitment to war. In China, Freudian theories were introduced and discussed widely among Chinese intellectuals in the 20s and 30s, but during the two wars, the War of Resistance against Japan and then the civil war, the Chinese interest in Freudian psychoanalysis passed its initial exploratory stage and remained more or less separate from the storms of public concern. The year 1949 marks a divergence from the past; it would require another volume to explore the fate of Freudian ideas in China since then.

I suppose that we need to be clear about one thing: that is, Freudian psychoanalysis is not, and should not be taken as, a branch of "natural science." Psychoanalysis is in large part an art of interpretation

---

1. Reuben Fine, *A History of Psychoanalysis* (New York: Columbia University Press, 1979), p. 97.
2. Ibid., p. 99.

whose mode of progress closely resembles that of literary criticism. In the field of psychoanalysis, terminological obscurities and complexities are abundant, not least because of the key role of metaphor both in analysis and in the theory of analysis. This is partly the reason why, in China as elsewhere, psychoanalysis has attracted literary people in particular. Insofar as psychoanalysis does make claims which are in principle subject to experimental confirmation or refutation, the enormous difficulty of an objective approach to interpretive questions leaves it still unproved, still legitimately open to important modifications. Many of Freud's successors have, for example, revised Freud's psychoanalytic concept of femininity, offered anthropological reconsiderations of the Oedipus complex, and pursued the Lacanian notion of linguistic models.

These developments are not, however, my present concern, which is Freudian thought in China between 1919 and 1949. From a historical perspective, Freudian theory indeed played a positive role in the "enlightenment" of Chinese intellectuals, particularly in deepening their understanding of human mind and behavior. Freud's view of the mind was and remains a radical departure from hitherto accepted views of the mind, because of its emphasis on irrationality and particularly on the developmental dynamics of sexuality. The concepts of repression, sexual desire, and the unconscious allowed Chinese intellectuals to question many social codes which had been held in esteem, and to call into question some fundamental assumptions of traditional Chinese culture, such as the belief in the inherent goodness of human beings. Under Freud's microscope, the human being is no longer seen as an autonomous unity, but as always in the process of reconstruction. As Ernest Jones has said,

> We are beginning to see man not as the smooth, self-acting agent he pretends to be, but as he really is--a creature only dimly conscious of the various influences that mold his thought and action and blindly resisting with all the means at his command the forces that are making for higher and fuller consciousness.[3]

In giving serious interpretive attention to what were previously seen (or unseen) as errors, animalities, breakdowns, violations and mere jests, psychoanalysis acted to blur the intellectual boundary between the normal and the pathological, between the significant and the insignificant, between common sense and nonsense. Freudian theory thus gave rise to new

---

3. Ernest Jones, *Papers on Psycho-analysis*, revised and enlarged edition (New York: William Wood & Co., 1918), Ch. ii, p. 15.

possibilities, for the Chinese writers, new ways to represent psychological conflict, desire and significance. Recognizing the existence of the unconscious, Chinese writers reinterpreted and explored at length some hitherto ignored themes such as dreams and moments of startling irrationality.

In discussing foreign influences on Chinese literature, few people have attempted to analyze the function that translation has played in their transmission. The common assumption is that we can somehow grasp the meaning of a concept without studying the medium in which the meaning is borne. It seems to me, however, that the role of translation in shaping people's reception of foreign ideas can never be overestimated. It is only within language that the production of meaning is possible. I have in this book tried to show that translation did play an important role in shaping people's understanding of Freudian theory. I wanted to show how the language actually **reconstructed** psychoanalysis in China, rather than just imperfectly reflecting it or slowing its movement. Translation is not just a secondary activity which transplants mechanically the original meanings across a semipermeable membrane. In order to see how psychoanalytic concepts are constructed in a Chinese milieu, we must study their actual transformations through an examination of translations. My own experience as a lecturer on and translator of Western literary theories in China reinforces my belief that translation presents an important, if not major, problem in people's response to foreign literary theories. Alternative translations can indeed yield different concepts. And the debate about the proper choice of psychoanalytic terms still goes on in contemporary China, over seventy years after the introduction of Freudian theory. For instance, there still exists the old question about the term "the unconscious"--some translate it as "wu yishi," and others translate it as "qian yishi"; and some use both in one article. "Wu yishi" and "qian yishi" have very different meanings in Chinese, as I have discussed in Chapter Two.[4]

The breaking down of moral prejudice against the subject of sex must be regarded as one of the most important achievements of Freud in China. For a long time, public discussion of sex had been taboo. Though of interest to all, sex was shrouded in secrecy and discussed with shame. The natural consequences were unhealthy furtiveness and appalling

---

4.   For a discussion of current controversy about the term "the unconscious," please see Li Yuntuan, "Yige lü jian bu xian que ling ren kunhuo de xianxiang: guanyu "qian yishi" yu "wu yishi" liang shuyu hun yong de zhiyi" [A common and yet confusing phenomenon: a question about the confusion in the use of "qian yishi" and "wu yishi"] , in *Xuexi yu tansuo* (Study and inquiry), No. 4, 1987.

ignorance. Freudian theory helped the Chinese to view sex as a natural part of human life and to understand the psychological development of children. And one of the major achievements of twentieth-century Chinese literature is to have taken up the topic of the psychology of sexuality. I have, however, not attempted to offer an extensive analysis of sexual desire in literature and have omitted discussion of many famous cases, such as Yu Dafu's "Nine Diaries," Ding Ling's "Diary of Miss Sophia," Zhang Ziping's numerous novels about love triangles, Zhang Jingsheng's efforts to discuss the history of sexual techniques, and so on. Granted, it was popular for writers to portray their sexual feelings; women writers, such as Feng Yuanjun, were very bold in their descriptions of female sexual desire. And granted, the personal is political, and sexual life consists in large part of individual and therefore social liberation. Still the popularity of such a theme did not result solely from the introduction of Freudian theories. Rather, these theories merely helped create an atmosphere of interest in and openness to the depiction of sexual drama. In studying Freudian theory in China, it would be a mistake to pay too much attention to the popular version of Freud, just as it would be a mistake to base one's conception of the relation between literature and psychoanalysis on the regrettable (worldwide) tendency in the psychoanalytic critical literature to engage in crude and mechanistic studies which reveal little more than their authors' obsession with sex. Freud's theory, even of the libido, is not about "sex" in the popular sense, and there is much else in Freudian theory with which Chinese intellectuals grappled. It is common to associate Freudian theory only with sexuality, but in so doing, one fails to pay attention to more intrinsic psychoanalytic concerns. Perhaps the right question here is very much a Foucaultian one: why did Chinese writers of that period talk so much about sex, given that the discourse on sexuality in the twentieth-century China often took the form of confession?

The psychoanalytic perspective in literary criticism is helpful because every study of literature involves assumptions of a psychological nature. No one is likely to deny that literature and emotion are closely related. Literary critics, as readers, must also ask questions about the narrative structure, and the ways in which a text was made and how it may be read. Literature is a product of complex processes; the study of a literary work is equally complicated and has to relate to the artist, the text, its multiple contexts, and finally also the reader. The simple and reductive early application of Freudian analysis to literature leaves a great deal to be desired in approaching these questions, but the psychoanalytic perspective itself is indispensable.

In many spheres in China, Freud's theories continue to be a source of challenge and controversy, as much now as when they first appeared seventy years ago. There has been a "rediscovery" of Freud in China since 1978. The many new translations of Freud's works into Chinese have attracted wide interest. A more sophisticated understanding of psychoanalysis is penetrating increasingly into the general culture. The implications of psychoanalytic ideas and assumptions for ideas about individuality and society have induced the government to view Freudian psychoanalysis as a threat to the socialist structure. Freud has been put on trial time and again, during almost all major official political campaigns against the infiltration of Western ideology into China. In literary spheres, Freudian influence has been blamed for the flourishing of explicit and graphic sexual descriptions. The literary application of Freudian theory is criticized as pernicious and rigid in its tendency to invent and promulgate Freudian codes and diagrams. However, in the broad range of academic literary criticism and on the grapevines of the educated, Freudian approaches have already become familiar. For instance, it is not enough to interpret the tension between a mother-in-law and her daughter-in-law purely in economic terms. People have to face the emotional complexities of human relations. Psychoanalysis has taught people to delve into the workings of the unconscious, and hence into certain questions about human behavior which are potentially deeply upsetting.

In the final analysis, Freudian theory has been criticized, but has not been successfully suppressed. Psychoanalysis presents a deep challenge to a vast range of traditional thought on human nature, a challenge extending from theoretical psychology in one direction to the social and political, and in another direction to the most intimately personal. Particularly with the rise of Chinese feminist criticism, the scope of psychoanalytic criticism is bound to expand and grow stronger.[5] Although psychoanalysis remains a radically disturbing subject of continuing debate, it is through such debate that psychoanalytic theory gains vitality in China.

---

5.   One of the finest combinations of feminism and psychoanalysis is a book by Meng Yue and Dai Jinhua, *Fu chu lishi dibiao* [Emerging from the Historical Horizon: Modern Chinese Women Writers] (Henan: Henan People's Press, 1989).

SELECTED BIBLIOGRAPHY

Abrams, M. H.. *Natural Supernaturalism: Tradition and Revolution in Romantic Literature*. New York: Norton, 1973.

Amabile, Teresa M. *The Social Psychology of Creativity*. New York: Springer-Verlag, 1983.

Ancona, Francesco Aristide. *Writing the Absence of the Father: Undoing Oedipal Structure in the Contemporary American Novel*. New York: University Press of America, 1987.

Auerbach, Erich. *Mimesis: The Representation of Reality in Western Literature*. Princeton: Princeton University Press, 1953.

Ba Jin. *Ba Jin xuan ji*. 10 vols. Chengdu: Sichuan People's Publishing House. 1982.

Balmary, Marie. *Psychoanalyzing Psychoanalysis: Freud and the Hidden Fault of the Father*. Trans. Ned Lukacher. Baltimore: The Johns Hopkins Press, 1979.

Becker, Raymond De. *The Understanding of Dreams*. London: George Allen & Unwin, 1968.

Benjamin, Walter. *Illuminations*. New York: Schocken Books, 1969.

Benvenuto, Bice and Roger Kennedy. *The Works of Jacques Lacan*. New York: St. Martin's Press, 1986.

Bernheimer, Charles and Claire Kahane, eds. *In Dora's Case: Freud-Hysteria-Feminism*. New York: Columbia University Press, 1985.

Bing Xin. *Bing Xin wenji*. 4 vols. Shanghai: Shanghai Press of Literature and Art, 1982.

Bloom, Harold. *The Anxiety of Influence A Theory of Poetry*. New York: Oxford University Press, 1973.

_____. *Modern Critical Views: Sigmund Freud*. New York: Chelsea House, 1985.

Borch-Jacobson, Mikkel. *The Freudian Subject*. Stanford: Stanford University Press, 1988.

Briére, O.. *Fifty Years of Chinese Philosophy 1898-1948*. Trans. Laurence G. Thompson. New York: Frederick A. Praeger, 1965.

Cao, Yu. *Yuan ye*. Hong Kong: Dongya, 1967.

Chase, Cynthia. "Oedipal Textuality: Reading Freud's Reading of *Oedipus*." *Diacritics*, Vol. 9, No. 1, 1979.

Cheng, Fangwu. *Cheng Fangwu wenji*. Jinan: Shangdong University Press, 1985.

Chin, Robert and Ai-li S. Chin, *Psychological Research in Communist China (1949-1966)*. Cambridge: MIT Press, 1969.

Chow, Tse-tsung. *The May Fourth Movement*. Cambridge: Harvard University Press, 1960.

Chu, Kwang-tsien. *The Psychology of Tragedy: A Criticial Study of Various Theories of Tragic Pleasure*. Strasbourg: Librairie Universitaire d'Alsace, 1933.

Culler, Jonathan. *On Deconstruction: Theory and Criticism after Structuralism*. Ithaca: Cornell University Press, 1983.

Davis, Robert Con. *The Fictional Father: Lacanian Readings of the Text*. Amherst: University of Massachusetts Press, 1981.

Deleuze, G. and Guattari, F.. *Anti-Oedipus*. New York: Viking, 1977.

De Man, Paul. *Allegories of Reading: Figural Language in Rousseau, Nietzsche, Rilke, and Proust*. New Haven: Yale University Press, 1979.

_____. *Blindness and Insight: Essays in the Rhetoric of Contemporary Criticism*. New York: Oxford University Press, 1971.

Derrida, Jacques. *The Ear of the Other: Otobiography, Transference, Translation*. New York: Schocken Books, 1982.

_____. "Freud and the Scene of Writing," in *Writing and Difference*. Trans. Alan Bass. Chicago: University of Chicago Press, 1978.

_____. "Speculations--on Freud." *Oxford Literary Review*. Trans. Ian McLeod. Vol. 3, No. 2 (1978): 78-97.

_____. *Dissemination.* Trans. Barbara Johnson. Chicago: University of Chicago Press, 1981.

Ducrot, Oswald and Tzvetan Todorov. *Encyclopedic Dictionary of the Sciences of Language.* Trans. Catherine Porter. Baltimore: The Johns Hopkins University Press, 1979.

Eagleton, Terry. *The Function of Criticism: From the Spectator to Post-Structuralism.* London: The Thetford Press, 1984.

_____. *Literary Theory: An Introduction.* Minneapolis: University of Minnesota Press, 1983.

_____. *Marxism and Literary Criticism.* Berkeley: University of California Press, 1976.

Edel, Leon. *The Modern Psychological Novel.* New York: Grove Press, 1955.

Edmunds, Lowell. *Oedipus: the Ancient Legend and Its Later Analogues.* Baltimore: The Johns Hopkins University Press, 1985.

Ellis, Havelock. *Studies in the Psychology of Sex .* New York: Random House, 1910.

Ellmann, Richard, ed. *The Modern Tradition.* New York: Oxford University Press, 1965.

Felman, Shoshana, ed. *Literature and Psychoanalysis: The Question of Reading: Otherwise.* Baltimore: The Johns Hopkins University Press, 1982.

Felman, Shoshana. *Jacques Lacan and the Adventure of Insight.* Cambridge: Harvard University Press, 1987.

Fine, Reuben. *A History of Psychoanalysis.* New York: Columbia University Press, 1979.

Fodor, Nandor, ed. *Freud: Dictionary of Psychoanalysis.* New York: Philosophical Library, 1950.

Fokkema, Douwe W.. *Literary History, Modernism, and Postmodernism.* Amsterdam: John Benjamins, 1984.

Forrester, John. *Language and the Origin of Psychoanalysis.* New York: Columbia University Press, 1980.

Foucault, Michel. *Madness and Civilization.* Trans. Richard Howard. London: Tavistock, 1973.

_____. *The History of Sexuality.* Vol. 1. Trans. Robert Hurley. New York: Vintage Books, 1980.

Friedman, Melvin. *Stream of Consciousness: A Study in Literary Method.* New Haven: Yale University Press, 1955.

Fromm, Erich. *The Crisis of Psychoanalysis.* Harmondsworth: Penguin, 1970.

_____. *The Forgotten Language.* New York: Rinehart, 1951.

Freud, Sigmund. *The Standard Edition of the Complete Psychological Works of Sigmund Freud.* 24 vols. London: Hogarth Press and the Institute of Psychoanalysis, 1957.

Frosh, Stephen. *The Politics of Psychoanalysis: An Introduction to Freudian and Post-Freudian Theory.* New Haven: Yale University Press, 1987.

Frye, Northrop. *Anatomy of Criticism: Four Essays.* Princeton: Princeton University Press, 1973.

Gálik, Marián. *The Genesis of Modern Chinese Literary Criticism 1917-1930.* London: Curzon Press, 1980.

Gallop, Jane. *Feminism and Psychoanalysis.* London: Macmillan, 1982.

Gilbert, Sandra M. and Susan Gubar. *The Madwoman in the Attic.* New Haven: Yale University Press, 1984.

Gunn, Edward M.. *Unwelcome Muse: Chinese Literature in Shanghai and Peking 1937-1945.* New York: Columbia University Press, 1980.

Guo, Moruo. *Moruo wenji.* 17 vols. Beijing: People's Literature Press, 1959.

_____. *Chuangzao shi nian.* Shanghai: Xiandai, 1932.

_____. *Chuangzao shi nian xu bian.* Shanghai: Beixin, 1946.

Habermas, J.. *Knowledge and Human Interest.* London: Heinemann, 1972.

Harari, Josué V.. *Textual Strategies: Perspectives in Post-Structuralist Criticism.* Ithaca: Cornell University Press, 1979.

Hermans, Theo, ed., *The Manipulation of Literature: Studies in Literary Translation.* New York: St. Martin's Press, 1985.

Hoffman, Frederick J.. *Freudianism and the Literary Mind.* Baton Rouge: Lousiana State University Press, 1957.

Hsia, C. T.. *A History of Modern Chinese Fiction.* New Haven: Yale University Press, 1971.

Humphrey, Robert. *Stream of Consciousness in the Modern Novel.* Berkeley: University of California Press, 1954.

Jameson, Fredric. *The Prison House of Language: A Critical Account of Structuralism and Russian Formalism.* Princeton: Princeton University Press, 1972.

_____. *The Political Unconscious: Narrative as a Socially Symbolic Act.* Ithaca: Cornell University Press, 1981.

Jones, Ernest. *The Life and Work of Sigmund Freud.* 3 vols. New York: Basic Books, 1981.

Kristeva, Julia. *Desire in Language: A Semiotic Approach to Literature and Art.* Ed. Leon S. Roudiez. New York: Columbia University Press, 1980.

Lacan, Jacques. *Speech and Language in Psychoanalysis.* Trans. Anthony Wilden. Baltimore: The Johns Hopkins University Press, 1981.

_____. *The Four Fundamental Concepts of Psycho-Analysis.* Ed. Jacques-Alain Miller. New York: Norton, 1981.

LaCapra, Dominick. *History, Politics, and the Novel.* Ithaca: Cornell University Press, 1987.

_____. *Rethinking Intellectual History: Texts, Contexts, Language.* Ithaca: Cornell University Press, 1983.

_____ and Steven L. Kaplan, eds. *Modern European Intellectual History: Reappraisals and New Perspectives.* Ithaca: Cornell University Press, 1982.

Lang, Olga. *Pa Chin & His Writing: Chinese Youth Between the Two Revolutions.* Cambridge: Harvard University Press, 1967.

Laplanche, Jean. and J. B. Pontalis. *The Language of Psychoanalysis.* New York: Norton, 1973.

Laplanche, Jean. *Life and Death in Psychoanalysis.* Trans. Jeffrey Mehlman. Baltimore: The Johns Hopkins University Press, 1976.

Lawrence, D. H. *Psychoanalysis and the Unconscious.* New York: Viking Press, 190.

Lee, Leo Ou-fan. ed. *Lu Xun and His Legacy.* Berkeley: University of California Press, 1985.

Lévi-Strauss, Claude. *The Elementary Structures of Kinship.* Trans. James Harle Bell. Boston: Beacon Press, 1969.

Liu, James J. Y.. *Chinese Theories of Literature.* Chicago: University of Chicago Press, 1975.

Lipshires, Sidney. *Herbert Marcuse: From Marx to Freud and Beyond.* Cambridge, Massachusetts: Schenkman, 1974.

Lowen, Alexander. *Narcissism: Denial of the True Self.* New York: Macmillan, 1983.

Lubot, Eugene. *Liberalism in an Illiberal Age: New Culture Liberals in Republican China 1919-1937.* Westport: Greenwood Press, 1982.

Lu Xun. *Lu Xun quan ji.* 20 vols. Shanghai: Lu Xun quan ji chubanshe, 1938.

MacAndrew, Elizabeth, *The Gothic Tradition in Fiction.* New York: Columbia University Press, 1979.

MacCannell, Juliet Flower, *Figuring Lacan: Criticism and the Cultural Unconscious.* Lincoln: University of Nebraska Press, 1986.

Mahony, Patrick. *Freud as a Writer.* New York: International Universities Press, 1982.

Malcolm, Janet. *Psychoanalysis: The Impossible Profession.* London: Picador, 1982.

Malmqvist, Göran, ed. *Modern Chinese Literature and Its Social Context.* Stockholm: Nobel Symposium Committee, 1975.

Mannoni, O.. *Freud: The Theory of the Unconscious.* London: New Left Books, 1971.

Marcuse, H.. *Eros and Civilisation.* Boston: Beacon Press, 1966.

Masson, Jeffrey Mousaieff. *The Assault on Truth: Freud's Suppression of the Seduction Theory.* New York: Farrar, Straus and Giroux, 1984.

McDougall, Bonnie. *The Introduction of Western Literary Theories into Modern China 1919-1925.* Tokyo: Center for East Asian Cultural Studies, 1971.

Mitchell, Juliet. *Psychoanalysis and Feminism.* Harmondsworth: Penguin, 1974.

Mordell, Albert. *The Erotic Motive in Literature.* New York: Boni & Liveright, 1919.

Morrison, Claudia C.. *Freud and the Critic: The Early Use of Depth Psychology in Literary Criticism.* Chapel Hill: University of North Carolina Press, 1968.

Munroe, Ruth. *Schools of Psychoanalytic Thought: An Exposition, Critique, and Attempt at Interpretation.* New York: Holt, Rinehart and Winston, 1955.

Mu, Shiying. *Public Cemetery* [Gong mu]. Shanghai: Xiandai, 1933.

_____. *Nan bei ji.* Shanghai: Xiandai, 1933.

Nietzsche, Friedrich Wilhelm. *The Use and Abuse of History*. Indianapolis: Bobbs-Merrill Education, 1957.

Norris, Christopher. *Deconstruction: Theory & Practice*. London and New York: Methuen, 1982.

O'Nell, Carl. *Dreams, Culture, and the Individual*. San Francisco: Chandler & Sharp, 1976.

Ong, Roberto. *The Interpretation of Dreams in Ancient China*. Germany: Studienverlag Brochmeyer, 1985.

Pierrot, Jean, *The Decadent Imagination 1880-1900*. Trans. Derek Coltman. Chicago: The University of Chicago Press, 1981.

Robert, Marthe. *The Psychoanalytic Revolution: Sigmun Freud's Life and Achievement*. Trans. Kenneth Morgan. New York: Avon Books, 1966.

_____. *From Oedipus to Moses: Freud's Jewish Identity*. New York: Anchor Books, 1976.

Robins, R. H.. *A Short History of Linguistics*. London: Longmans, 1967.

Roustang, Francois. *Dire Mastery: Discipleship from Freud to Lacan*. Trans. Ned Lukacher. Baltimore: The Johns Hopkins University Press, 1976.

Rudnytsky, Peter. L.. *Freud and Oedipus*. New York: Columbia University Press, 1987.

Russell, Bertrand. *The Analysis of Mind*. London: George Allen and Unwin, 1921.

Schneiderman, Stuart, ed. *Returning to Freud: Clinical Psychoanalysis in the School of Lacan*. New Haven: Yale University Press, 1980.

Sheleff, Leon Shaskolsky. *Generations Apart: Adult Hostility to Youth*. New York: McGraw-Hill, 1981.

Shen, Congwen, *Shen Congwen wenji*. 12 vols. Hong Kong: Sanlian, 1982.

Shen, Yanbing. *Mao Dun quan ji*. 15 vols. Beijing: People's Literature Press, 1984.

Shi, Zhecun. *Jiangjun de tou*. Shanghai: Xin Zhonghua, 1933.

Skura, Meredith Anne. *The Literary Use of the Psychoanalytic Process*. New Haven: Yale University Press, 1981.

Sloane, Paul. *Psychoanlytic Understanding of the Dream*. New York: Jason Aronson, 1979.

Solomon, Richard. *Mao's Revolution and the Chinese Political Culture*. Berkeley: University of California Press, 1971.

Sophocles. *Oedipus the King*. Trans. Thomas Gould. London: Prentice-Hall International, 1970.

Stacy, R. H.. *Defamiliarization in Language and Literature*. Syracuse: Syracuse University Press, 1977.

Steinberg, Erwin R., ed. *The Stream-of-Consciousness Technique in the Modern Novel*. Port Washington, New York: Kennikat Press, 1979.

Stevens, William Oliver. *The Mystery of Dreams*. London: George Allen & Unwin, 1950.

Sulloway, Frank. *Freud: Biologist of the Mind*. New York: Basic Books, 1979.

Tennenhouse, Leonard, ed. *The Practice of Psycholoanalytic Criticism*. Detroit: Wayne State University Press, 1976.

Todorov, Tzvetan. *The Fantastic*. Ithaca: Cornell University Press, 1975.

Turkle, Sherry. *Psychoanalytic Politics: Freud's French Revolution*. London: Burnett, 1978.

Volosinov, V. N.. *Freudianism: A Marxist Critique*. Trans. I. R. Titunik. New York: Academic Press, 1976.

Wang, Jingyuan. "Foreign Literary Trends and the May-Fourth New Literature" [Wailai wenyi sichao he wu si xin wen], *Wenxue pinglun congkan*, Vol. 1, No. 21, August 1984.

Watt, Ian. *The Rise of the Novel*. Berkeley: University of California Press, 1957.

Weber, Samuel. *The Legend of Freud*. Minneapolis: University of Minnesota Press, 1983.

Woolf, Virginia. *The Captain's Death Bed and Other Essays*. New York: Harcourt, 1950.

_____. *The Second Common Reader*. New York: Harvest, 1986.

Wright, Elizabeth. *Psychoanalytic Criticism: Theory in Practice*. London and New York: Methuen, 1984.

Yan, Jiayan. *Selected Works of the School of New Sensibilities* [Xin ganjue pai xiaoshuo xuan]. Beijing: People's Literature Press, 1985.

Ye, Lingfeng. *Lingfeng xiaoshuo ji*. Shanghai: Xiandai, 1931.

Yu, Dafu. *Yu Dafu wenji*. 12 vols. Hong Kong: Sanlian, 1982.

Yu, Fenggao. "Psychological Schools and Modern Chinese Fiction" [Xinlixue pai yu Zhongguo xiandai xiaoshuo], *Wenxue pinglun*, September 1985.

Yuan, Changying. *Kongque dong nan fei ji qi ta dumuju*. Changsha: The Commercial Press, 1930.

Zheng, Zhenduo. *Zheng Zhenduo wenji*. Beijing: People's Publishing House, 1985.

Zhou Zuoren. *Yishu yu shenghuo*. Hong Kong: Xinhua, no date.

_____. *Zhitang hui xiang lu*. Hong Kong: Tingtao chubanshe, 1970.

_____. *Ziji de yuandi*. Shanghai: Beixin, 1927.

Zhu, Shaozhi, ed. *Zhongguo dangdai shi da nü zuojia jia zuo ji*. Shanghai: Dafang shuju, 1939.

CHINESE PUBLICATIONS ON SIGMUND FREUD

有关心理分析学论文索引
（按发表日期排列，不包括文学作品）

1919年以前出版的一些论文

王国维译，Harold Höffding著 《心理学概论》，1907.

章锡琛，〈群众心理之特征〉，《东方杂志》，10卷4期，
　　1913/10/1.

卢可封，〈中国催眠术〉，《东方杂志》，14卷3期，1917/3/15.

陈大齐，〈辟灵学〉，《新青年》，4卷5期，1918/5/15.

1919

陈家蔼，〈新〉，《新潮》，1卷1期，1991/1/1.

张崧年，〈男女问题〉，《新青年》，6卷3期，1919/3/15.

1920

张崧年，〈近代心理学〉，《新青年》，7卷3期，1920/2/1.

若木译，桑田芒藏原著〈群众心理〉，《东方杂志》，17卷19期，
　　1920/10/10.

Y，〈弗洛特新心理学之一斑〉，《东方杂志》，17卷22期，
　　1920/11/25.

独秀，〈无意识的举动〉，《新青年》，8卷4期，1920/12/1.

罗素，〈心底分析〉，《民国日报·觉悟副刊》，1920—1921.

1921

朱光潜，〈福鲁德的隐意识说与心理分析〉，《东方杂志》，
　　18卷14期，1921/7/25.

张东荪，〈论精神分析〉，《民铎杂志》，2卷5期，1921.

张东荪，〈论精神分析〉，《时事新报·学灯》，1921/5/12.

小峰记录，罗素讲演〈心的分析〉，《时事新报·学灯》，
　　3－4期，1921.

郑振铎，〈肉欲横行中国〉，《文学旬刊》，9期，1921/7/30.

郭沫若，〈《西厢记》艺术上的批判与其作者的性格〉（1921），
　　《文艺论集》（上海：光华书局，1929）.

1 9 2 2

仲密(周作人)，〈沉沦〉，《晨报副镌》，1922/3/26.

张耀翔，〈文学家之想象〉，《心理杂志》，1卷3期，1922/7.

陈大齐，《迷信与心理》(北京大学出版部，1922/8，再版).

张崧年，〈男女问题不成问题的解决〉，《少年中国》，3期，
　　1922/10/1.

潘光旦，〈冯小青考〉，《妇女杂志》，1922.

王靖译，〈论现代小说〉，《东方杂志》，19卷19期，
　　1922/10/10.　[H. G. Wells, "Modern Novels"].

王平陵，〈现代心理学的派别及其研究法〉，《东方杂志》，
　　19卷19期，1922/10/10.

罗素讲演，孙伏虞笔记，《心之分析》(北平：新知书社，1922).

1 9 2 3

佚名，〈精神分析与文艺〉，《时事新报·学灯》，
　　1923/1/1-2/11.

成仿吾，〈新文学之使命〉，《创造周报》，1923/2.

西谛(郑振铎)，〈精神分析学与文艺〉，《文学旬刊》，64期，
　　1923/2.

汤澄波，〈析心学论略〉，《东方杂志》，20卷6期，1923/3/25.

甘蛰仙，〈唯美的人格主义〉，《晨报副镌》，1923/5/4.

郭沫若，〈批评与梦〉，《创造季刊》，2卷1期，1923/5/10.

倪文宙，〈变态心理学之基本观－癔症〉，《教育杂志》，
　　15卷5期，1923/5/20.

〈心理学的范围〉，《东方杂志》，20卷10期，1923/5/25.

吴颂皋，〈精神分析的起源和派别〉，《东方杂志》，20卷11期，
　　1923/6/19.

周作人，《自己的园地》（上海：北新书局，1923）.

1 9 2 4

邱景尼，〈性欲的升华〉，《晨报副镌》，1924/12/23.

庄泽宣编，《心理学名词汉译》（北平：中华教育改进社，1924）.

张耀翔，〈新诗人之情绪〉，《心理》，3卷2期，1924/4.

鲁迅译，厨川白村《苦闷的象征》（北新书局，1924）.

1 9 2 5

郝耀东译，《自知之术》（上海：黎明，1925）
　　[D. H. Bonus, Association Tests Used in Psychoanalysis].

作人，〈蔼理斯感想录抄〉，《语丝》，30期，1925/2/9.

陈贤德，〈语言心理〉，《东方杂志》，22卷6期，1925/3/25.

W生，〈读心术〉，《东方杂志》，22卷6期，1925/3/25.

李宗武，〈近代文学上之两性问题〉，《晨报副镌》，
　　1925/4/22-4/29.

顺风，〈蔼理斯与福来尔〉，《语丝》，26期，1925/5/11.

王季平，〈近代心理学的潮流〉，《学林》，1卷11期，
　　1925/5/15.

谢循初，〈弗洛德传略及其思想之进展〉，《心理杂志》，
　　3卷4期，1925/7.

仲云译，厨川白村著〈病的性欲与文学〉，《小说月报》，16卷
　　5期，1925/5.

仲云译，厨川白村著，〈文艺与性欲〉，《小说月报》，
　　16卷7期，1925/7/10.

高卓（高觉敷）译，〈心之分析的起源与发展〉，《教育杂志》，
　　17卷10-11期，1925/10-11. [Sigmund Freud, On the
　　History of the Psycho-Analytic Movement].

1 9 2 6

章士钊，〈再答稚晖先生〉，《甲寅周刊》，1卷27号，
　　1926/1/26.

余文伟，〈佛洛伊特派心理学及其批评〉，《民铎杂志》，
　　7卷4期，1926/4/1.

崔载阳编，《近代六大家心理学》(上海：商务，1926).

高觉敷，《心理学论文集》(上海：商务，1926).

徐庆誉，〈心是脑的产物吗？〉，《东方杂志》，23卷24期，
　　1926/12.

沈雁冰，〈中国文学内的性欲描写〉，《小说月报》，17卷号外，
　　1926/6.

高卓，〈所谓兽性问题〉，《一般》，1卷，1926.

鲁迅，〈狗·猫·鼠〉，《朝花夕拾》，1926.

1 9 2 7

张东民，《性的崇拜》(上海：北新，1927).

岂明，〈读《性的崇拜》〉，《语丝》，147期，1927/9/3.

叶作舟，〈妇女与歇私的里亚〉，《妇女杂志》，13卷，1927/10.

赵演译，《弗洛特心理分析》(上海：商务，1927)
　　[Barbara Low, Psycho-Analysis: A Brief Account of
　　the Freudian Theory].

谢六逸译，松村武雄著《文艺与性爱》(上海：新月，1927).

潘光旦，《小青之分析》(上海：新月，1927).

1 9 2 8

赵景深，〈中国新文艺与变态性欲〉，《一般》，4卷1期，
　　1928/1/5.

潘菽，〈心理学的过去与将来〉，《学艺》，9卷1期，1928/1/15.

鹤逸，〈变态性欲与文艺〉，《晨报副镌》，1928/2/14-15.

甘师禹，〈性爱在文学中的活动〉，《世界日报副刊》，
　　1928/5/22、6/5/、7/30.

觉敷，〈谈谈弗洛伊特〉，《一般》，6期，1928.

契可亲，〈耶的卜司错综与文艺〉，《北新月刊》，2卷14期，
　　　1928／7／1．

国新，〈从文艺中看东方人的亲子之爱〉，《益世报》，
　　　1928／8／4-18．

赵演，〈现代变态心理学之大派〉，《教育杂志》，20卷12期，
　　　1928／12．

黄维荣，《变态心理学》（上海：世界书局，1928）．

胡秋原，〈文艺起源论〉，《北新》，2卷22期，1928．

侍桁译，〈生之要求与艺术〉，《北新》，2卷21期，1928／9／16．

1 9 2 9

张东荪，《精神分析学ABC》（上海：世界出版社，1929）．

黄维荣，《变态心理ABC》（上海：世界，1929）．

陈东原，《群众心理ABC》（上海：ABC丛书社，1929）．

高觉敷，《心理学概论》（上海：商务，1929）．

韦，〈成对〉，《新月》，1卷12期，1929／1／10．

汪德全，〈心理冲突与压制〉，《民铎》，10卷3期，1929／3．

夏斧心译，《群众心理与自我分析》（上海：开明书店，1929年5
　　　月初版、10月再版）．[Sigmund Freud, Group Psychology
　　　and the Analysis of the Ego].

张东荪，〈由自利的假我到移欲的真我〉，《新哲学论丛》（上
　　　海：商务，1929）．

蒋径三，〈心理主义的美学说〉，《民铎》，10卷5期，1929／11．

孙席珍，〈变态性欲的林和靖〉，《文学周报》，7卷，合订本，
　　　1929．

刘穆，〈文学中性的表现〉，《文学周报》，8卷，合订本，1929．

1 9 3 0

章士钊译，《菲罗乙德叙传》（上海：开明书店，1930）
　　　[Sigmund Freud, Selbstdarstellung].

朱光潜，《变态心理学派别》（上海：开明书店，1930）．

夏斧心译，《群众心理与自我分析》（上海：开明书店， 1930年铅印再版本） [Sigmund Freud, Group Psychology and the Analysis of the Ego].

刘穆译，〈现代文学中的性的解放〉，《小说月报》，21卷3期，1930/3.

秦含章，〈梦的行为〉，《国立劳大月刊》，1卷3期，1930/3.

张振镛，〈青年烦闷心理之分析〉，《教育建设》，3期，1930.

邱鹤，〈笑之分析〉，《教育建设》，4期，1930.

高觉敷，〈心理学与自然科学，《教育杂志》，22卷3期，1930/3/20.

高觉敷，〈弗洛伊特的心理学〉，《学生杂志》，17卷6期，1930/6.

陈剑修，〈心理学是鬼的科学还是人的科学〉，《北大学生》，1卷1期，1930/7/1.

胡文博，〈现代心理学之四大潮流及其对于教育之影响〉，《中华教育界》，18卷8期，1930/8.

高觉敷译，《精神分析引论》（上海：商务，第三版，1930/10） [Sigmund Freud, Introductory Lectures on Psycho-analysis].

章颐年，〈联想反应之应用问题〉，《教育季刊》，1卷2期，1930/12.

许则骧，〈群众心理的特征〉，《大夏期刊》，1卷1期，1930/12.

高觉敷，〈心理学界的现状〉，《学生杂志》，17卷1期，1930.

许杰，《火山口·新序》（上海：乐华读书公司，1930）.

伊卡，〈青年的苦闷〉，《学生杂志》，17卷5期，1930.

1931

芒，〈佛洛德对于人类思想之影响〉，《东方杂志》，28卷17期，1931.

张书延，〈美国心理社会学派〉，《新北方》，1卷1期，1931/1/20.

高觉敷，〈弗洛伊特及其精神分析的批判〉，《教育杂志》，23卷3期，1931/3.

张竞生译，弗鲁特著〈心理分析纲要〉，《读书杂志》，
　　1卷2期，1931.

张竞生译，弗鲁特著〈心理分析纲要与梦的分析〉，《读书杂志》，
　　1卷，特刊号，1931.

沈有乾，〈关于心理学和不关心理学的杂记〉，《新月》，
　　3卷5／6期，1931.

沈绮雨，〈所谓新感觉派者〉，《北斗》，1卷4期，1931／12／20.

潘菽，〈意识的研究〉，《教育杂志》，23卷3期，1931.

贺昌年，〈语言的缺陷〉，《民铎》，11卷1期，1931.

摩台尔，《近代文学与性爱》（上海：开明，1931）.

朱光潜，《变态心理学派别》（上海：开明，1931）.

1 9 3 2

曹佴千，〈变态心理学在教育上的价值〉，《中华教育界》，
　　19卷7期，1932／1.

宋阳（瞿秋白），〈论弗理契〉，《文学月报》，1卷4／5／6期，1932.

觉敷，〈弗洛伊德说与性教育〉，《中学生》，22期，1932／2.

张竞生译，弗鲁特著〈梦的分析〉，《读书杂志》，1卷6期，1932.

张竞生，〈写在《精神分析学与艺术》之尾巴！〉，《读书杂志》，
　　2卷10期，1932.

周起应（周扬）译，弗理契著〈弗洛伊特主义与艺术〉，　《文学月
　　报》，1期，1932／7／10.

胡秋原译，佛理采著〈精神分析学与艺术〉，《读书杂志》，2卷
　　6期，1932.

施蛰存译，〈新的浪漫主义〉，《现代》，9期，1932.

胡雪译，卡尔弗登著　《文学与性的表现》（上海：神州国光社，
　　1932）.

1 9 3 3

朱光潜，《变态心理学》（写于1930年，1933年出版），收在《朱
　　光潜美学文集》（上海：文艺出版社，1983），1卷.

周作人，〈性的心理〉，《现代》，4卷1期，1933／1／11.

郭任远著，吴颂皋译，〈取消心理学上的本能学〉，《学艺》，
　　1933／3／1.

鲁迅，〈听说梦〉，《南腔北调集》，1933.

胡秋原，〈Phallisism 狂时代〉，《现代》，3卷2期，1933.

曹葆华译，Hebert Read 著〈心理分析与文学批评〉，《北平
　　晨报·学园》，549号、550号、551号、1933／8／3、8／4、8／7.

天放，〈什么是‘梦’〉，《清华周刊》，40卷2期，1933／10.

赵究灵，〈我也来谈谈‘心理’与‘科学’〉，《独立评论》，
　　75期，1933／11／5.

高觉敷译，《精神分析引论》（上海：商务，合订本，1933）
　　[Sigmund Freud, Introductory Lectures on Psycho-
　　analysis].

朱光潜（Chu Kwang-Tsien），The Psychology of Tragedy；A
　　Critical Study of Various Theories of Tragic Pleasure
　　（Strasbourg；Librarie Universitaire d'Alsace, 1933）.

　　　　　　　　　　1 9 3 4

张耀翔，〈中国历代名人变态行为考〉，《东方杂志》，　31卷1
　　期，1934／1.

吴福元，〈佛洛以特心理学的重要理论及其对于教育的贡献〉，
　　《心理半年刊》，1卷1期，1934／1／1.

郭祖超译，Wexberg著〈个性心理学的历史背景〉，　《心理半年
　　刊》，1卷1期，1934／1／1.

箫孝嵘，〈现代变态心理学之分析及其批评〉，《心理半年刊》，
　　1卷1期，1934／1／1.

张德培，　〈从近四年来杂志论文上观察中国心理学的趋势〉，
　　《师大月刊》，16卷25期，1934.

李威深　，〈二重人格〉，《大公报》，1934／3.

叶青，〈佛洛伊德梦论批判〉，《新中华》，2卷9-10期，1934／5-6.

赵钦武，〈关于心理分析及佛洛依特之批评〉，《中法大学月刊》，
　　5卷2期，1934／6.

钟鲁齐，〈现代各派心理学之比较的研究〉，《民族杂志》，
　　　2卷7期，1934／7．

大学用书，《变态心理学》（南京：中正书店，1934／7）．

虞于道，〈心理学研究法〉，《出版周刊》，91期，1934／8／25．

叶麟，〈由心理学的观点试论小说中景物写法〉，《大公报》，
　　　文艺副刊，102期，1934／9／15－19．

周先庚，〈心理学与心理技术〉，《独立评论》，1934／9．

郑沛缪，〈我们需要怎样的心理学〉，《独立评论》，1934／9．

谢循初，〈二十世纪新心理学〉，《出版周刊》，1934／9．

吴福元译，B. Hart著〈精神病理学之发展及其在医学上之位置〉，
　　　《心理半年刊》，1－3卷，1934．

谢循初译，《现代心理学之派别》（上海：国立编译馆， 1934年
　　　初版，1935年再版）[R. S. Woodworth, Contemporary
　　　Schoots of Psychology].

弗罗依德序，章衣萍，章铁民合译，《少女日记》（上海：现代，
　　　1934）．

孔真，〈心理学述要〉，《新中华》，1卷1期，1934／10／10．

陈德荣译，《解心术学说》（上海：商务，1934年9月初版，12月
　　　再版）[John Carl Flugel, Theories of Psychoanalysis].

　　　　　　　　　　1 9 3 5

汪馥泉译，中村古峡著〈精神分析与现代文学〉，《文艺月刊》，
　　　7卷1／2期，1935／1．

高觉敷，〈弗洛伊特主义怎样应用在文学上〉，载于郑振铎和付
　　　东华合编《文学百题》（上海：生活书店，1935）．

陈思烈，〈佛洛德的梦的心理〉，《文化与教育》，44期，1935／1．

陈思烈，〈佛洛德的生平及其心理学之背景〉，《文化与教育》，
　　　49期，1935／3．

叶青，〈佛洛伊德心理学之哲学的结论〉，《科学论丛》，
　　　3期，1935．

思毅，〈精神病与现代社会〉，《新华周刊》，43卷4期，1935／6．

何子恒，〈国际非战运动与青年心理〉，《新中华》，23卷11期，
　　1935／6／10.
陈思烈，〈佛洛德的过失心理〉（上、下），《文化与教育》，
　　60／61期，1935／6－7.
钱蘋，〈抑郁儿童之个案研究〉，《心理半年刊》，2卷2期，
　　1935／7／1.
叶青，〈精神分析派心理学批判〉，《新中华》，23卷15期，
　　1935／8／10.
华超译，Brown著《心理学与精神疗法》（上海：商务，1935）.
高觉敷，《现代心理学》（上海：商务，1935）.

1 9 3 6
高觉敷译，《精神分析引论新编》（上海：商务，1936）[Sigmund
　　Freud, New Introductory Lectures on Psychoanalysis]
虞心远译，《精神分析学之批判》（上海：辛垦书局，1936／3）
　　[Wilhelm Reich, "Dialektischer Materialismus und
　　Psychoanalyse" and W. Jurinetz, "Psychoanalyse und
　　Marxismus"].
朱道俊著，《人格心理学》（上海：商务，1936）.
海天，〈语文性欲化〉，《宇宙风》，1936／1／6.
咏琴，〈佛洛依德的精神分析学与性问题〉，《东方杂志》，
　　33卷7期，1936.
朱光潜，〈文艺与道德问题的略史〉，《东方杂志》，33卷1期，
　　1936／1／1.
李长之，〈现代中国青年几种病态心理的分析〉，《自由评论》，
　　10－11期，1936／2.
朱光潜，〈诗的起源〉，《东方杂志》，33卷7期，1936／4／1.
萧孝嵘，〈现代心理学派的分析〉，《中华教育界》，23卷10期，
　　1936／4／1.
朱光潜，〈文艺与道德有何关系〉，《中山文化》，3卷2期，1936／4.
虞心远，〈精神分析学之批判的研究〉，《研究与批判》，2卷1
　　期，1936／4.

高觉敷，〈从心理学观点解释中国悲惨的现状－中国民族心理的
　　五种缺陷〉，《观察》，2卷18期，1936/6/28.

苏雪林，〈读《将军的头》〉，《大公报》，1936/10/4.

赵景深，〈中国新文艺与精神分析〉，《文学讲话》（上海：国
　　光印书局，第六版，1936）.

周作人，〈猥亵的歌谣〉，《周作人近作精选》（文林书店，1936）.

铁怀刚，〈心理失常的检举〉，《心理季刊》，1期，1936.

钱怀刚，〈心理学在文学作品的势力〉，《心理季刊》，3期，1936.

潘光旦，〈中国文献中同性恋举例〉，潘光旦译《性心理学》
　　（上海：商务，1936）[Havelock Ellis, Studies in the
　　Psychology of Sex].

方重译，A. Ramsay著〈心理学与文学批评〉，《文哲季刊》，
　　6卷2期，1936.

1 9 3 7

卢怡昌，〈精神分析未来之展望〉，《中华教育界》，24卷7期，
　　1937/1.

星，〈大可注意之儿童变态心理〉，《大公报》，家庭栏，
　　272/273期，1937/1/24-26.

宗亮东，〈心理分析与本能论〉，《中华教育界》，24卷8期，
　　1937/2.

朱光潜，〈心理上个别的差异与诗的欣赏〉，《好文章》，7期，
　　1937/4/10.

高觉敷，〈心理学的向量〉，《东方杂志》，34卷12期，1937.

1 9 3 8

郭沫若，《创造十年续篇》（上海：北新，1938）.

高觉敷，〈心理学家的动员〉《东方杂志》，35卷13期，1938/7/1.

高觉敷，〈法西斯蒂主义与心理测验〉，《东方杂志》，35卷16
　　期，1938/8/16.

陈德荣译，《民族心理与国际主义》（上海：商务，1938）[W.B.
　　Phillsturg, The Psychology of Nationality and
　　Internationalism].

何邦，〈战时的心理神经病〉，《东方杂志》，35卷22期，
　　1938/11/16.

　　　　　　　　　1 9 3 9
林传鼎，《唐宋以来三十四个历史人物心理特质的估计》（上海：
　　辅仁大学，1939）.
吴汝康，〈欲望的合理化〉，《学生杂志》，19卷2期，1939/2.

　　　　　　　　　1 9 4 0
楚之译，《精神分析与唯物史观》（上海：世界，1940）.
《变态心理学》（上海：西风社，1940）.

　　　　　　　　　1 9 4 1
唐钺译，《心理学与军人》（长沙：商务，1941）　[Frederic
　　Charles Bartlett, Psychology and the Soldier].

　　　　　　　　　1 9 4 2

　　　　　　　　　1 9 4 3
钱能新，〈心理战与闪击战〉，《新中华》，复刊，1卷6期，1943/6.

　　　　　　　　　1 9 4 4
陈节坚，《变态心理学》（上海：商务，1944）.
唐钺译，《论习惯》（重庆：商务，1944）[William James, Habit].
冯明章译，《性心理》（重庆：文摘出版社，1944）[Havelock Ellis,
　　Studies in the Psychology of Sex].
吴江霖，〈论心理学作为生物社会科学之一〉，《新中华》，复
　　刊，2卷4/5期，1944/4-5.

　　　　　　　　　1 9 4 5
周作人，《立春以后》（太平书局，1945）.

1 9 4 6

唐钺译，《论情绪》（上海：商务，1946） [William James, Principles of Psychology].

陈汝懋，〈论心理事件的原因〉，《东方杂志》，42卷3期，1946/2/1.

刘永和，〈侵略行为的心理因素〉，《东方杂志》，42卷12期，1946/6/15.

朱有瓛，〈最近之心理学界〉，《学艺》，14卷7期，1946/7.

1 9 4 7

卫译，〈为什么不运用你的下意识〉，《文摘》，11卷2期，1947/2.

钱钟书，〈说回家〉，《观察》，2卷1期，1947/3/1.

季季译，罗素著《心的分析》（上海：中华，1947）.

曹日昌，〈心理学史的问题〉，《学艺》，17卷11期，1947/11.

1 9 4 8

陶菊隐，〈精神病的意义及其对于社会的影响〉，《新中华》，6卷2期，1948/1/16.

冯鸿，〈下意识与精神病〉，《新中华》，6卷8期，1948/4/16.

1 9 4 9

楚之译，《精神分析与唯物史观》（上海：世界，1949，再版） [Reuben Osborn, Freud and Marx, A Dialectic Study].

潘光旦译，《性心理学》（上海：商务，1949，再版） [Havelock Ellis, Studies in the Psychology of Sex].

GLOSSARY

Ah Q　阿Q

Ah Q jingshen　阿Q精神

Aitisi de shidai　蔼理斯的时代

Ba Jin　巴金

Ba Jin xuan ji　巴金选集

baihua wen　白话文

Baijin de nü ti suxiang　白金的女体塑像

Baike zhishi　百科知识

Ban Gu　班固

Bao Ji　鲍羿

Beixin yuebao　北新月报

Bi Yan　毕严

Biantai xingyu de Lin Hejing　变态性欲的林和靖

Biantai xinli ABC　变态心理ABC

Biantai xinlixue paibie　变态心理学派别

Biaozhun hanzi waiguo renming diming biao
　　标准汉字外国人名地名表

Bing Xin　冰心

Bing Xin wenji　冰心文集

Bu Ning　不佞

Bu tian　补天

Buzhou shan　不周山

Can chun　残春

Cao Yu　曹禺

Chang ming deng　长明灯

Chen Derong　陈德荣

Chen Dongyuan　陈东原

Chen Jia'ai　陈家蔼

Chen Jingzhi　陈敬之

gong shou er bie 拱手而别
Gong mu 公墓
gou bian jia 媾变家
Gu du zhe 孤独者
gu wen 古文
Guancha 观察
Guanyu fanyi 关于翻译
Guanyu xinli fenxi ji Fuluoyite zhi piping
    关于心理分析及佛洛依特之批评
Guo chou 国仇
Guo Moruo 郭沫若
Guo Renyuan 郭任远
Guomin ribao 国民日报
Guoyu 国语

Han shu 汉书
Hao Yaodong 郝耀东
He Bang 何邦
he qi mei zi 鹤妻梅子
Hei mudan 黑牡丹
Henan 河南
Hu Qiuyuan 胡秋原
Hu Shensheng 胡申生
Hu Shi 胡适
Hua 化
hua xia 华夏
Huang Weirong 黄维荣
Huanqiu 环球
huaxu hua 华胥化
huaxu kuang 华胥狂
Huaxu shi 华胥氏
Hui Zong 徽宗
Hui zhi feng 惠之风

Huiyi wo bian de di yi bu cheng tao shi
回忆我编的第一部成套史

Ji Ji　季季
ji guang tun　吉光屯
Ji liu　激流
Jia　家
Jia Rui　贾瑞
jian　奸
jianghu pai dawang　江湖派大王
Jiangjun de tou　将军的头
jiaoji de meng　焦急的梦
Jiaoyu jie　教育界
Jiaoyu xinli yanjiu　教育心理研究
Jiaoyu zazhi　教育杂志
Jie jia zhi ye　姐嫁之夜
Jie xin shu xueshuo　解心术学说
jieshao de piping　介绍的批评
Jiliang yu naizi　脊梁与奶子
Jin di　禁地
Jin suo ji　金锁记
Jingquhouren　敬渠后人
Jingshen fenxi pai xinlixue pipan
　精神分析派心理学批判
Jingshen fenxi xue ABC　精神分析学ABC
Jingshen fenxi xue pipan　精神分析学批判
Jingshen fenxi xue yu yishu　精神分析学与艺术
Jingshen fenxi yin lun　精神分析引论
Jingshen fenxi yu weiwu shi guan
　精神分析与唯物史观
Jingshen yujie　精神郁结
Jiulümei　鸠绿媚
Jiu wen si pian　旧文四篇

jiyi de quexian huo yiwang 记忆的缺陷或遗忘
jiyi zhe de yishi 记忆着的意识
Juefu 觉敷

Kaiming 开明
Kang Youwei 康有为
Kexue luncong 科学论丛
Kongque dong nan fei ji qita dumuju
　　孔雀东南飞及其它独幕剧
Ku cha sui bi 苦茶随笔
Kuang jie 况颉
kumen de xiangzheng 苦闷的象征

Lang tao sha 浪淘沙
Li 礼
Li Jingbin 李景彬
li xue 理学
Li Yuntuan 李运抟
Liang ge shijian de bu gan zheng zhe
　　两个时间的不感症者
Liang Qichao 梁启超
Liang Shiqiu 梁实秋
Liangyou 良友
Liaozhai zhi yi 聊斋志异
Liezi/Huangdi 列子·黄帝
Lin Hejing 林和靖
Lin Shu 林纾
Lin Yutang 林语堂
Lingfeng xiaoshuo ji 灵凤小说集
Liu Na'ou 刘呐鸥
Liu Shousong 刘绶松
Liu Xie 刘勰
Liuxing xing ganmao 流行性感冒

Qinlüe xingwei de xinli yinsu
侵略行为的心理因素
qiuzi zhi dao 龟兹之道
Qu Qiubai 瞿秋白
Qu Yuan 屈原
Qunzhong xinli zhi tezheng 群众心理之特征

ren 韧
Renlei de xingwei 人类的行为
ri you suo si, ye you suo meng
日有所思，夜有所梦
Rou pu tuan 肉蒲团
Ru lin wai shi 儒林外史

San guo yanyi 三国演义
seqing kuang 色情狂
seyu 色欲
Shan nüren xingpin 善女人行品
Shanghai guji chubanshe 上海古籍出版社
Shaonü riji 少女日记
Shen Congwen wenji 沈从文文集
Shen Yanbing 沈雁冰
shenjing shuairuo 神经衰弱
shengming li 生命力
Shi hao li 石壕吏
Shi Nai'an 施耐庵
Shi se xing hu fei xing hu 食色性乎非性乎
Shi Xiu 石秀
Shi Zhecun 施蛰存
Shi Zhecun tan "Xiandai zazhi" ji qita
施蛰存谈《现代杂志》及其他
Shida yuekan 师大月刊
Shiheng 侍桁

Shijie　世界
shishi　时时
shiyu　食欲
Shishi xinbao　时事新报
shou nüe dai kuang　受虐待狂
shu shi ren　书是人
Shu Xincheng　舒新城
Shu yan lie qi lu　书艳猎奇录
Shui hu　水浒
Shuo hui jia　说回家
Si ren du qiaocui　斯人独憔悴
Sixizi de shengyi　四喜子的生意
Su Xuelin　苏雪林
Sun Fuyu　孙伏虞
Sun Xizhen　孙席珍
suo zhu de　所住的

Taiping guang ji　太平广记
Tang Chengbo　汤澄波
Tantan Fuluoyite　谈谈弗洛伊特
Ti juan xie　啼鹃血
Tianma xing kong shi de da jingshen
　　天马行空式的大精神
Ting shuo meng　听说梦
"Ting shuo meng" shi zenyang piping Fuluoyide de
　　〈听说梦〉是怎样批评弗洛伊德的
Tong shi tian ya lun luo ren　同是天涯沦落人
Tongcheng　桐城
tongxing jian　同性奸
tongxing lian　同性恋
Tou mianbao de mianbao shi　偷面包的面包师
tufan　吐番
tujin he tiaoyue　突进和跳跃

tuoxie 妥协

Tushu pinglun 图书评论

Waitai wenyi sichao he wu si xin wenxue
外来文艺思潮和五四新文学

Waiyu jiaoxue yu yanjiu chubanshe
外语教学与研究出版社

Wang Guowei 王国维

Wang Jingzhi 汪静之

Wang Jinyuan 王锦园

Wang Tongzhao 王统照

Wanyou wenku 万有文库

Wen Yiduo 闻一多

wenti zuojia 文体作家

Wenxin diaolong 文心雕龙

Wenxue bai ti 文学百题

Wenxue pinglun congkan 文学评论丛刊

Wenxue xun kan 文学旬刊

Wenxue yue bao 文学月报

Wenxuejia zhi xiangxiang 文学家之想象

Wenyi bao 文艺报

Wenyi yuekan 文艺月刊

Wo de chuangzuo shenghuo zhi licheng
我的创作生活之历程

Wo de wenyi sixiang zhong de fandong fangmian
我的文艺思想中的反动方面

Wu Fuyuan 吴福元

wu yishi 无意识

Wu Zimin 吴子敏

Wugui lieche 无轨列车

Xi Di 西蒂

Xi xin xue lünlue 析心学论略

Xi you bu　西游补

Xia Fuxin　夏斧心

Xia Ji'an xiansheng jinian ji
　　夏济安先生纪念集

Xia yishi yu jingshenbing　下意识与精神病

Xiandai　现代

Xiandai biantai xinli xueshuo zhi fenxi jiqi piping
　　现代变态心理学说之分析及其批评

Xiandai Zhongguo xiaoshuo zhong ji zhong qingxiang
　　现代中国小说中几种倾向

Xiao hun ji　销魂记

Xiao Xiaorong　萧孝嵘

Xiaoqing zhi fenxi　小青之分析

Xiaoshuo shi bao　小说时报

Xiaoshuo yuebao　小说月报

Xie Liuyi　谢六逸

Xie Xunchu　谢循初

xiesidili zheng　歇斯底里症

Xin　新

xin　心

Xin chao　新潮

Xin de fenxi　心的分析

xin ganjue　新感觉

Xin ganjue pai xiaoshuo xuan
　　新感觉派小说选

Xin jing　心经

xin ling li　心灵力

Xin qingnian　新青年

Xin shi nao de chanwu ma?　心是脑的产物吗？

Xin shiren zhi qingxu　新诗人之情绪

Xin wenxue de zuli　新文学的阻力

Xin wenxue shiliao　新文学史料

Xin zhi fenxi　心之分析

Xin Zhonghua　新中华
xinli fenxi xiaoshuo　pai　心理分析小说派
xinli xiaoshuo　心理小说
Xinlixue zai wenxue zuopin zhong de shili
　　心理学在文学作品中的势力
Xinlixue zazhi　心理学杂志
xing de fadong　　性的发动
Xing shi　性史
Xinken shuju　辛垦书局
Xinli ban nian kan　心理半年刊
Xinli xuebao　心理学报
Xinli zhan yu shanji zhan　心理战与闪电战
xinlixue　心理学
Xinlixue de paibie　心理学的派别
Xinlixue gailun　心理学概论
Xinlixue gaiyi　心理学概议
Xinlixue lunwen ji　心理学论文集
Xinlixue rumen　　心理学入门
Xinlixue wenji　心理学文集
Xinlixuejia de dongyuan　心理学家的动员
Xinlixuepai yu Zhongguo xiandai xiaoshuo
　　　心理学派与中国现代小说
xinxing　　心性
Xinyi　新艺
Xinyue　新月
Xiyu　西域
Xu Qingyu　徐庆誉
xu xu dao dao　絮絮叨叨
xuanxue　玄学
xue cang shuo　穴藏说
Xue deng　学灯
Xue Li　薛礼
Xue Li huan jia　薛礼还家

Xue Rengui　薛仁贵

xuesheng zazhi　学生杂志

Xuexi yu tansuo　学习与探索

Yan Fu　严复

Yan Jiayan　严家炎

Yan Yongjing　颜永京

yanping　烟瓶

yanzhi　言志

Ye　夜

Ye Lingfeng　叶灵凤

Ye Qing　叶青

Yezonghui li de wu ge ren　夜总会里的五个人

Yi ban　一般

yi bing　癔病

Yi ge lü jian bu xian que ling ren kunhuo de
　　xianxiang, guanyu "qian yishi" yu "wu
　　yishi" liang shuyu hun yong de zhiyi
　　一个屡见不鲜却令人困惑的现象――关于"潜意识"与
　　"无意识"两术语混用的质疑

Yi meng　异梦

Yi wenxueshu fangfa de taolun
　　译文学书方法的讨论

Yi zhu tong　遗珠痛

Yishu yu shenghuo　艺术与生活

Yiwen guan　译文馆

Yiyu ertong zhi ge an yanjiu
　　抑郁儿童之个案研究

yizhi zuoyong　移植作用

Yongqin　咏琴

You Zhiwu　由稚吾

Youguan "Xin ling xue" yi shu de yanjiu
　　有关《心灵学》一书的研究

yu 欲
Yu 浴
Yu Dafu 郁达夫
Yu Dafu wenji 郁达夫文集
Yu Fenggao 余风高
Yu Min 于民
Yu Xingyuan 虞心远
Yuan Changying 袁昌英
Yuan ye 原野
yuanyang 鸳鸯
Yuzhi shuhui 誊智书会

zaidao 载道
zarou 杂糅
Zhang Ailing 张爱玲
Zhang Depei 张德培
Zhang Dongsun 张东荪
Zhang Jingsheng 张竟生
Zhang Shizhao 章士钊
zhang taiye 长太爷
Zhang Tianyi 张天翼
Zhang Tiemin 章铁民
Zhang Xichen 章锡琛
Zhang Yaoxiang 张耀翔
Zhang Yiping 章衣萍
Zhang Ziping 张资平
Zhanshi de xinli shenjing bing
　　战时的心理神经病
Zhao Jiabi 赵家璧
Zhao Jingshen 赵景深
Zhao Liru 赵莉如
Zhao Qinwu 赵钦武
Zhao Yan 赵演

Zheng Xinling　郑心伶

Zheng Zhenduo　郑振铎

Zhitang hui xiang lu　知堂回想录

Zhongfa daxue yuekan　中法大学月刊

zhonggou　中媾

Zhongguo cuimian shu　中国催眠术

Zhongguo dangdai shi da nü zuojia jia zuo ji
　　中国当代十大女作家佳作集

Zhongguo er san shi nian dai zuojia
　　中国二三十年代作家

Zhongguo funü shenghuo shi　中国妇女生活史

Zhongguo gudai meixue sixiangjia juyao
　　中国古代美学思想家举要

Zhongguo jindai jiaoyushi ziliao
　　中国近代教育史资料

Zhonguo lidai ming ren biantai xingwei kao
　　中国历代名人变态行为考

Zhongguo xin wenxue dasi，xiaoshuo
　　中国新文学大系：小说

Zhongguo xin wenxueshi chugao　中国新文学史初稿

Zhonggue xin wenyi yu biantai xingyu
　　中国新文艺与变态性欲

Zhongguo xinlixue fazhanshi lüe
　　中国心理学发展史略

Zhongshan wenhua jiaoyu guan jikan
　　中山文化教育馆季刊

zhongyong　中庸

Zhou li　周礼

Zhou Qiying　周起应

Zhou Zuoren　周作人

Zhou Zuoren pingxi　周作人评析

Zhu Guangqian　朱光潜

Zhu Xi　朱熹

Zhu Ziqing 朱自清

Zhushu shang guanchan wan jin Zhongguo
xinlixue zhi yanjiu 著述上观察晚近中国
心理学之研究

zi bu wang 字不枉

zi wo lian 自我恋

Zi zhi zhi shu 自知之术

Ziji de yuandi 自己的园地

CORNELL EAST ASIA SERIES

For ordering information, please contact the *Cornell East Asia Series*, East
Asia Program, Cornell University, 140 Uris Hall, Ithaca, NY 14853-7601
USA, (607) 255-6222.

6-92/.6M/BB

Lightning Source UK Ltd.
Milton Keynes UK
UKHW011817070622
404079UK00001B/94